Science
& Religion

Science
& Religion

AN INTRODUCTION

Alister E. McGrath

First published 1999

2   4   6   8   10   9   7   5   3   1

Blackwell Publishers Ltd
108 Cowley Road
Oxford OX4 1JF
UK

Blackwell Publishers Inc.
350 Main Street
Malden, Massachusetts 02148
USA

British Library Cataloguing in Publication Data
A CIP catalogue record for this book is available from the British Library.

Library of Congress Cataloguing-in-Publication Data
McGrath, Alister E., 1953–
    Science and religion : an introduction / Alister E. McGrath.
        p.   cm.
    Includes bibliographical references and index.
    ISBN 0-631-20841-0 (hardcover : alk. paper). —
ISBN 0-631-20842-9 (pbk. : alk. paper)
    1. Religion and science.   I. Title.
BL240.2.M413   1998   98-23477
                                                                                        CIP

Typeset in 10½ on 13pt Galliard
by York House Typographic Ltd, London
Printed in Great Britain by T.J. International, Padstow, Cornwall

This book is printed on acid-free paper

Contents

Preface

The study of science and religion is one of the most fascinating areas of human inquiry. The remarkable interest in books and documentaries dealing with God and physics, spirituality and science, and the great mysteries of human nature and destiny are a clear sign that there is growing interest in this area. Many colleges, seminaries and universities now offer courses dealing with the general theme of science and religion, which often attract large and appreciative audiences.

A major difficulty, however, concerns the extent of prior knowledge of those interested in this area of study. To appreciate the complex interaction of the natural sciences and religion, it is necessary to have at least a good general working knowledge of at least one religion and one major natural science, preferably physics or biology. Many of those who would like to explore this fascinating field find themselves discouraged through this lack of prior knowledge. This book aims to deal with this situation by assuming that its readers know little, if anything, about the natural sciences or religion, and aims to introduce everything on the basis of the assumption of zero prior knowledge on the part of its readers.

This book thus aims to introduce its readers to the main themes and issues in the study of religion and the natural sciences. Those with some previous knowledge in the areas of science or religion will therefore find that they are from time to time presented with material with which they are already familiar. It is hoped that this will not prove tedious. In any case, the particular concern of this volume is to explore the interface of science and religion. Those already with some knowledge of science or religion should therefore find that material with which they are already familiar is handled in new ways, so that its connections with our theme become clear.

My own interest in this field goes back more than twenty years. I began my studies at Oxford University by studying Chemistry, focussing on quantum theory, before going on to gain my doctorate in molecular biophysics. After this, I studied theology at Oxford and Cambridge, focussing particularly on the historical interaction of science and religion, particularly during the sixteenth and nineteenth centuries. It is my hope that my own experience of relating the two areas of study may be of value to others seeking to do the same.

In writing this book, I have been enormously helped by many others working in the fields of science and religion, whether specializing in one or the other, or their mutual relationship. As they are too many to name, I hope that they will accept this acknowledgement of their assistance, encouragement, and support. I am also grateful to the John Templeton Foundation for support throughout the writing of this book.

Alister McGrath
Oxford, June 1998

How to Use this Book

This book aims to introduce you to some of the major themes in the study of science and religion. It assumes that you know little or nothing about either of them, and tries to explain as much as possible in the space available.

1 Read the material in the order in which it is set out. Later sections of the book assume that you know about the material which is presented in earlier chapters.
2 It is essential that you become familiar with three major historical landmarks in the relation of science and religion. These are: the astronomical debates of the sixteenth and early seventeenth centuries; the rise of the Newtonian worldview in the later seventeenth and eighteenth centuries; and the Darwinian controversy of the nineteenth century. These landmark debates are widely regarded as fundamental to the development of the relation of the sciences and religion, and you must understand their basic themes if you are to appreciate later developments and debates.
3 This book aims to equip you for further reading, and for further study. At the end of every chapter there are suggestions for further reading. These references allow you to follow through any matters of interest to the level you think is appropriate for your needs. By the time you have worked through all the material in this book, you should be able to handle the more advanced monographs and articles detailed in the Bibliography, as well as having a good overall knowledge of the issues involved in this fascinating area of study.

All important citations in the text have been sourced to allow users to read them in their original content and in greater depth. Sources of citations are detailed on pp. 240–7.

4 Remember that this book is only an introduction! It should whet your appetite to know more, and offers you guidance about further reading so that you can find out more. There are severe limits of space within an introductory work of this kind, with the inevitable result that many important themes have to be treated in a much shorter space than they deserve!

1

Historical Landmarks

Anyone wishing to understand the interaction of science and religion needs to become familiar with three major landmarks – the astronomical debates of the sixteenth and early seventeenth centuries; the rise of the Newtonian worldview in the late seventeenth and eighteenth century; and the Darwinian controversy of the nineteenth. This chapter aims to introduce these landmark debates, indicating the points at issue and their significance for our theme. As these three debates are constantly referred to in the literature concerning the theme of "science and religion" – as they are also in the present text – the reader must regard it as essential to master the basic ideas and developments which are discussed in this chapter.

We begin by considering how the intellectual foundations for modern science were laid in the Middle Ages, which sets the context for what follows.

The Medieval Synthesis

It is often suggested that the scientific revolution which emerged in the sixteenth and seventeenth centuries owed little, if anything positive, to the Middle Ages. This view, which is widely encountered in the older literature dealing with the history of science, has recently come under criticism from specialists in medieval intellectual history, such as Edward Grant, who have pointed out that the origins of the scientific revolution can indeed be traced back to the Middle Ages. For Grant, the medieval period created an intellectual context within which the natural sciences could develop as serious intellectual disciplines, and also furnished ideas and methods which would prove of major importance to that development.

The three medieval developments that may be regarded as establishing a context within which the natural sciences were to develop are the following.

1   The Middle Ages saw the translation into Latin – the common language of the western European scholarly community – of a series of scientific texts which had their origins in the Greco-Arabian tradition. Arabian commentators on the text of Aristotle, as well as the original Aristotelian texts themselves, became available to western thinkers. The rediscovery of Aristotle had a major impact on medieval theology and philosophy, with writers such as Thomas Aquinas finding him a major stimulus to philosophical and theological reflection. These texts – by no means limited to the writings of Aristotle – also proved to be a major stimulus to wrestling with the questions of the natural sciences. While it is possible to argue that the natural sciences could have developed without these texts, that development would unquestionably have taken place much later than it did.

2   The Middle Ages saw the foundation of the great universities of western Europe. These would prove to be of central importance in the development of the natural sciences. Courses in logic, natural philosophy, geometry, music, arithmetic, and astronomy were prescribed for all those wishing to gain any qualification from a typical medieval university. The introduction of natural philosophy into the medieval university curriculum ensured that a significant number of scientific issues were addressed as a routine part of higher education. A typical medieval university would have four faculties: the faculty of arts, and the three "higher faculties" of medicine, law, and theology. The faculty of arts was seen as laying the foundation for more advanced study, and it is important to note how much "natural philosophy" was included in that foundational course.

3   A class of "theologians–natural philosophers" emerged, often within a university context, who were convinced that the study of natural world was theologically legitimate. Although Aristotle was widely regarded as a pagan philosopher (and hence of limited value to Christians), he was nevertheless seen as a resource to allow a greater understanding of the natural world, and hence to learn more of the God who had created that world. It is therefore important to

note that many of the greatest names in the world of medieval natural science – such as Robert Grosseteste, Nicolas Oresme, and Henry of Langenstein – were all active theologians who did not see a contradiction between their faith and the investigation of the natural order.

This growing emphasis on "natural philosophy" proved to be of major importance to the emergence of the natural sciences in western Europe. Yet it is also important to appreciate that the Middle Ages saw considerable attention being paid to an issue which would prove to be of major importance in the sixteenth century – the question of biblical interpretation. At least on the basis of a superficial reading, the Bible seemed to suggest an earth-centred (geocentric) universe, which was created in six days, with humanity being created on the sixth day. In view of the considerable discussion as to how the opening chapters of the book of Genesis are to be interpreted, it is of considerable important to note the way in which medieval biblical commentators opened the way to reading these texts in significantly different ways, more amenable to the insights which were emerging from the natural sciences.

Every text demands to be interpreted; the Christian Bible is no exception to this rule. There is a sense in which the history of Christian theology can be regarded as the history of biblical interpretation. In view of the importance of the question as to whether certain passages are to be interpreted literally, and others in a non-literal or allegorical manner, we may consider the development of this issue in the Middle Ages.

It is important to appreciate that the foundations of this discussion were laid centuries earlier, in the patristic period. Two major schools of biblical interpretation developed, one associated with the city of Alexandria, the other with Antioch. The Alexandrian school of biblical interpretation drew on the methods devised by the Jewish writer Philo of Alexandria (*c.*30 BC–*c.*45 AD). Drawing on earlier Jewish traditions, which allowed the literal interpretation of scripture to be supplemented by an appeal to allegory. But what is an allegory? The Greek philosopher Heracleitus had defined it as "saying one thing, and meaning something other than what is said." Philo argued that it was necessary to look beneath the surface meaning of scripture, to discern a deeper meaning which lay beneath the surface of the text. These ideas were taken upon by a group of theologians based in Alexandria, of which the most important are generally agreed to be Clement, Origen, and Didymus the Blind. Indeed, Jerome playfully referred to the last-mentioned as "Didymus the Sighted," on account of the spiritual insights which resulted from his application of the allegorical method of biblical interpretation. The scope of the allegorical method can be seen from Origen's interpretation of key Old Testament images. Joshua's conquest of the promised land, interpreted allegorically, referred to Christ's conquest of sin upon the cross, just as the sacrificial legislation in Leviticus pointed ahead to the spiritual sacrifices of Christians.

In contrast, the Antiochene school placed an emphasis upon the interpretation of Scripture in the light of its historical context. This school, especially associated with writers such as Diodore of Tarsus, John Chrysostom and Theodore of Mopsuestia, gave an emphasis to the historical location of Old Testament prophecies, which is quite absent from the writings of Origen and other representatives of the Alexandrian tradition. Thus Theodore, in dealing with Old Testament prophecy, stresses that the prophetic message was relevant to those to whom it was directly addressed, as well as having a developed meaning for a Christian readership. Every prophetic oracle is to be interpreted as having a single consistent historical or literal meaning. In consequence, Theodore tended to interpret relatively few Old Testament passages as referring directly to Christ, whereas the Alexandrian school regarded Christ as the hidden content of many Old Testament passages, both prophetic and historical.

In the western church a slightly distinct approach can be seen to have developed. In many of his writings, Ambrose of Milan developed a threefold understanding of the senses of Scripture: in addition to the natural sense, the interpreter may discern a moral and rational or theological sense. Augustine chose to to follow this approach, and instead argued for a twofold sense – a literal–fleshly–historical approach and an allegorical–mystical–spiritual sense, although Augustine allows that some passages can possess both senses. "The sayings of the prophets are found to have a threefold meaning, in that some have in mind the earthly Jerusalem, others the heavenly city, and others refer to both." To understand the Old Testament at a purely historical level is unacceptable; the key to its understanding lies in its correct interpretation.

This distinction between the literal or historical sense of Scripture on the one hand, and a deeper spiritual or allegorical meaning on the other, came to be generally accepted within the church during the early Middle Ages. The standard method of biblical interpretation used during the Middle Ages is usually known as the *Quadriga*, or the "four-fold sense of

Scripture". The origins of this method lie specifically in the distinction between the literal and spiritual senses. Scripture possesses four different senses. In addition to the literal sense, three non-literal senses could be distinguished: the allegorical, defining what Christians are to believe; the tropological or moral, defining what Christians are to do; and the anagogical, defining what Christians were to hope for. The four senses of Scripture were thus the following:

1 The literal sense of Scripture, in which the text could be taken at face value.
2 The allegorical sense, which interpreted certain passages of Scripture to produce statements of doctrine. Those passages tended to be either obscure, or to have a literal meaning which was unacceptable, for theological reasons, to their readers.
3 The tropological or moral sense, which interpreted such passages to produce ethical guidance for Christian conduct.
4 The anagogical sense, which interprets passages to indicate the grounds of Christian hope, pointing toward the future fulfillment of the divine promises in the New Jerusalem.

A potential weakness was avoided by insisting that nothing should be believed on the basis of a non-literal sense of Scripture, unless it could first be established on the basis of the literal sense. This insistence on the priority of the literal sense of Scripture may be seen as an implied criticism of the allegorical approach adopted by Origen, which virtually allowed interpreters of Scripture to read into any passage whatever "spiritual" interpretations they liked.

By the high noon of the Middle Ages, a sophisticated approach to biblical interpretation had therefore been set in place, which allowed some biblical passages to be interpreted literally, and others in non-literal senses. Augustine stressed the importance of respecting the conclusions of the sciences in relation to biblical exegesis. As Augustine himself stressed in his commentary on Genesis, certain passages were genuinely open to diverse interpretations; it was therefore important to allow further scientific research to assist in the determination of which was the most appropriate mode of interpretation for a given passage:

In matters that are so obscure and far beyond our vision, we find in Holy Scripture passages which can be interpreted in very different ways without prejudice to the faith we have received. In such cases, we should not rush in headlong and so firmly take our stand on one side that, if further progress in the search for truth justly undermines our position, we too fall with it. We should not battle for our own interpretation but for the teaching of the Holy Scripture. We should not wish to conform the meaning of Holy Scripture to our interpretation, but our interpretation to the meaning of Holy Scripture.

Augustine therefore urged that biblical interpretation should take due account of what could reasonably be regarded as established facts.

In some ways, this approach to biblical interpretation may be seen as ensuring that Christian theology never became trapped in a pre-scientific worldview. Edward Grant has shown the importance of this point in relation to the development of medieval cosmology over the period 1200–1687, noting especially the manner in which Augustine's approach was endorsed and developed by Thomas Aquinas. The general approach set out by Augustine was adopted by several influential Roman Catholic theologians of the sixteenth century, including a highly significant commentary on Genesis, which is known to have influenced Galileo's developing views on biblical interpretation.

As we shall see, these approaches would be put to good use during the first major controversy to develop in relation to science and religion – the astronomical debates of the sixteenth and seventeenth centuries, focusing on the theories of Copernicus and Galileo. We shall consider these in what follows.

The New Astronomy: The Copernican and Galileian Controversies

Every age is characterized by a series of settled beliefs, which undergird its worldview. The Middle Ages is no exception. One of the more important elements in the medieval worldview was the belief that the sun and other celestial bodies – such as the moon and the planets – rotated around the earth. This geocentric view of the universe was treated as self-evidently true. The Bible was interpreted in the light of this belief, with geocentric assumptions being brought to the interpretation of a number of passages. Most living languages still bear witness to this geocentric worldview. For example, even in modern English, it is perfectly acceptable to state that "the sun rose at 7.33 a.m." – despite the fact that this reflects the belief that the sun rotates around the earth. As the truth or falsity of the geocentric made little difference to everyday life anyway, there was little popular interest in challenging it.

The model of the universe which was most widely accepted during the early Middle Ages was devised by Claudius Ptolemy, an astronomer who worked in the Egyptian city of Alexandria during the first half of the second century. In his *Amalgest*, Ptolemy brought together existing ideas concerning the motions of the moon and planets, and argued that these could be understood on the basis of the following assumptions:

1 The earth is at the centre of the universe;
2 All heavenly bodies rotate in circular paths around the earth;
3 These rotations take the form of motion in a circle, the centre of which in turn moves in another circle. This central idea, which was originally due to Hipparchus, is based on the idea of *epicycles* – that is, circular motion imposed upon circular motion.

Increasingly detailed and precise observation of the movement of the planets and stars caused increasing difficulties for this theory. Initially, the discrepancies could be accommodated by adding additional epicycles. By the end of the fifteenth century, the model was so complex and unwieldy that it was close to collapse. But what could replace it?

During the sixteenth century, the geocentric model of the solar system was abandoned in favour of a heliocentric model, which depicted the sun as lying at its centre, with the earth being seen as one of a number of planets orbiting around it. This represented a radical departure from the existing model, and must be regarded as one of the most significant changes in the human perception of reality to have taken place in the last millennium. Although it is customary to refer to this shift in thinking as "the Copernican revolution," it is generally agreed that three individuals were of major importance in bringing about the acceptance of this change.

1 Nicholas Copernicus (1473–1543), a Polish scholar, argued that the planets moved in concentric circles around the sun. The earth, in addition to rotating about the sun, also rotated on its own axis. The apparent motion of the stars and planets was thus due to a combination of the rotation of the earth on its own axis, and its rotation around the sun. The model possessed a simplicity and elegance which compared favourably with the increasingly cumbersome

Ptolemaic model. Nevertheless, it still proved incapable of explaining all known observational data. The theory would require further modification before it would find acceptance.

2　The Danish scholar Tycho Brahe (1546–1601), based at an observatory on an island near Copenhagen, carried out a series of precise observations on planetary motion over the period 1576–92. These observations would form the basis for Kepler's modified model of the solar system. Kepler acted as assistant to Tycho when the latter was forced to relocate to Bohemia following the death of Frederick II of Denmark.

3　Johannes Kepler (1571–1630) focused his attention on the observation of the motion of the planet Mars. The Copernican model, which assumed that planets orbit in circles around the sun, was unable to account for the observed motion of the planet. In 1609, Kepler was able to announce that he had uncovered two general laws governing the motion of Mars. First, Mars rotated in an elliptical orbit, with the sun at one of its two foci. Second, the line joining Mars to the sun covers equal areas in equal periods of time. By 1619, he had extended these two laws to the remaining planets, and uncovered a third law: the square of the periodic time of a planet (that is, the time taken by the planet to complete one orbit around the sun) is directly proportional to the cube of its mean distance from the sun.

Kepler's model represented a significant modification of Copernicus' ideas. It must be stressed that Copernicus' radical new model was simply not able to explain the observational data, despite its conceptual elegance and simplicity, on account of his flawed assumption that orbits were necessarily circular. This assumption, interestingly, seems to have derived from classical Euclidian geometry; Copernicus never really freed himself completely from classic Greek ways of thinking.

The publication of Copernicus' *de revolutionibus orbium coelestium* ("on the revolutions of the heavenly bodies") in May 1543 thus caused a mild sensation, although the final acceptance of the model would have to wait for the detailed work by Kepler in the first two decades of the seventeenth century. As we noted, the older model (often referred to as a "geocentric" theory) was widely accepted by theologians of the Middle Ages, who had become so familiar with reading the text of the Bible through geocentric spectacles that they had some difficulty coping with the new approach.

Early published defenses of the Copernican theory (such as G. J. Rheticus's *Treatise on Holy Scripture and the Motion of the Earth*, which is widely regarded as the earliest known work to deal explicitly with the relation of the Bible and the Copernican theory) thus had to deal with two issues. First, they had to set out the observational evidence which led to the conclusion that the earth and other planets rotated around the sun. Second, they had to demonstrate that this viewpoint was consistent with the Bible, which had long been read as endorsing a geocentric view of the Bible. As we noted above, the observational evidence was only finally accounted for in the light of Kepler's modification of Copernicus's model. But what of the theological aspects of that model? What of the radical shift which it proposed from an earth-centred universe?

There is no doubt that the rise of the heliocentric theory of the solar system caused theologians to re-examine the manner in which certain biblical passages were interpreted. We noted earlier some of the issues of biblical interpretation involved (see pp. 4–6), however, at this stage, we may distinguish three broad approaches within the Christian tradition of biblical interpretation. In what follows, we shall note these, and consider their importance to the science and religion dialogue. In general terms, the three broad types of approach are:

1 A *literal* approach, which argues that the passage in question is to be taken at its face value. For example, a literal interpretation of the first chapter Genesis would argue that creation took place in six periods of twenty-four hours.

2 A non-literal or *allegorical* approach, which stresses that certain sections of the Bible are written in a style which it is not appropriate to take absolutely literally. During the Middle Ages, three non-literal senses of Scripture were recognized; this was regarded by many sixteenth-century writers as somewhat elaborate. This view regards the opening chapters of Genesis as poetic or allegorical accounts, from which theological and ethical principles can be derived; it does not treat them as literal historical accounts of the origins of the earth.

3 An approach based on the idea of *accommodation*. This has been by far the most important approach in relation to the interaction of biblical interpretation and the natural sciences. The approach argues that revelation takes place in culturally and anthropologically conditioned manners and forms, with the result that it needs to be appropriately interpreted. This approach has a long tradition of use

within Judaism and subsequently within Christian theology, and can easily be shown to have been influential within the patristic period. Nevertheless, it mature development can be found within the sixteenth century. This approach argues that the opening chapters of Genesis use language and imagery appropriate to the cultural conditions of its original audience; it is not to be taken "literally," but is to be interpreted to a contemporary readership by extracting the key ideas which have been expressed in forms and terms which are specifically adapted or "accommodated" to the original audience.

The third approach proved to be of especial importance during the debates over the relation between theology and astronomy during the sixteenth and seventeenth centuries. The noted reformer John Calvin (1509–64) may be regarded as making two major and positive contributions to the appreciation and development of the natural sciences. First, he positively encouraged the scientific study of nature; second, he eliminated a major obstacle to the development of that study, through his understanding of the way in which the Bible was to be interpreted in terms of "accommodation" (as explained above). His first contribution is specifically linked with his stress upon the orderliness of creation; both the physical world and the human body testify to the wisdom and character of God.

In order than no one might be excluded from the means of obtaining happiness, God has been pleased, not only to place in our minds the seeds of religion of which we have already spoken, but to make known his perfection in the whole structure of the universe, and daily place himself in our view, in such a manner that we cannot open our eyes without being compelled to observe him. . . . To prove his remarkable wisdom, both the heavens and the earth present us with countless proofs – not just those more advanced proofs which astronomy, medicine and all the other natural sciences are designed to illustrate, but proofs which force themselves on the attention of the most illiterate peasant, who cannot open his eyes without seeing them.

Calvin thus commends the study of both astronomy and medicine. They are able to probe more deeply than theology into the natural world, and thus uncover further evidence of the orderliness of the creation and the wisdom of its creator. It may thus be argued that Calvin gave a new religious motivation to the scientific investigation of nature. This was now seen as a means of discerning the wise hand of God in creation. The *Confessio Belgica* (1561), a Calvinist statement of faith which exercised particular influence in the Lowlands (an area which would become particularly noted for its botanists and physicists), declared that nature is "before our eyes as a most beautiful book in which all created things, whether great or small, are as letters showing the invisible things of God to us." God can thus be discerned through the detailed study of the creation through the natural sciences.

Calvin's second major contribution was to eliminate a significant obstacle to the development of the natural sciences – biblical literalism. Calvin points out that the Bible is primarily concerned with the knowledge of Jesus Christ. It is not an astronomical, geographical, or biological textbook. And when the Bible is interpreted, it must be borne in mind that God "adjusts" to the capacities of the human mind and heart. God has to come down to our level if revelation is to take place. Revelation thus presents a scaled-down or "accommodated" version of God to us, in order to meet our limited abilities. Just as a human mother stoops down to reach her child, so God stoops down to come to our level. Revelation is an act of divine condescension.

In the case of the biblical accounts of the creation (Genesis 1), Calvin argues that they are accommodated to the abilities and horizons of a relatively simple and unsophisticated people; they are not intended to be taken as literal representations of reality. The author of Genesis, he declares, "was ordained to be a teacher of the unlearned and primitive, as well as the learned; and so could not achieve his goal without descending to such crude means of instruction." The phrase "six days of creation" does not designate six periods of twenty-four hours, but is simply an accommodation to human ways of thinking to designate an extended period of time. The "water above the firmament" is simply an accommodated way of speaking about clouds.

The impact of both these ideas upon scientific theorizing, especially during the seventeenth century, was considerable. For example, the English writer Edward Wright defended Copernicus' heliocentric theory of the solar system against biblical literalists by arguing, in the first place, that Scripture was not concerned with physics, and in the second, that its manner of speaking was "accommodated to the understanding and way of speech of the common people, like nurses to little children." Both these arguments derive directly from Calvin, who may be argued to have made a fundamental contribution to the emergence of the natural sciences in this respect.

Fresh controversy broke out over the heliocentric model of the solar system in Italy during the early decades of the seventeenth century. This eventually led to the Roman Catholic church condemning Galileo Galilei (1564–1642), in what is widely regarded as a clear error of judgment on the part of some ecclesiastical bureaucrats. Galileo mounted a major defense of the Copernican theory of the solar system. Galileo's views were initially received sympathetically within senior church circles, partly on account of the fact that he was held in high regard by a papal favorite, Giovanni Ciampoli. Ciampoli's fall from power led to Galileo losing support within papal circles, and is widely regarded as opening the way to Galileo's condemnation by his enemies.

Although the controversy centering on Galileo is often portrayed as science versus religion, or libertarianism versus authoritarianism, the real issue concerned the correct interpretation of the Bible. Appreciation of this point is thought to have been hindered in the past on account of the failure of historians to engage with the theological (and, more precisely, the hermeneutical) issues attending the debate. In part, this can be seen as reflecting the fact that many of the scholars interested in this particular controversy were scientists or historians of science, who were not familiar with the intricacies of the debates on biblical interpretation of this remarkably complex period. Nevertheless, it is clear that the issue which dominated the discussion between Galileo and his critics was that of how to interpret certain biblical passages. The issue of accommodation was of major important to that debate, as we shall see.

To explore this point, we may turn to a significant work published in January 1615. In his *Lettera sopra l'opinione de' Pittagorici e del Copernico* ("Letter on the opinion of the Pythagoreans and Copernicus"), the Carmelite friar Paolo Antonio Foscarini argued that the heliocentric model of the solar system was not incompatible with the Bible. Foscarini did not introduce any new principles of biblical interpretation in his analysis; rather, he sets out and applies traditional rules of interpretation:

When Holy Scripture attributes something to God or to any other creature which would otherwise be improper and incommensurate, then it should be interpreted and explained in one or more of the following ways. First, it is said to pertain metaphorically and proportionally, or by similitude. Second, it is said . . . according to our mode of consideration, apprehension, understanding, knowing, etc. Thirdly, it is said according to vulgar opinion and the common way of speaking.

The second and third ways which Foscarini identifies are generally regarded as types of "accommodation," the third model of biblical interpretation noted above. As we have seen, this approach to biblical interpretation can be traced back to the first Christian centuries, and was not regarded as controversial.

Foscarini's innovation did not lie in the interpretative method he adopted, but in the biblical passages to which he applied it. In other words, Foscarini suggested that certain passages, which many had interpreted literally up to this point, were to be interpreted in an accommodated manner. The passages to which he applied this approach were those which seemed to suggest that the earth remained stationary, and the sun moved. Foscarini argued as follows:

Scripture speaks according to our mode of understanding, and according to appearances, and in respect to us. For thus it is that these bodies appear to be related to us and are described by the common and vulgar mode of human thinking, namely, the earth seems to stand still and to be immobile, and the sun seems to rotate around it. And hence Scripture serves us by speaking in the vulgar and common manner; for from our point of view it does seem that the earth stands firmly in the center and that the sun revolves around it, rather than the contrary.

Galileo's growing commitment to the Copernican position led him to adopt an approach to biblical interpretation similar to Foscarini's.

The real issue was how to interpret the Bible. Galileo's critics argued that some biblical passages contradicted him. For example, they argued, Joshua 10: 12 spoke of the sun standing still at Joshua's command. Did not that prove beyond reasonable doubt that it was the sun which moved around the earth? In his *Letter to the Grand Countess Christina*, Galileo countered with an argument that this was simply a common way of speaking. Joshua could not be expected to know the intricacies of celestial mechanics, and therefore used an "accommodated" way of speaking.

The official condemnation of this viewpoint was based on two considerations:

1   Scripture is to be interpreted according "to the proper meaning of the words." The accommodated approach adopted by Foscarini is

thus rejected in favor of a more literal approach. As we have stressed, both methods of interpretation were accepted as legimitate, and had a long history of use within Christian theology. The debate centered on the question of which was appropriate to the passages in question.

2   The Bible is to be interpreted "according to the common interpretation and understanding of the Holy Fathers and of learned theologians." In other words, it was being argued that nobody of any significance had adopted Foscarini's interpretation in the past; it was therefore to be dismissed as an innovation.

It therefore followed that the views of both Foscarini and Galileo were to be rejected as innovations, without any precedent in Christian thought.

This second point is of major importance, and needs to be examined more carefully, in that it is to be set against the long-standing and bitter debate, fuelled during the seventeenth century by the Thirty Years War (1618–48), between Protestantism and Roman Catholicism over whether the former was an innovation or a recovery of authentic Christianity. The idea of the unchangeability of the catholic tradition became an integral element of Roman Catholic polemic against Protestantism. As Jacques-Bénigne Bossuet (1627–1704), one of the most formidable apologists for Roman Catholicism, put this point in 1688:

The teaching of the church is always the same . . . The gospel is never different from what it was before. Hence, if at any time someone says that the faith includes something which yesterday was not said to be of the faith, it is always heterodoxy, which is any doctrine different from orthodoxy. There is no difficulty about recognizing false doctrine; there is no argument about it. It is recognized at once, whenever it appears, simply because it is new.

These same arguments were widely used at the opening of the century, and are clearly reflected and embodied in the official critique of Foscarini. The interpretation which he offered had never been offered before – and it was, for that reason alone, wrong.

It will therefore be clear that this critical debate over the interpretation of the Bible must be set against a complex background. The highly charged and politicized atmosphere at the time seriously prejudiced theological debate, for fear that the concession of any new approach might be seen as an indirect concession of the Protestant claim to legitimacy. To allow that Roman Catholic teaching on any matter of significance had "changed" was potentially to open the floodgates which would inevitably lead to demands for recognition of the orthodoxy of central Protestant teachings – teachings that the Roman Catholic church had been able to reject as "innovations" up to this point.

It was thus inevitable that Galileo's views would meet with resistance. They key factor was that of theological innovation: to concede Galileo's interpretation of certain biblical passages would seriously undermine the catholic criticisms of Protestantism, which involved the assertion that Protestantism introduced new (and therefore erroneous) interpretations of certain biblical passages. It was only a matter of time before his views would be rejected. It is generally agreed that Galileo's positive reputation in ecclesiastical circles until a surprisingly late date was linked to his close relationship with the papal favourite, Giovanni Ciampoli. When Ciampoli fell from grace in the spring of 1632, Galileo found his position seriously weakened, perhaps to the point of being fatally compromised. Without the protection of Ciampoli, Galileo was vulnerable to the charges of "heresy through innovation" which were levelled against him by his critics.

The Heliocentric Worldview

Key Feature:
The older geocentric (= "earth-centered") worldview was found incapable of explaining planetary motion. These difficulties were relieved (but not entirely resolved) by Copernicus' suggestion that the earth and other planets moved around the sun in circular orbits. The final development, which allowed most aspects of planetary motion to be understood, was Kepler's hypothesis that the earth and planets revolved around the sun in elliptical, rather than circular, orbits.

Key names:
Nicholas Copernicus (1473–1543)
Tycho Brahe (1546–1601)
Johannes Kepler (1571–1630)
Galileo Galilei (1564–1642)

Religious significance:
Challenged the traditional view that the earth stood at the center of the universe, which had been held to be supported by certain biblical passages, and by the writings of a number of influential theologians.

The Mechanistic Universe: Newton and Deism

The rise of the heliocentric model of the solar system had clarified issues of geometry; issues of mechanics, however, remained unresolved. Kepler had established that the square of the periodic time of a planet is directly proportional to the cube of its mean distance from the sun. But what was the basis of this law? What deeper significance did it possess? Could the motion of the earth, moon, and planets all be accounted for on the basis of a single principle? Part of the genius of Isaac Newton (1642–1727) lay in his demonstration that a single principle could be seen as lying behind "celestial mechanics."

Newton's particular contribution can be seen as lying in noticing the connection between observations which had hitherto not been considered to be related in any way, and giving increasing precision to ideas which had until then been discussed in a generally vague manner. Such was the force of Newton's demonstration of the mechanics of the solar system that the poet Alexander Pope was moved to write the following lines as Newton's epitaph:

> Nature and Nature's Law lay hid in Night
> God said, let Newton be, and all was Light.

Newton used the basic concepts of mass, space, and time. Each of these concepts can be measured, and are capable of being handled mathematically. Although Newton's emphasis on mass has now been replaced by an interest in momentum (the product of mass and velocity), these basic themes continue to be of major significance in classical physics. On the basis of his three fundamental concepts, he was able to develop precise ideas of acceleration, force, momentum, and velocity.

The most helpful way to understand Newton's demonstration of the laws of planetary motion is to think of Newton establishing a series of principles which govern the behavior of objects on earth, and subsequently extrapolating these same principles to the motion of the planets. For example, consider the famous story of Newton noticing an apple falling to the earth. The same force which attracted the apple to the earth could, in Newton's view, operate between the sun and the planets. The gravitational attraction between the earth and an apple is precisely the same force which operates between the sun and a planet, or the earth and the moon.

Newton initally concentrated his attention on uncovering the laws which governed motion. His three laws of motion established the general principles relating to terrestial motion. The critical development lay in his assumption that these same laws could be applied to celestial as much as to terrestial mechanics. Newton began work on his planetary theory as early as 1666. Taking his laws of motion as his starting point, he addressed Kepler's three laws of planetary motion. It was a relatively simple matter to demonstrate that Kepler's second law could be understood if there exists a force between the planet and the sun, directed towards the sun. The first law could be explained if it was assumed that the force between the planet and sun was inversely proportional to the square of the distance between them. This force could be determined mathematically, on the basis of what would later be termed "the Law of Universal Gravitation," which can be stated as follows:

Any two material bodies, P and P', with masses m and m', attract each other with a force F, given by the formula $F = Gmm'/d^2$

where d is their distance apart, and G is the Constant of Gravitation. It should be noted that Newton did not need to determine the precise value of G to explain Kepler's laws.

Newton applied the laws of motion to the orbit of the moon around the earth. On the basis of the assumption that the force which attracted an apple to fall to the earth also held the moon in its orbit around the earth, and that this force was inversely proportional to the square of the distance between the moon and the earth, Newton was able to calculate the period of the moon's orbit. It proved to be incorrect by a factor of roughly 10 per cent. In fact, the error arose through an inaccuracy in relation to the distance between the earth and the moon. Newton had simply used the prevailing estimate of this distance; on using a value which was more accurate, determined by the French astronomer Jean Picard in 1672, theory and observation proved to be in agreement.

It is not our intention to provide a full historical analysis of precisely how and when Newton arrived at his conclusions, nor to set them out in detail. The important point to appreciate is that Newton was able to demonstrate that a vast range of observational data could be explained on the basis of a set of universal principles. Newton's successes in explaining terrestial and celestial mechanics led to the rapid development of the idea that the universe could be thought of as a great machine, acting according to fixed laws. This is often referred to as a "mechanistic worldview," in that the operation of nature is explained on the assumption that it is a machine operating according to fixed rules.

The religious implications of this will be clear. The idea of the world as a machine immediately suggested the idea of *design*. Newton himself was supportive of this interpretation. Although later writers tended to suggest that the mechanism in question was totally self-contained and self-sustaining – and therefore did not require the existence of a God – this view was not widely held in the 1690s. Perhaps the most famous application of Newton's approach is found in the writings of William Paley, who compared the complexity of the natural world with the design of a watch. Both implied design and purpose, and thus pointed to a creator.

The success of Newton's mechanistic worldview led to a significant religious development, of considerable importance to our theme. It can be shown without difficulty that Newton's emphasis on the regularity of nature encouraged the rise of "Deism." The term "deism" (from the Latin *deus*, "god") is often used in a general sense to refer to that view of God which maintains God's creatorship, but denies a continuing divine involvement with, or special presence within, that creation. It is thus often contrasted with "theism" (from the Greek *theos*, "god"), which allows for continuing divine involvement within the world. Deism can be regarded as a form of Christianity which placed particular emphasis on the regularity of the world, yet which was widely regarded by its critics as having reduced God to a mere clockmaker.

The term "Deism" is used to refer to the views of a group of English thinkers during the "Age of Reason," in the late seventeenth century and early eighteenth centuries. In his influential study *The Principal Deistic Writers* (1757), John Leland grouped together a number of writers – including Lord Herbert of Cherbury, Thomas Hobbes, and David Hume – under the broad and newly-coined term "deist." Whether these writers would have approved of this designation is questionable. Close examination of their religious views shows that they have relatively little in common, apart from a general scepticism concerning several specifically Christian ideas, most notably concerning aspects of the traditional views of the nature of revelation and salvation. The Newtonian worldview offered Deism a highly sophisticated way of defending and developing their views, by allowing them to focus on the wisdom of God in creating the world.

The nature of Deism can be grasped to some extent from John Locke's *Essay concerning Human Understanding* (1690). This developed an idea of God which became characteristic of much later Deism. Indeed, Locke's *Essay* can be said to lay much of the intellectual foundations of Deism. Locke argued that "reason leads us to the knowledge of this certain and evident truth, that there is an eternal, most powerful and most knowing Being." The attributes of this being are those which human reason recognizes as appropriate for God. Having considered which moral and rational qualities are suited to the deity, Locke argues that "we enlarge every one of these with our idea of infinity, and so, putting them together, make our complex idea of God." In other words, the idea of God is made up of human rational and moral qualities, projected to infinity.

Matthew Tindal's *Christianity as Old as Creation* (1730) argued that Christianity was nothing other than the "republication of the religion of nature." God is understood as the extension of accepted human ideas of justice, rationality and wisdom. This universal religion is available at all times and in every place, whereas traditional Christianity rested upon the idea of a divine revelation which was not accessible to those who lived before Christ. Tindal's views were propagated before the modern discipline of the sociology of knowledge created scepticism of the idea of "universal reason," and are an excellent model of the rationalism characteristic of the movement, and which later became influential within the Enlightenment.

The ideas of English Deism percolated through to the continent of Europe through translations (especially in Germany), and through the writings of individuals familiar with and sympathetic to them, such as Voltaire's *Philosophical Letters*. Enlightenment rationalism is often considered to be the final flowering of the bud of English Deism. For our purposes, however, it is especially important to note the obvious consonance between deism and the Newtonian worldview; indeed, it is possible to argue that deism owed its growing intellectual acceptance in part to the successes of the Newtonian mechanical view of the world.

The amalgam of Newtonian natural philosophy and certain forms of Anglican theology proved popular and plausible in post-revolutionary England (see further pp. 98–102). Nevertheless, it was an unstable amalgam. As has often been pointed out, it was not long before the estrangement of celestial mechanics and religion began to set in. Celestial mechanics seemed to many to suggest that the world was a self-sustaining mechanism which had no need for divine governance or sustenance for its day-to-day operation. This danger had been recognized at an early stage by one of Newton's interpreters, Samuel Clark. In his correspondence with Leibniz, Clark expressed concern over the potential implications of the growing emphasis on the regularity of nature:

The notion of the world's being a great machine, going on without the interposition of God, as a clock continues to go on without the assistance of a clockmaker; is the notion of materialism and fate, and tends (under the pretence of making God a supramundane intelligence) to exclude providence, and God's government in reality of the world.

The image of God as a "clockmaker" (and the associated natural theology which appealed to the regularity of the world) was thus seen as potentially leading to a purely naturalist understanding of the universe, in which God had no continuing role to play.

The Mechanistic Worldview

Key Feature:
The solar system can be treated as a mechanism which operates according to certain definite universal principles. The same principles which govern the motion of bodies on earth can also be shown to govern the movements of the planets.

Key name:
Isaac Newton (1642–1727)

Religious significance:
Newtonianism created a new interest in natural theology for a while, in that the regularity of the world was seen as being evidence for the divine design of nature. As time progressed, Newtonianism came to be seen as eliminating the need for God at many levels. The universe was seen as a self-governing and self-sustaining mechanism which does not require God's involvement. The religious movement now known as "Deism" was influenced by Newtonian ideas.

If God was being excluded from the mechanics of the world, there were many who suggested that divine design and activity was still to be found in the biological realm. It is at this point that we need to turn to consider the nineteenth-century Darwinian controversy, which opened up a new area of scientific debate, not least in relation to religious beliefs.

The Origins of Humanity: The Darwinian Controversy

In the previous section, we suggested that the various components of Newton's theory of planetary motion had already been identified by other scholars; Newton's genius lay in relating observations which others had not regarded as having any connection with each other. It is possible to argue that something similar applies to the case of Charles Darwin (1809–82). Among the studies which prepared the way for Darwin's theory, particular attention should be paid to Charles Lyell's *Principles of Geology* (1830). The prevailing popular understanding of the history of the earth from its creation took the form of a series of catastrophic changes. Lyell argued for "uniformitarianism" (a term which was coined by James Hutton in 1795), in which the same forces which can now be observed at work within the natural world are argued to have been active over huge expanses of time in the past. Darwin's theory of evolution works on a related assumption: that forces which lead to the development of new breeds of plants or animals in the present operate over very long periods of time in the past.

The major rival to Darwin's theory was due to the eighteenth-century Swedish naturalist Carl von Linné (1707–78), more generally known by the Latinized form of his name, "Carolus Linnaeus." Linnaeus argued for the "fixity of species." In other words, the present range of species which can be observed in the natural world represents the way things have been in the past, and the way they will remain. Linnaeus' detailed classification of species conveyed the impression to many of his readers that nature was fixed from the moment of its origination. This seemed to fit in rather well with a traditional and popular reading of the Genesis creation accounts, and suggested that the botanical world of today more or less corresponded to that established in creation. Each species could be regarded as having been created separately and distinctly by God, and endowed with its fixed characterisics.

The difficulty which was pointed out, particularly by Buffon, was that the fossil evidence suggested that certain species had become extinct. In other words, fossils were found which contained the preserved remains of plants (and animals) which now had no known counterpart on the earth. Did not this seem to contradict the assumption of the fixity of species? And if old species died out, might not new ones arise to replace them? Other issues seemed to cause some difficulty for the theory of special creation – for example, the irregular geographical distribution of species.

It will be helpful to set out the specific observations which needed to be explained. For Darwin, the issues which required to be explained included the following:

1 The problem of explaining adaptation; that is, the manner in which organism's forms are adapted to their needs. A ready explanation of one type was available from the doctrine of special creation, which posited that the creator caused each organism's form to be related to its environmental needs.

2 The question of why some species die out. It is known that Darwin's discovery of Thomas Malthus' theories on population growth had a significant impact on his thinking on this issue. It was not initially clear how the extinction of seemingly well-adapted and successful species could be explained without recourse to "catastrophe" theories.

3 The uneven geographical distribution of life-forms throughout the world. Darwin's personal research trips on the *Beagle* convinced him of the importance of developing a theory which could explain the peculiarities of island populations.

4 Vestigial structures – such as the nipples of male mammals – were difficult to accommodate on the basis of the concept of special creation, in that they appeared to be redundant and serve no apparent purpose.

Darwin's task was to develop an explanation which would account for these observations more satisfactorily than the alternatives which were then available, especially the theory of special creation. The story of how Darwin arived at these insights, partly through his voyage on the *Beagle*, is fascinating, and worth following through in greater detail. Although the historical account of how Darwin arrived at his theory has perhaps been subject of a degree of romantic embellishment, it is clear that the driving force behind his reflections was the belief that the morphological and geographical phenomena could be convincingly accounted for by a single theory of natural selection. Darwin himself was quite clear that his explanation of the biological evidence was not the only one which could be adduced. He did, however, believe that it possessed greater explanatory power than its rivals, such as the doctrine of special creation. "Light has been shown on several facts, which on the theory of special creation are utterly obscure."

The basic elements of Darwin's theory are the following. Darwin argues that a process of "natural selection" takes place within nature. The opening chapters of *The Origin of Species* notes the way in which new breeds of plants and animals are developed by commercial breeders. A similar process, he argues, can be seen to operate within nature. Variations arise within nature; the question is then whether the new variant is better adapted for survival than those which preceded it. If they are better adapted, they are more likely to survive, with the result that their characteristics will be inherited by their successors. The phase "the survival of the fittest" (originally coined by Herbert Spencer) would later be used to describe this process.

The notion of a competition within nature for survival reflects Darwin's reading of the writings of Thomas Malthus (1766–1834) on populations. Competition means that those species that are bested adapted will be more likely to survive. In his earlier thinking on the origins of species, Darwin had experienced some difficulty in accounting for why certain species had died out when they seemed to be successful and well-adapted. Darwin's initial hypothesis had been that it was necessary to invoke some form of "catastrophe theory" to explain their extinction. Malthus' theories of population growth, set out in his *Essay on the Principle of Population* (1798), offered another and more persuasive explanation – that competition for survival meant that a well-adapted species would be overwhelmed by a better-adapted species. Darwin thus set out what he term "the doctrine of Malthus applied with manifold force to the whole animal and vegetable kingdoms."

In the end, Darwin's theory had many weaknesses and loose ends. For example, it required that the emergence of new species (generally referred to as "speciation") should take place; yet the evidence for this was conspicuously absent. Darwin himself devoted a large section of *The Origin of Species* to detailing difficulties with his theory, noting in particular the "imperfection of the geological record," which gave little indication of the existence of intermediate species, and the "extreme perfection and complication" of certain individual organs, such as the eye. Nevertheless, he was convinced that these were difficulties which could be tolerated on account of the clear explanatory superiority of his approach. Yet even though Darwin did not believe that he had adequately dealt with all the problems which required resolution, he was confident that his explanation was the best available:

A crowd of difficulties will have occurred to the reader. Some of them are so grave that to this day I can never reflect on them without being staggered; but, to the best of my judgement, the greater number are only apparent, and those are are real are not, I think, fatal to my theory.

Those theories were set out in two major works: *The Origin of Species* (1859) and *Descent of Man* (1871). Taken together, the two works argue that all species – including humanity – result from a long and complex process of biological evolution. The religious implications of this will be clear. Traditional Christian thought regarded humanity as being set apart from the rest of nature, created as the height of God's creation, and alone endowed with the "image of God." Darwin's theory suggested that human nature emerged gradually, over a long period of time, and that no fundamental biological distinction could be drawn between human beings and animals in terms of their origins and development.

The popular account of the Darwinian controversy at this point focuses on the meeting of the British Association at Oxford on June 30, 1860. The British Association had always seen one of its most significant objectives as being to popularize science. As Darwin's *Origin of Species* had been published the previous year, it was natural that it should be a subject of discussion at the 1860 meeting. Darwin himself was in ill health, and was unable to attend the meeting in person. According to the popular legend, Samuel Wilberforce, Bishop of Oxford, attempted to pour scorn on the theory of evolution by suggesting that it implied that humans were recently descended from monkeys. He was then duly rebuked by T. H. Huxley, who turned the tables on him, showing him up to be an ignorant and arrogant cleric. The classic statement of this legend dates from 1898, and takes the form of an autobiographical memory from Mrs Isabella Sidgewick, published in *Macmillan's Magazine*:

I was happy enough to be present on the memorable occasion at Oxford when Mr Huxley bearded Bishop Wilberforce ... The Bishop rose, and in a light scoffing tone, florid and fluent, he assured us that there was nothing in the idea of evolution; rock pigeons were what rock pigeons had always been. Then, turning to his antagonist with a smiling insolence, he begged to know, was it through his grandfather or his grandmother that he claimed descent from a monkey?

The account, which dates from 1898, contradicts accounts published or in circulation closer to the meeting itself. The truth of the matter was that Wilberforce had written an extensive review of the *Origin of Species*, pointing out some serious weaknesses. Darwin regarded this review as significant, and modified his discussion at several points in response to Wilberforce's criticisms. The review shows no trace of "ecclesiastical obscurantism". Nevetheless, by 1900 the legend was firmly established, and went some way towards reinforcing the "conflict" or "warfare" model of the interaction of science and religion – a theme to which we shall return in the following chapter.

Darwinianism

Key theme:
The various types of plant and animal life (including human beings) came into existence through a process of natural selection, in which those species which were better adapted for survival displaced others, which gradually became extinct.

Key name:
Charles Darwin (1809–82)

Religious significance:
Darwinianism challenged the traditional Christian idea that all life owed its specific characteristics to individual acts of divine creation. More particularly, it called into question the unique and privileged position of humanity as the apex of God's creation.

The present chapter has explored three major issues in the history of the interaction of science and religion, focusing on Christianity. It must be stressed that the issues raised relate to most religions, particularly Judaism and Islam, and not simply to Christianity. As we have stressed, Christianity was particularly involved in these disputes on account of its dominance in the areas in which the natural sciences developed.

But is that an historical accident? Or is there some reason for suggesting that Christianity has some connection with the development of the natural sciences? In the next chapter, we shall consider some further historical and theoretical issues relating to the theme of science and religion.

For further reading

Biagioli, M. *Galileo, Courtier: The Practice of Science in the Culture of Absolutism*. Chicago: University of Chicago Press, 1993.

Blackwell, R. J. *Galileo, Bellarmine and the Bible*. Notre Dame, IN: University of Notre Dame Press, 1991.

Brotóns, V. N. "The Reception of Copernicus in Sixteenth-Century Spain: The Case of Diego de Zúñiga." *Isis* 86 (1995): 52–78.

Clagett, M. *Giovanni Marliani and Late Medieval Physics*. New York: Columbia University Press, 1941.

Cohen, I. B. *The Newtonian Revolution*. Cambridge: Cambridge University Press, 1980.

Durant, J. *Darwinism and Divinity*. Oxford and New York: Basil Blackwell, 1985.

Gale, B. G. *Evolution without Evidence: Charles Darwin and The Origin of Species*. Albuquerque: University of New Mexico Press, 1982.

Garrison, J. W. "Newton and the Relation of Mathematics to Natural Philosophy." *Journal of the History of Ideas* 48 (1987): 609–27.

Gillespie, N. C. *Charles Darwin and the Problem of Creation*. Chicago: University of Chicago Press, 1979.

Glick, T. F. *The Comparative Reception of Darwinism*. Austin: University of Texas Press, 1972.

Grant, E. *The Foundations of Science in the Middle Ages: Their Religious, Institutional and Intellectual Contexts*. Cambridge: Cambridge University Press, 1996.

——. *Planets, Stars and Orbs: The Medieval Cosmos, 1200–1687*. Cambridge: Cambridge University Press, 1996.

Hall, A. R. *Isaac Newton: Adventurer in Thought*. Cambridge: Cambridge University Press, 1996.

Hooykaas, R. "Calvin and Copernicus." *Organon* 10 (1974): 139–48.

Hull, D. L. *Darwin and his Critics*. Cambridge: Harvard University Press, 1973.

Jacob, M. C. *The Newtonians and the English Revolution 1689–1720*. London: Harvester, 1976.

Lucas, J. R. "Wilberforce and Huxley: A Legendary Encounter." *Historical Journal* 22 (1979): 313–30.

Manuel, F. E. *The Religion of Isaac Newton*. Oxford: Clarendon Press, 1974.

McGuire, J. E. "Force, Active Principles and Newton's Invisible Realm." *Ambix* 15 (1968): 154–208.

Moore, J. R. *The Post-Darwinian Controversies: A Study of the Protestant Struggle to come to terms with Darwin in Great Britain and America, 1870–1900*. Cambridge: Cambridge University Press, 1979.

Murdin, L. *Under Newton's Shadow: Astronomical Practices in the Seventeenth Century*. Bristol: Adam Hilger, 1985.

Pedersen, O. *Galileo and the Council of Trent*. Vatican City: Specolo Vaticana, 1983.

Richards, R. J. *Darwin and the Emergence of Evolutionary Theories of Mind and Behaviour*. Chicago: University of Chicago Press, 1987.

Schaffer, S. "Glass Works: Newton's Prism and the Uses of Experiment." *The Uses of Experiment: Studies in the Natural Science*. Ed. David Gooding, Trevor Pinch and Simon Schaffre. Cambridge: Cambridge University Press, 1989, pp. 67–104.

Sylla, E. D. "The a posteriori Foundations of Natural Science. Some Medieval Commentaries on Aristotle's *Physics*." *Synthese* 40 (1979): 147–87.

Westfall, R. S. "Galileo and the Jesuits." *Metaphysics and Philosophy of Science in the Seventeenth and Eighteenth Centuries*. Ed. R. S. Woolhouse. Dordrecht: Kluwer, 1988, pp. 45–72.

Westman, R. S. "Proof, Poetics and Patronage: Copernicus' Preface to *De Revolutionibus*." *Reappraisals of the Scientific Revolution*. Ed. David C. Lindberg and Robert S. Westman. Cambridge: Cambridge University Press, 1990, pp. 167–205.

White, R. "Calvin and Copernicus: The Problem Reconsidered." *Calvin Theological Journal* 15 (1980): 233–43.

Wilson, C. A. "Rheticus, Ravetz and the 'Necessity' of Copernicus' Innovation." *The Copernican Achievement*. Ed. Robert S. Westman. London: University of California Press, 1975, pp. 17–39.

2
Religion: Ally or Enemy of Science?

In the previous chapter, we explored some of the historical debates which focused on the relation of science and religion. That brief discussion raises a significant question, which we can state as follows: is religion a stimulus or a hindrance to the development of the natural science? It is tempting to offer a simple answer to the question of whether religion is the ally or enemy of science. The question, however, demands a complex answer, for the following reasons:

1 The question presupposes that there is some uniform entity called "science," whereas in fact there are a number of scientific disciplines, each with its own distinctive sphere of study and associated method of investigation. As we shall explore later in this study, the inter-action of physics and religion is significantly different from that of biology and religion. The term "science" needs to be qualified or further defined before the question can be answered properly.
2 The question also assumes that "religion" is some easily defined and homogeneous phenomenon. In fact, this is not the case. It is remarkably difficult to offer a viable definition of what consitutes a religion. A number of significantly different understandings of the nature of religion, each claiming to be "scientific" or "objective," has emerged during the last century. Certain of these attempts (most notably those of Karl Marx, Sigmund Freud and Emile Durkheim) have been strongly reductionist, generally reflecting the personal or institutional agendas of those who developed them. These reductive approaches have been subjected to severe criticism by writers such as Mircea Eliade on account of their obvious inadequacies. More significantly, different religions would seen to encourage different

approaches to the sciences, requiring the religion in question to be specified before a meaningful answer can be given. The relation between Christianity and physics cannot be assumed to be the same as that between Islam or Hinduism and physics.

3 Even within a single religion, a number of different strands of thought need to be discerned. It is unwise to assume that each of these strands adopts an identical approach to the issue. For example, we shall be considering four different strands in modern Christian theology later in this chapter, and noting the significantly different responses which they offer to the question.

Our attention is first claimed by the question of what the elusive word "religion" actually means.

Defining "Religion": Some Clarifications

It must be stressed that definitions of religion are rarely neutral, but are often generated to favor beliefs and institutions with which one is in sympathy and penalize those to which one is hostile. Definitions of religions often depend on the particular purposes and prejudices of individual scholars. Thus a writer who has a particular concern to show that all religions give access to the same divine reality will develop a definition of religion which embodies this belief (for example, F. Max Mueller's famous definition of religion as "a disposition which enables men to apprehend the Infinite under different names and disguises"). A similar agenda underlies more recent writings which are committed to the view that all religions are simply local culturally-conditioned responses to the same basic transcendent ultimate reality.

In order to appreciate the historical complexities of the interaction of science and religion, it is essential to treat each religion on its own terms. Christianity is not the same as Buddhism, and the differences between them may well be of critical importance in helping us understand why the natural sciences developed in a Christian rather than a Buddhist context. The historical investigation of such questions will be seriously prejudiced by the unwarranted assumption that "all religions say the same thing."

Perhaps the wisest approach is to respect the integrity of the different religions of the world, rather than attempt to homogenize their ideas or force them into a common mould. There is a growing consensus that it is seriously misleading to regard the various religious traditions of the world as variations on a single theme. "There is no single essence, no one content of enlightenment or revelation, no one way of emancipation or liberation, to be found in all that plurality" (David Tracy). John B. Cobb Jr. also notes the enormous difficulties confronting anyone wishing to argue that there is an "essence of religion."

Arguments about what religion truly is are pointless. There is no such thing as religion. There are only traditions, movements, communities, peoples, beliefs, and practices that have features that are associated by many people with what they mean by religion.

Cobb stresses that the assumption that religion has an essence has bedevilled and seriously misled recent discussion of the relation of the religious traditions of the world. For example, he points out that both Buddhism and Confucianism have "religious" elements – but that does not necessarily mean that they can be categorized as "religions." Many "religions" are, according to Cobb, better understood as cultural movements with religious components.

The idea of some universal notion of religion, of which individual religions are subsets, is a very western idea, which appears to have emerged at the time of the Enlightenment. To use a biological analogy, the assumption that there is a genus of religion, of which individual religions are species, is a very western idea, without any real parallel outside western culture – except on the part of those who have been educated in the west, and uncritically absorbed its presuppositions.

Writers specializing in fieldwork anthropology (such as E. E. Evans-Pritchard and Clifford E. Geertz) have offered more complex and reflective models of religion. A major debate within contemporary anthropology and sociology of religion concerns whether religion is to be defined "functionally" (religion has to do with certain social or personal functions of ideas and rituals) or "substantially" (religion has to do with certain beliefs concerning divine or spiritual beings). Despite widespread differences in terminology (many writers disagreeing over the propriety of key terms such as "supernatural", "spiritual", and "mystical"), there appears to be at least some measure of genuine agreement that religion, however conceived, in some way involves belief and behavior linked with a supernatural realm of divine or spiritual beings.

For our purposes, we shall not attempt to resolve this debate. The important thing is to note that the term "religion" is less easily defined that one would like. It is considerably more productive and valuable to compare individual religions (such as Christianity or Islam) in their relationships to the natural sciences. However, it is important to appreciate that there are significant variations within religions, as will become clear from what follows.

Varieties within a Religion: The Case of Christianity

As we have stressed in the present chapter, the religion which has been most deeply involved in the interaction between religion and natural science is Christianity. Nevertheless, the term "Christian" can refer to a wide variety of intellectual positions, requiring further clarification. Protestant, Roman Catholic, and Eastern Orthodox forms of Christianity are, for example, quite distinct. Our attention, however, particularly concerns the more academic levels of discussion within western Christianity, on account of its close interaction with the natural sciences over the last few centuries.

Any attempt to understand the complex relationship of Christian theology and the sciences requires at least some degree of familiarity with the main schools of Christian thought in the modern period. In what follows, we shall outline four major schools of thought within western Christianity which have all been of major importance in relation to their interaction with the natural sciences. There exist significant differences within western Christianity over a number of issues, and that these issues often have a direct bearing on their attitude towards the natural sciences. For example, Liberal Protestantism has tended to have a very positive attitude towards the natural sciences, whereas Neo-Orthodoxy has tended to insist that religion and science belong to totally different spheres of activity.

Liberal protestantism

Liberal Protestantism is unquestionably one of the most important movements to have arisen within modern Christian thought. Its origins are complex. However, it is helpful to think of it as having arisen in response to the theological programme set out by F. D. E. Schleiermacher (1768–1834), especially in relation to his emphasis upon human "feeling," and the need to relate Christian faith to the human situation. Classic liberal Protestantism had its origins in the Germany of the mid-nineteenth century, amidst a growing realization that Christian faith and theology alike require reconstruction in the light of modern knowledge. In England, the increasingly positive reception given to Charles Darwin's theory of natural selection (popularly known as the "Darwinian theory of evolution") created a climate in which some traditional Christian theology (such as the doctrine of the seven days of creation) seemed to be increasingly untenable. From its outset, liberalism was committed to bridging the gap between Christian faith and modern knowledge.

Liberalism's program required a significant degree of flexibility in relation to traditional Christian theology. Its leading writers argued that reconstruction of belief was essential if Christianity was to remain a serious intellectual option in the modern world. For this reason, they demanded a degree of freedom in relation to the doctrinal inheritance of Christianity on the one hand, and traditional methods of biblical interpretation on the other. Where traditional ways of interpreting Scripture, or traditional beliefs, seemed to be compromised by developments in human knowledge, it was imperative that they should be discarded or reinterpreted to bring them into line with what was now known about the world.

The theological implications of this shift in direction were considerable. A number of Christian beliefs came to be regarded as seriously out of line with modern cultural norms; these suffered one of two fates:

1 They were abandoned as resting upon outdated or mistaken presuppositions. The doctrine of original sin is a case in point; this was put down to a misreading of the New Testament in the light of the writings of St Augustine, whose judgment on these matters had become clouded by his overinvolvement with a fatalist sect (the Manichees).
2 They were reinterpreted, in a manner more conducive to the spirit of the age. A number of central doctrines relating to the person of Jesus Christ may be included in this category, including his divinity (which was reinterpreted as an affirmation of Jesus exemplifying qualities which humanity as a whole could hope to emulate).

Alongside this process of doctrinal reinterpretation (which continued in the "history of dogma" movement) may be seen a new concern to ground Christian faith in the world of humanity – above all, in human experience and modern culture. Sensing potential difficulties in grounding Christian faith in an exclusive appeal to Scripture or the person of Jesus Christ, liberalism sought to anchor that faith in common human experience, and interpret in ways that made sense within the modern worldview.

Liberalism was inspired by the vision of a humanity which was ascending upwards into new realms of progress and prosperity. The doctrine of evolution gave new vitality to this belief, which was nurtured by strong evidence of cultural stability in western Europe in the late nineteenth century. Religion came increasingly to be seen as relating to the spiritual needs of modern humanity, and giving ethical guidance to society. The strongly ethical dimension of liberal Protestantism is especially evident in the writings of Albrecht Benjamin Ritschl.

For Ritschl, the idea of the "kingdom of God" was of central importance. Ritschl tended to think of this as a static realm of ethical values, which would undergird the development of German society at this point in its history. History, it was argued, was in the process of being divinely guided towards perfection. Civilization is seen as part of this process of evolution. In the course of human history, a number of individuals appear who are recognized as being the bearers of special divine insights. One such individual was Jesus. By following his example and sharing in his inner life, other human beings are able to develop. The movement showed enormous and unbounded optimism in human ability and potential. Religion and culture were, it was argued, virtually identical. Later critics of the movement dubbed it "culture Protestantism," on account of their belief that it was too heavily dependent upon accepted cultural norms.

Many critics – such as Karl Barth in Europe and Reinhold Niebuhr in North America – regarded liberal Protestantism as based upon a hopelessly optimistic view of human nature. They believed that this optimism had been destroyed by the events of the First World War, and that liberalism would henceforth lack cultural credibility. This has proved to be a considerable misjudgment. At its best, liberalism may be regarded as a movement committed to the restatement of Christian faith in forms which are acceptable within contemporary culture. Liberalism has continued to see itself as a mediator between two unacceptable alternatives: the mere restatement of traditional Christian faith (usually described as "traditionalism" or "fundamentalism" by its liberal critics), and the rejection of Christianity in its totality. Liberal writers have been passionately committed to the search for a middle road between these two stark alternatives.

Perhaps the most developed and influential presentation of liberal Protestantism is to be found in the writings of Paul Tillich (1886–1965), who rose to fame in the United States in the late 1950s and early 1960s, towards the end of his career, and who is widely regarded as the most influential American theologian since Jonathan Edwards.

Tillich's programme can be summarized in the term "correlation." By the "method of correlation," Tillich understands the task of modern theology to be to establish a conversation between human culture and Christian faith. Tillich reacted with alarm to the theological program set out by Karl Barth, seeing this as a misguided attempt to drive a wedge between theology and culture. For Tillich, existential questions – or "ultimate questions," as he often terms them – are thrown up and revealed by human culture. Modern philosophy, writing, and the crea- tive arts point to questions which concern humans. Theology then formulates anwers to these questions, and by doing so, it correlates the gospel to modern culture. The gospel must speak to culture, and it can do so only if the actual questions raised by that culture are heard.

For David Tracy (Chicago), the image of a dialogue between the gospel and culture is controlling: that dialogue involves the mutual correction and enrichment of both gospel and culture. There is thus a close relation between theology and apologetics, in that the task of theology is understood to be that of interpreting the Christian response to the human needs disclosed by cultural analysis. It will be clear that this approach of "correlation" encourages a dialogue between religion and science, on the grounds that the latter is a significant element of modern western culture.

The term "liberal" is thus probably best interpreted as "a theologian in the tradition of Schleiermacher and Tillich, concerned with the reconstruction of belief in response to contemporary culture." Liberal- ism has been criticized on a number of points, of which the following are typical.

1   It tends to place considerable weight upon the notion of a universal human religious experience. Yet this is a vague and ill-defined notion, incapable of being examined and assessed publicly. There are also excellent reasons for suggesting that "experience" is shaped by interpretation to a far greater extent than liberalism allows.

2   Liberalism is seen by its critics as placing too great emphasis upon transient cultural developments, with the result that it often appears to be uncritically driven by a secular agenda.

3   It has been suggested that liberalism is too ready to surrender distinctive Christian doctrines in an effort to become acceptable to contemporary culture.

Liberal Protestantism is of considerable importance to our study, in that it adopts a generally positive attitude towards the religious significance of the natural sciences. This was especially clear in the case of the Darwinian theory of evolution, which was seen by many Liberal Protestant writers as illustrating the way in which human nature and society were developing upwards. Liberalism was generally inclined to interpret potentially difficult passages of the Bible in ways which reduced their supernatural significance, and found little difficulty in harmonizing the biblical accounts of creation with the Darwinian theory of evolution. Although liberalism retained traditional Christian ideas (where modernism, which we shall discuss presently, was happy to abandon them), they reinterpreted them in a manner which was conducive to the emerging consensus on biological evolution.

Similarly positive attitudes towards the natural sciences are associated with the movement generally known as "Modernism," to which we now turn.

Modernism

The term "modernist" was first used to refer to a school of Roman Catholic theologians operating toward the end of the nineteenth century, which adopted a critical and sceptical attitude to traditional Christian doctrines, especially those relating to Christology and soteriology. The movement fostered a positive attitude to radical biblical criticism, and stressed the ethical, rather than the more theological, dimensions of faith. In many ways, modernism may be seen as an attempt by writers within the Roman Catholic church to come to terms with the outlook of the Enlightenment which had, until that point, largely been ignored by that church.

"Modernism" is, however, a loose term, which should not be understood to imply the existence of a distinctive school of thought, committed to certain common methods or indebted to common teachers. It is certainly true that most modernist writers were concerned to integrate Christian thought with the spirit of the Enlightenment, especially the new understandings of history and the natural sciences which were then gaining the ascendency. Equally, some modernist writers drew inspiration from writers such as Maurice Blondel (1861–1949), who argued that the supernatural was intrinsic to human existence, or Henri Bergson (1859–1941), who stressed the importance of intuition over intellect. Yet there is not sufficient commonality between the French, English and American modernists, nor between Roman Catholic and Protestant modernism, to allow the term to be understood as designating a rigorous and well-defined school.

Among Roman Catholic modernist writers, particular attention should be paid to Alfred Loisy (1857–1940) and George Tyrrell (1861–1909). During the 1890s, Loisy established himself as a critic of traditional views of the biblical accounts of creation, and argued that a real development of doctrine could be discerned within scripture. His most significant publication, *L'évangile et l'église* ("The Gospel and the Church"), appeared in 1902. This important work was a direct response to the views of Adolf von Harnack, published two years earlier as *What is Christianity?*, on the origins and nature of Christianity. Loisy rejected Harnack's suggestion that there was a radical discontinuity between Jesus and the church; however, he made significant concessions to Harnack's liberal Protestant account of Christian origins, including an acceptance of the role and validity of biblical criticism in interpreting the gospels. As a result, the work was placed upon the list of prohibited books by the Roman Catholic authorities in 1903.

The British Jesuit writer George Tyrrell followed Loisy in his radical criticism of traditional catholic dogma. In common with Loisy, he criticized Harnack's account of Christian origins in *Christianity at the Crossroads* (1909), dismissing Harnack's historical reconstruction of Jesus as "the reflection of a Liberal Protestant face, seen at the bottom of a deep well." The work also included a defence of Loisy's work, arguing that the official Roman Catholic "hostility to the book and its author have created a general impression that it is a defence of Liberal Protestant against Roman Catholic positions, and that "Modernism" is simply a protestantizing and rationalizing movement."

In part, this perception may be due to the growing influence of modernist attitudes within the mainstream Protestant denominations. In England, the Churchmen's Union was founded in 1898 for the advancement of liberal religious thought; in 1928, it altered its name to the Modern Churchmen's Union. Among those especially associated with this group may be noted Hastings Rashdall (1858–1924), whose *Idea of Atonement in Christian Theology* (1919) illustrates the general tenor of English modernism. Drawing somewhat uncritically upon the earlier writings of liberal Protestant thinkers such as Ritschl, Rashdall argued that the theory of the atonement associated with the medieval writer Peter Abelard was more acceptable to modern thought forms than traditional theories which made an appeal to the notion of a substitutionary sacrifice. This strongly moral or exemplarist theory of the atonement, which interpreted Christ's death virtually exclusively as a demonstration of the love of God, made a considerable impact upon English, and especially Anglican, thought in the 1920s and 1930s. Nevertheless, the events of the Great War (1914–18), and the subsequent rise of fascism in Europe in the 1930s, undermined the credibility of the movement. It was not until the 1960s that a renewed modernism or radicalism became a significant feature of English Christianity.

The rise of modernism in the United States follows a similar pattern. The growth of liberal Protestantism in the late nineteenth and early twentieth centuries was widely perceived as a direct challenge to more conservative evangelical standpoints. Newman Smyth's *Passing Protestantism and Coming Catholicism* (1908) argued that Roman Catholic modernism could serve as a mentor to American Protestantism in several ways, not least in its critique of dogma and its historical understanding of the development of doctrine. The situation became increasingly polarized through the rise of the movement now known as "fundamentalism" in response to modernist attitudes.

Modernism is of major importance to our study, in view of its strong support for Darwinian theories of evolution. Always more radical than liberalism, modernism saw no difficulty in eliminating those aspects of Christian thought which they found inconvenient. This is perhaps most clearly seen in relation to its attitude to biological evolution. Modernism seemed to deify evolution, by investing the evolutionary process with supernatural significance through an appeal to spiritual or cosmic forces which guided that process towards its goal. This is particularly clear in the writings of Henri Bergson, whose *Creative Evolution* developed the idea of the evolutionary process being guided by a "vital impulse (*élan vital*) within nature. Bergson detected within nature an immanent force which caused it to strive upwards, reaching out for as yet unacheived goals. While Bergson was decidedly vague about the precise nature of this "vital impulse" (or how it might be observed), it possessed a certain

Romantic attraction which captured the imaginatiobn of many of his contemporaries. George Tyrrell is known to have been sympathetic to an idea of divine immanence within nature similar to that of Bergson.

For the modernists, much traditional Christian theology rested on a series of misunderstandings or mistakes. The rise of the natural sciences offered a corrective to these mistakes, and thus allowed Christian theologians the opportunity to correct these errors. For Lyman Abbott, religion was always in the process of developing. In his *Theology of an Evolutionist* (1897), he argued that the Bible portrayed the gradual dawning of an incomplete understanding of the world and God in humanity. That understanding was still in the process of development and correction, and the natural sciences were to be seen as an important element in this process of development.

However, we must now turn back to the opening of the twentieth century, to consider an earlier reaction against liberalism, which is especially associated with the name of Karl Barth: neo-Orthodoxy. As we shall see, this movement was much less positive in its estimation of the religious role of the natural sciences.

Neo-orthodoxy

The First World War witnessed a disillusionment with, although not a final rejection of, the liberal theology which had come to be associated with Schleiermacher and his followers. A number of writers argued that Schleiermacher had, in effect, reduced Christianity to little more than religious experience, thus making it a human-, rather than God-centered, affair. The First World War, it was argued, destroyed the credibility of such an approach. Liberal theology seemed to be about human values – and how could these be taken seriously, if they led to global conflicts on such a massive scale? By stressing the "otherness" of God, writers such as Karl Barth (1886–1968) believed that they could escape from the doomed human-centered theology of liberalism.

These ideas were given systematic exposition in Barth's *Church Dogmatics* (1936–69), probably the most significant theological achievement of the twentieth century. Barth never lived to finish this enterprise, so that his exposition of the doctrine of redemption is incomplete. The primary theme which resonates throughout the *Church Dogmatics* is the need to take seriously the self-revelation of God in Christ through Scripture. Although this might seem to be little more than a reiteration of themes already firmly associated with Calvin or

Luther, Barth brought a degree of creativity to his task which firmly established him as a major thinker in his own right.

The work is divided into five volumes, each of which is further subdivided. Volume I deals with the Word of God – for Barth, the source and starting point of Christian faith and Christian theology alike. Volume II deals with the doctrine of God, and Volume III with the doctrine of the creation. Volume IV deals with the doctrine of reconciliation or "atonement," and the incomplete Volume V with the doctrine of redemption.

Apart from the predictable (and relatively non-informative) "Barthianism," two terms have been used to describe the approach associated with Barth. The term "dialectical theology" has been used, taking up the idea, found especially in Barth's 1919 commentary on Romans, of a "dialectic between time and eternity," or a "dialectic between God and humanity." The term draws attention to Barth's characteristic insistence that there is a contradiction or dialectic, rather than a continuity, between God and humanity. The second term is "neo-Orthodoxy," which draws attention to the affinity between Barth and the writings of the period of Reformed Orthodoxy, especially during the seventeenth century. In many ways, Barth can be regarded as entering into dialogue with several leading Reformed writers of this period.

Perhaps the most distinctive feature of Barth's approach is his "theology of the Word of God." According to Barth, theology is a discipline which seeks to keep the proclamation of the Christian church faithful to its foundation in Jesus Christ, as he has been revealed to us in Scripture. Theology is not a response to the human situation or to human questions; it is a response to the word of God, which demands a response on account of its intrinsic nature.

Neo-Orthodoxy became a significant presence on the North American scene during the 1930s, especially through the writings of Reinhold Niebuhr and others, which criticized the optimistic assumptions of much liberal Protestant social thinking of the time.

Neo-Orthodoxy has been criticized at a number of points. The following criticisms are of especial importance:

1 Its emphasis upon the transcendence and "otherness" of God leads to God being viewed as distant and potentially irrelevant. It has often been suggested that this leads to extreme scepticism.
2 There is a certain circularity to its claim to be based only upon divine

revelation, in that this cannot be checked out by anything, other than an appeal to that same revelation. In other words, there are no recognized external reference points, by which neo-Orthodoxy's truth claims can be verified. This has led many of its critics to suggest that it is a form of fideism – that is to say, a belief system which is impervious to any criticism from outside.

3   Neo-Orthodoxy has no helpful response to those who are attracted to other religions, which it is obliged to dismiss as distortions and perversions. Other theological approaches are able to account for the existence of such religions, and place them in relation to the Christian faith.

Our concern lies especially with the manner in which Neo-Orthodoxy relates to the natural sciences. Barth insisted that theology was a discipline with its own distinct approach to its subject – God. God is to be regarded as radically distinct from the world, and methods which are used to study the world are totally inappropriate for the study of God. Science is about the human investigation of the world; theology is about responding to God's self-revelation. For Barth, the natural sciences can neither confirm or contradict theology, in that they relate to different subjects, use different methods of investigation, and speak different languages. Barth shows little interest in the natural sciences, and tends to adopt an understanding of the sciences which rests on nineteenth-, rather than twentieth-, century assumptions. In particular, it should be noted that Barth vigorously rejects any idea that something can be known of God from nature. The idea of "natural theology" is seen by Barth as contradicting the priority of divine revelation.

Nevertheless, it must be noted that not all of those who share Barth's commitment to the priority of God's self-revelation adopt such a negative approach to the natural sciences. Thomas F. Torrance, one of Barth's most significant interpreters, adopts a strongly positive attitude to the natural sciences, on the basis of a different interpretation of the place of natural theology. We shall consider Torrance's contribution later in this work.

Evangelicalism

The term "evangelical" dates from the sixteenth century, and was then used to refer to catholic writers wishing to revert to more biblical beliefs and practices than those associated with the late medieval church. The term is now used widely to refer to a transdenominational trend in theology and spirituality, which lays particular emphasis upon the place of Scripture in the Christian life. Evangelicalism now centers upon a cluster of four assumptions:

1 The authority and sufficiency of Scripture.
2 The uniqueness of redemption through the death of Christ upon the cross.
3 The need for personal conversion.
4 The necessity, propriety, and urgency of evangelism.

All other matters have tended to be regarded as matters upon which a substantial degree of diversity may be accepted.

Of particular importance is the question of evangelical understandings of the nature of the church. Historically, evangelicalism has never been committed to any particular theory of the church, regarding the New Testament as being open to a number of interpretations in this respect, and treating denominational distinctives as of secondary importance to the gospel itself. This most emphatically does not mean that evangelicals lack commitment to the church, as the body of Christ; rather, it means that evangelicals are not committed to any one theory of the church. A corporate conception of the Christian life is not understood to be specifically linked with any one denominational understanding of the nature of the church. In one sense, this is a "minimalist" approach to "ecclesiology" (as the doctrine of the church is often termed); in another, it represents an admission that the New Testament itself does not stipulate with precision any single form of church government, which can be made binding upon all Christians. This has had several major consequences, which are of central importance to an informed understanding of the movement.

1 Evangelicalism is transdenominational. It is not confined to any one denomination, nor is it a denomination in its own right. There is no inconsistency involved in speaking of "Anglican evangelicals," "Presbyterian evangelicals," "Methodist evangelicals," or even "Roman Catholic evangelicals."

2 Evangelicalism is not a denomination in itself, possessed of a distinctive ecclesiology, but is a trend within the mainstream denominations.

3   Evangelicalism itself represents an ecumenical movement. There is a natural affinity amongst evangelicals, irrespective of their denominational associations, which arises from a common commitment to a set of shared beliefs and outlooks. The characteristic evangelical refusal to allow any specific ecclesiology to be seen as normative, while honoring those which are clearly grounded in the New Testament and Christian tradition, means that the potentially divisive matters of church ordering and government are treated as of secondary importance.

An essential question which demands clarification at this point concerns the relation between fundamentalism and evangelicalism. Fundamentalism arose as a reaction within some of the American churches to the rise of a secular culture. It was from its outset, and has remained, a counter-cultural movement, using central doctrinal affirmations as a means of defining cultural boundaries. Certain central doctrines – most notably, the absolute literal authority of Scripture and the second coming of Christ before the end of time (a doctrine usually referred to as "the premillenial return of Christ") – were treated as barriers, intended as much to alienate secular culture as to give fundamentalists a sense of identity and purpose. A siege mentality became characteristic of the movement; fundamentalist counter-communities viewed themselves as walled cities, or (to evoke the pioneer spirit) circles of wagons, defending their distinctives against an unbelieving culture.

The emphasis upon the premillenial return of Christ is of especial significance. This view has a long history; it never attained any especial degree of significance prior to the nineteenth century. However, fundamentalism appears to have discerned in the idea an important weapon against the liberal Christian idea of a kingdom of God upon earth, to be achieved through social action. "Dispensationalism," especially of a premillenarian type, became an integral element of Fundamentalism.

Yet disquiet became obvious within American fundamentalism during the late 1940s and early 1950s. Neo-evangelicalism (as it has subsequently come to be known) began to emerge, committed to redressing the unacceptable situation created by the rise of fundamentalism. Fundamentalism and evangelicalism can be distinguished at three general levels.

1   Biblically, fundamentalism is totally hostile to the notion of biblical criticism, in any form, and is committed to a literal interpretation of

Scripture. Evangelicalism accepts the principle of biblical criticism (although insisting that this be used responsibly), and recognizes the diversity of literary forms within Scripture.

2   Theologically, fundamentalism is narrowly committed to a set of doctrines, some of which evangelicalism regards as at best peripheral (such as those specifically linked with Dispensationalism), and at worst an utter irrelevance. There is an overlap of beliefs (such as the authority of Scripture), which can too easily mask profound differences in outlook and temperament.

3   Sociologically, fundamentalism is a reactionary countercultural movement, with tight criteria of membership, and is especially associated with a "blue-collar" constituency. Evangelicalism is a cultural movement with increasingly loose criteria of self-definition, which is more associated with a professional or "white-collar" constituency. The element of irrationalism often associated with fundamentalism is lacking in evangelicalism, which has produced significant writings in areas of the philosophy of religion and apologetics.

The break between fundamentalism and neo-evangelicalism in the late 1940s and early 1950s changed both the nature and the public perception of the latter. Billy Graham, perhaps the most publicly visible representative of this new evangelical style, became a well-known figure in English society, and a role model for a younger generation of evangelicals. The public recognition in America of the new importance and public visibility of evangelicalism dates from the early 1970s. The crisis of confidence within American liberal Christianity in the 1960s was widely interpreted to signal the need for the emergence of a new and more publicly credible form of Christian belief. In 1976, America woke up to find itself living in the "Year of the Evangelical," with a born-again Christian (Jimmy Carter) as its President, and an unprecedented media interest in evangelicalism, linked with an increasing involvement on the part of evangelicalism in organized political action.

The attitude of evangelicalism to the natural science is complex. Many evangelicals argue that the biblical understanding of creation rests on a literal interpretation of the first two chapters of the book of Genesis. For this reason, they argue that it is not possible to speak of "evolution," in that the biblical account seems to speak of all forms of biological life, including humanity, being created within the space of several days. This would be inconsistent with any evolutionary view of the origins of human nature. The movement known as "scientific creationism" has its origins in an evangelical context.

Other evangelicals, however, argue that evolution is consistent with the idea of the providence of God guiding the emergence of humanity. Although critical of any idea that biological evolution is due to random factors (where "random" is understood as meaning "outside the control of God"), writers such as Benjamin B. Warfield held that evolution was consistent with the biblical view of the origins of human nature. As evangelicalism becomes an increasingly significant presence in western Christianity, the divergencies within the movement in relation to the natural sciences will become of increasing importance.

We are now in a position to begin exploring some of the understandings of the relation between religion and the natural sciences which have been influential in the last two centuries.

Models of the Interaction of Science and Religion

A survey of the vast literature devoted to the relationship between science and religion suggests that a number of different understandings of that relationship exist. The question of how these understandings may be categorized is therefore clearly of some importance. Perhaps the simplest way of approaching this issue is to ask two questions, in the following order:

1 Do science and religion relate to the same reality?
2 Are the insights of science and religion contradictory or complementary?

While fully conceding that this approach runs the risk of being simplistic, it allows some broad features of the main approaches to be identified.

Confrontational models

Historically, the most significant understanding of the relation between science and religion is that of "conflict," or perhaps even "warfare." This strongly confrontational model continues to be deeply influential at the popular level, even if its appeal has diminished considerably at a more scholarly level. In view of its continuing importance, we shall explore it in some detail, considering its historical origins in particular.

The general tone of the encounter between religion (especially Christianity) and the natural sciences can be argued to have been set by two works published in the final section of the nineteenth century – John William Draper's *History of the Conflict between Religion and Science* (1874) and Andrew Dickson White's *History of the Warfare of Science with Theology in Christendom* (1896). Both works reflect a strongly positivist and "Whiggish" view of history, and a determination to settle old scores with organized religion, which contrasts sharply with the much more settled and symbiotic relationship between the two typical of both North America and Great Britain up to around 1830.

John William Draper's *History of the Conflict between Religion and Science* argued that the natural sciences were to be welcomed as the liberators of humanity from the oppression of traditional religious thought and structures, particularly Roman Catholicism. "The history of science is not a mere record of isolated discoveries; it is a narrative of the conflict of two contending powers, the expansive force of the human intellect on one side, and the compression arising from traditionary faith and human interests on the other." Draper was particularly offended by developments within the Roman Catholic church, which he regarded as pretentious, oppressive, and tyrannical. The rise of science (and especially Darwinian theory) was, for Draper, the most significant means of "endangering her position," and was thus to be encouraged by all means available. Like many polemical works, the work is notable more for the stridency of its assertions rather than the substance of its arguments; nevertheless, the general tone of its approach would help create a mindset, which is admirably summarized in the famous epitaph of Sir Richard Gregory:

> My grandfather preached the gospel of Christ
> My father preached the gospel of socialism
> I preach the gospel of science.

The origins of Andrew Dickson White's *History of the Warfare of Science with Theology in Christendom* (1896) lie in the circumstances surrounding the foundation of Cornell University. Many denominational schools felt threatened by the establishment of the new university, and encouraged attacks on the fledgling school and White, its first president, accusing both of atheism. Angered by this unfair treatment, White decided to launch an offensive against his critics in a lecture delivered in New York on December 18, 1869, entitled "The Battle-Fields of Science." Once more, science was portrayed as a liberator in the quest for academic freedom. The lecture was gradually expanded until it was published in 1876 as *The Warfare of Science*. The material gathered in this book was supplemented by a further series of "New Chapters in the Warfare of Science," published as articles in the *Popular Science Monthly* over the period 1885–92. The two-volumed book of 1896 basically consists of the material found in the 1876 book, to which this additional material was appended.

White himself declared that the "most mistaken of mistaken ideas" was that "religion and science are enemies." Nevertheless, this was precisely the impression created by his work, whether he himself intended it or not. The crystallization of the "warfare" metaphor in the popular mind was unquestionably catalyzed by White's vigorously polemical writing, and the popular reaction to it. The popular late nineteenth-century interpretation of the Darwinian theory in terms of "the survival of the fittest" also lent weight to the imagery of conflict; was this not how nature itself determined matters? Was not nature itself a spectacular battlefield, on which the war of biological survival was fought? Was it not therefore to be expected that the same battle for survival might take place between religious and scientific worldviews, with the victor sweeping the vanquished from existence, the latter never to appear again in the relentless evolutionary development of human thought and knowledge?

A significant social shift can be discerned as lying behind the emergence of this "conflict" model. From a sociological perspective, scientific knowledge can be seen as a cultural resource which was constructed and deployed by particular social groups toward the achievement of their own specific goals and interests. This approach casts much light on the growing competition between two specific groups within English society in the nineteenth century: the clergy and the scientific professionals. The clergy were widely regarded as an elite at the beginning of the century, with the "scientific parson" a well-established social stereotype.

With the appearance of the "professional scientist," however, a struggle for supremacy began, to determine who would gain the cultural ascendancy in the second half of the century. The "conflict" model can be understood in terms of the specific conditions of the

Victorian era, in which an emerging professional intellectual group sought to displace a group which had hitherto occupied the place of honour. The rise of Darwinian theory appeared to give added scientific justification to this model: it was a struggle for the survival of the intellectually most able. In the early nineteenth century, the British Association had many members who were clergy; indeed, the "naturalist-parson" was an accepted social category of the time. By the end of the century, the clergy tended to be portrayed as the enemies of science – and hence of social and intellectual progress. As a result, there was much sympathy for a model of the interaction of the sciences and religion which portrayed religion and its representatives in uncomplimentary and disparaging terms.

It is often suggested, especially by those with a religious way of thinking, that the continuing popularity of "warfare" imagery is due to the propagandist methods of certain natural scientists. It is therefore important to note that certain types of fundamentalist religious belief are implacably opposed to the natural sciences, and actively promote the concept of conflict. Consider, for example, the title of a work recently published by Henry Morris, President of the Institute for Creation Research, with the title *The Long War against God*, which represents a sustained critique of modern evolutionary theory.

In an appreciative foreword to the book, a conservative Baptist pastor declares that "modern evolutionism is simply the continuation of Satan's long war against God." This proves to be a fair summary of the general thrust of the work, which seems to assume that Darwinian evolution brings together the occult, magic, and every conceivable human depravity. In a remarkably speculative and exegetically dubious analysis, Morris invites us to imagine Satan planning the idea of evolution as a means of dethroning God. It will be clear that it is thus quite improper to suggest that the persistence of "warfare" imagery is solely due to a group of anti-religious scientists. A significant minority of religious activists insist that science has declared war on religion, and that a vigorous counterattack is the most appropriate form of defense.

The plausibility of warfare imagery is especially linked with a style of North American Protestant Christianity which is generally known as "fundamentalism." In view of the importance of this movement, it is important to understand its origins and development. As we noted earlier, "fundamentalism" arose as a religious reaction within American Protestant culture during the 1920s to the rise of a secular culture in society at large. It derived its name from a series of twelve books entitled

The Fundamentals, which set out a conservative Protestant perspective on cultural and theological developments at this time.

Despite the wide use of the term to refer to religious movements within Islam and Judaism, "fundamentalism" originally and properly designates a movement within Protestant Christianity in the United States, especially during the period 1920–40, noted for its determination to confront secular culture wherever possible. This inbuilt propensity towards confrontation inevitably led to the reinforcement of a "warfare" model of the relation of religion and society – with the natural sciences (and supremely the theory of biological evolution) being seen as the advance guard of the secularizing trend within society as a whole.

The incident which has since become an icon of this confrontationalism was the infamous Scopes Trial of 1925. Thus caused the "warfare" image to gain further credibility, not least on account of the tactics used inside and outside the courtroom by anti-evolutionists. In May 1925, John T. Scopes, a young high-school science teacher, fell foul of a recently adopted statute which prohibited the teaching of evolution in Tennessee's public schools. The American Civil Liberties Union moved in to support Scopes, while William Jennings Bryan served as prosecution counsel. It proved to be the biggest public relations disaster of all time for fundamentalism.

Bryan, who had unwisely declared that the trial was a "duel to the death" (note again the explicit use of conflict imagery) between Christianity and atheism, was totally wrongfooted by the celebrated agnostic attorney Clarence Darrow. The legal move was as simple as it was brilliant: Bryan was called to the stand as a witness for the defense, and interrogated concerning his views on evolution. Bryan was forced to admit that he had no knowledge of geology, comparative religions or ancient civilizations, and showed himself to have hopelessly naive religious views. The "monkey trial" (as it is widely known) came to be seen as a symbol of reactionary religious thinking in the face of scientific progress.

The "conflict" or "warfare" model remains influential, even today, particularly in popular media presentations of the relation of science and religion. "Science disproves religion!" is a common theme in much western media analysis of this important topic. However, there are other models which need to be considered. In what follows, we shall set out a broad-brush picture of the main approaches which will be encountered in the literature today.

Non-confrontational models

In the previous section, we considered the "conflict" or "warfare" models of the interaction of science and religion. These remain influential. However, two other significant approaches to the relation between religion and the natural sciences can be identified, although it must be stressed that each of these can be divided into any number of subcategories. They have the common feature that they avoid any idea of "conflict" or "warfare" between the disciplines.

Science and religion are convergent A number of strands within western Christian theology have stressed that "all truth is God's truth." On the basis of this assumption, all advances and developments in a scientific understanding of the universe are to be welcomed, and accommodated within the Christian faith. Inevitably, this approach requires adjustments to the content of that faith at several points. The origins of this trend are often traced back to English Deism during the seventeenth century, although it is generally agreed that the trend was at its most marked during the nineteenth century.

Liberal Protestantism was the dominant force within western Protestant Christianity during the nineteenth century. F. D. E. Schleiermacher (1768–1834), widely regarded as the father of the movement, argued for the reinterpretation of the Christian faith in terms which were consistent with the accepted wisdom of the age. Although Schleiermacher died a quarter of a century before the publication of Darwin's *The Origin of Species*, his general approach was applied to this issue by his successors, including Albrecht Ritschl. Liberal Protestantism argued that evolutionary theories allowed theology to appreciate the particular manner in which God was present and active within the world. Evolution was thus seen to be consistent and continuous with God's existence and activity.

Process theology (see pp. 105–9) is a particularly good example of a form of religious thought which has actively sought to adapt the Christian tradition to the insights of the natural sciences. Drawing on the insights of writers such as Alfred North Whitehead and Charles Hartshorne, process theology has stressed the way in which God can be said to work within the natural process. A related approach can be seen in the writings of the noted French Jesuit palaeontologist Pierre Teilhard de Chardin, who envisages the entire process of evolution as being guided by the hand of God towards more complex structures and levels of existence (see pp. 221–5).

A related understanding of the way in which science and religion interact can be found in the writings of the Cambridge theologian Charles Raven, particularly his *Natural Religion and Christian Theology* (1953). For Raven, the same basic methods had to be used in every aspect of the human search for knowledge, whether religious or scientific. "The main process is the same, whether we are investigating the structure of an atom or a problem in animal evolution, a period of history or the religious experience of a saint." Raven vigorously resists any attempt to divide the universe into "spiritual" and "physical" components, and insists that we must "tell a single tale which shall treat the whole universe as one and indivisible."

Science and religion are distinct   A second broad category of approaches stresses the distinctiveness of science and religion. This is particularly the case within Neo-orthodoxy, a movement which is widely regarded as a reaction against Liberal Protestantism, especially its tendency to "accommodate" itself to the prevailing culture. Perhaps the most noted representative of this school is Karl Barth. For Barth, the natural sciences have no bearing on the Christian. They cannot be invoked to support or contradict faith, in that the sciences and theology operate on the basis of very different assumptions.

This emphasis on the distinctiveness of science and religion is found in the writings of many North American writers influenced by Neo-Orthodoxy. A good example is provided by Langdon Gilkey. In his 1959 work *Maker of Heaven and Earth*, Gilkey argues that theology and the natural sciences represent independent and different ways of approaching reality. The natural sciences are concerned with asking "how" questions, where theology asks "why" questions. The former deals with secondary causes (that is, interactions within the sphere of nature), while the latter deals with primary causes (that is, the ultimate origin and purpose of nature).

Religion and the Development of the Natural Sciences

As we have noted, this question has to be addressed with particular reference to Christianity, on account of the emergence of the natural sciences within the specifically Christian context of western Europe. Nevertheless, the discussion can be broadened out beyond this specific religion. In what follows, we shall consider some of the general factors – some positive, others negative – which seem to be involved in this interaction. We may begin by considering two ways in which religion may be seen as a hindrance to scientific advance.

The conservatism of traditional religion

Our first point concerns the generally conservative character of much traditional religion. It needs to be noted that, in the specific context of western Europe from about 1100–1900, the Christian churches tended to be seen as guardians of tradition, opposed to radical new ideas. This is not necessarily a result of Christian theology, but reflects the social role which the churches played over a long period in western European history. On the other hand, the natural sciences were often seen as radical, calling into question received wisdom.

Yet the point in question has wider validity, going beyond both Christianity and western Europe. As Freeman Dyson points out in an essay entitled "The Scientist as Rebel," a common element of most visions of science is that of "rebellion against the restrictions imposed by the local prevailing culture." Science is thus a subversive activity, almost by definition – a point famously stated in a lecture delivered to the "Society of Heretics" at Cambridge by the biologist J. B. S. Haldane in February 1923. For the Arab mathematician and astronomer Omar Khayyam, science was a rebellion against the intellectual constraints of Islam; for nineteenth century Japanese scientists, science was a rebellion against the lingering feudalism of their culture; for the great Indian physicists of the twentieth century, their discipline was a powerful intellectual force directed against the fatalistic ethic of Hinduism (not to mention British imperialism, which was then dominant in the region). And in western Europe, scientific advance inevitably involved confrontation with the culture of the day – including its political, social, and religious elements. In that the West has been dominated by Christianity, it is thus unsurprising that the tension between science and western culture has often been viewed as a confrontation between science and Christianity.

The scientific worldview challenges traditional religious views

Although there is a danger of overstatement involved, the rise of the scientific worldview called into question many traditional religious views. For example, the rise and gradual acceptance of the Copernican model of the solar system posed a serious challenge to an earth-centered view of the universe, which had become implicit in much traditional religious thinking. It is, however, arguable whether such geocentric approaches should have become so deeply embedded in traditional religious thinking. As we have noted, the general view that the Bible supports such a geocentrism rests largely on the implicit assumption that, as the earth is at the center of everything, the Bible must say the same thing. Techniques of biblical interpretation which allowed for the "stripping out" of culturally conditioned elements in the Bible or on the part of the biblical interpreter proved able to deal with this difficulty.

In the case of the Newtonian worldview, it initially seemed that advances in scientific understanding confirmed some central themes of traditional religious teaching, most notably the doctrine of creation. As Newtonianism was further developed, it began to take on anti-religious tones, most notably in that it was interpreted as implying that there was no further need for God in the working of the universe.

It is the Darwinian controversy, however, which posed the most radical threat to traditional religious beliefs, in that it posed a direct challenge to the belief that God created each species directly (the idea of "special creation"), and particularly the idea that humanity was the apex of God's creation, created in such a manner that it was set apart from the rest of the animal kingdom. Darwin's ideas (which, aware of their sensitivity, he tended to state rather cautiously) clearly implied that human beings were rather less special than they might like to think.

Where Copernicanism called into challenge one aspect of the traditional interpretation of the Genesis creation narrative, Darwinism called another into question. Although there were many who believed that it was perfectly possible to reconcile the Bible, Copernicus and Darwin (and the idea of "theistic evolution" needs to be noted here), the general perception arose that there was a fundamental, perhaps even fatal, contradiction between the two disciplines of science and religion. Although this was polarized by social and political factors typical of western Europe (and especially England) in the later nineteenth century, the fact remains that some such tension exists – and thus potentially makes religion hostile to scientific advance.

Yet the picture is more complex than these negative factors might suggest. Having noted two negative factors, we may now consider two positive factors. We shall be considering them in more detail later in this work, and it is necessary simply to note them at this early stage.

To study nature is to study God

The insight that God created the world is widely agreed to offer a fundamental motivation for scientific research. Three broad positions on the question of the status of the natural order could be distinguished:

1 The natural world is divine.
2 The natural world is created, and bears some resemblance to its creator.
3 The natural world has no relation to God.

Clearly, a degree of simplification has been introduced here. However, it allows us to make a point of fundamental importance. Suppose that someone is strongly religious. If the natural world has no relation to God, there will be no motivation to study it. On the other hand, if the natural world does bear some relation to God, there will clearly be a very good reason for studying it, in that it offers to allow deeper insights into the nature of the God who created it. It is clearly therefore of considerable interest to explore the way in which a doctrine of creation – such as that associated with Judaism or Christianity – establishes a connection between God and the natural order.

A point which is stressed by many religious writers of the sixteenth and seventeenth centuries is that the invisible God can be studied through the visible creation. This idea (which is sometimes expressed in terms of the "two books" of Scripture and Nature) gave additional impetus to the study of nature. If God could not be seen, yet had somehow imprinted his nature on the creation, it would be possible to gain an enhanced appreciation of the nature and purpose of God by studying the natural order.

The divine ordering of nature

A second related issue concerns the order of nature. One of the fundamental themes of a doctrine of creation (such as that associated with Christianity and Judaism) is that in creation God imposes order, rationality, and beauty upon nature. The doctrine of creation leads directly to the notion that the universe is possessed of a regularity which is capable of being uncovered by humanity. This theme, which is expressed in terms of "the laws of nature," is of fundamental importance to the emergence and the development of the natural sciences. This religious undergirding of the notion of the regularity of nature is known to have been of major historical importance to the emergence of the natural sciences, and will be considered further later in this work.

It will therefore be clear that any analysis of the historical interaction of science and religion which portrays the matter in purely negative or purely positive terms is being unacceptably selective in its approach. The simple fact is that the historical interaction has been ambivalent. Religious belief has both encouraged and discouraged the emergence of the natural sciences.

Our analysis thus far, however, has been primarily historical in nature. In order to gain a fuller appreciation of the issues, it is necessary to consider more theoretical issues in greater detail. We may begin a more theoretical analysis by beginning to explore some of the philosophical issues associated with science and religion.

For further reading

Barbour, I. G. *Issues in Science and Religion*. Englewood Cliffs: Prentice-Hall, 1966.

——. *Myths, Models and Paradigms: A Comparative Study in Science and Religion*. New York: Harper & Row, 1974.

——. "Experiencing and Interpreting Nature in Science and Religion." *Zygon* 29 (1994): 457–87.

Barth, K., and E. Brunner. *Natural Theology*. London: SCM Press, 1947.

Brooke, J. H. *Science and Religion: Some Historical Perspectives*. Cambridge and New York: Cambridge University Press, 1991.

——. *Telling the Story of Science and Religion: A Nuanced Account*. Cambridge: Cambridge University Press, 1991.

Cosslett, T. *Science and Religion in the Nineteenth Century*. Cambridge and New York: Cambridge University Press, 1984.

Gilbert, J. "Burhoe and Shapley: A Complementarity of Science and Religion." *Zygon* 30 (1995): 531–9.

Gilkey, L. "Nature, Reality and the Sacred: A Meditation in Science and Religion." *Zygon* 24 (1989): 283–98.

Gilley, S., and A. Loades. "Thomas Henry Huxley: The War between Science and Religion." *Journal of Religion* 61 (1981): 285–308.

Lindberg, D. C., and R. L. Numbers. "Beyond War and Peace: A Reappraisal of the Encounter between Christianity and Science." *Church History* 55 (1984): 338–54.

——, and ——. *God and Nature: Historical Essays on the Encounter between Christianity and Science.* Berkeley: University of California Press, 1986.

McGrath, A. E. *Evangelicalism and the Future of Christianity.* Downers Grove, IL: InterVarsity Press, 1995.

——. *A Passion for Truth: The Intellectual Coherence of Evangelicalism.* Downers Grove, IL: InterVarsity Press, 1996.

Numbers, R. L. "Creationism in 20th-Century America." Science 218 (1982): 538–44.

——. "Science and Religion." *Osiris* 1 (1985): 59–80.

——. *The Creationists: The Evolution of Scientific Creationism.* New York: Knopf, 1992.

Olshewsky, T. M. "Between Science and Religion." *Journal of Religion* 62 (1982): 243–60.

Peters, T. "Theology and the Natural Sciences." *The Modern Theologians: An Introduction to Christian Theology in the Twentieth Century.* Ed. David F. Ford. 2nd edn. Oxford/Cambridge, MA: Blackwell, 1997, pp. 649–68.

Pinnock, C. H. "Climbing out of a Swamp: The Evangelical Struggle to Understand the Creation Texts." *Interpretation* 43 (1989): 143–55.

Robbins, J. W. "Science and Religion: Critical Realism or Pragmatism?" *International Journal for Philosophy of Religion* 21 (1987): 83–94.

Rolston, H. *Science and Religion: A Critical Survey.* Philadelphia: Temple University Press, 1987.

Rudwick, M. J. S. "Senses of the Natural World and Senses of God: Another Look at the Historical Relation of Science and Religion." *The Sciences and Theology in the Twentieth Century.* Ed. Arthur R. Peacocke. London: Oriel Press, 1981, pp. 241–61.

Rumschiedt, H. M. *Revelation and History: An Analysis of the Barth-Harnack Correspondence of 1923.* Cambridge: Cambridge University Press, 1972.

Schilling, H. K. *Science and Religion.* New York: Charles Scribner's Sons, 1962.

Torrance, T. F. "The Problem of Natural Theology in the Thought of Karl Barth." *Religious Studies* 6 (1970): 121–35.

Turner, F. M. "Rainfall, Plagues and the Prince of Wales: A Chapter in the

Conflict of Science and Religion." *Journal of British Studies* 13 (1974): 46–65.

——. "The Victorian Conflict between Science and Religion: A Professional Dimension." *Isis* 69 (1978): 356–76.

Watts, F. "Are Science and Religion in Conflict?" *Zygon* 32 (1997): 125–38.

Westfall, R. S. *Science and Religion in Seventeenth-Century England*. Ann Arbor: University of Michigan Press, 1973.

3

Religion and the Philosophy of Science

The discipline of the philosophy of science deals, in very general terms, with the philosophical issues associated with the natural sciences. Some of those issues overlap with the traditional themes of philosophy. For example, consider the major issue of the "laws of nature," which attempt to represent the regularity or ordering which appears to exist within nature. Is this "regularity" really present within nature itself? Or is it imposed upon nature by the human mind? This debate, which was given particular stimulus during the late eighteenth century by the Scottish philosopher David Hume, is of general philosophical interest, but has particular significance for the natural sciences.

Other issues have a more specific relation to the natural sciences. For example, suppose a certain experiment is carried out, which suggests that a type of particle exists. This particle cannot itself be observed, but its existence seems to be implied by the behaviour of other aspects of the system. The philosophy of science will aim to clarify the status of this hypothetical and unobserved particle. Can it really be said to "exist"? For some writers, the only things can can be said to "really exist" are the experimental observations. For many of them, the theoretical particle is just a "useful fiction," a helpful way of explaining the phenomena.

The present chapter aims to deal with some of leading themes in the philosophy of science, and explore their particular relevance to religion. The following chapter will explore the converse of this issue, looking at the way in which the philosophy of religion has drawn on insights from the natural sciences. We begin our discussion by considering the difference between "rationalism" and "empiricism."

Rationalism and Empiricism

One of the most significant philosophical distinctions of relevance to the development of the natural sciences concerns "rationalism" and "empiricism." The terms are used in significantly different ways by different writers, and it is important to appreciate that a degree of simplification has been necessary for the purposes of the present study. Nevertheless, the distinction which will be drawn is helpful in allowing us to understand one of the most significant aspects of the rise of the natural sciences – the appeal to our experience of the world as the basis for knowledge.

The term "rationalism" derives from the Latin term *ratio* ("reason"), and is generally understood to refer to the view that all truth has its origins in human thought, unaided by any form of supernatural intervention or an appeal to the experience of the senses. The phase "the autonomy of human thought" is sometimes used to refer to this position, which stresses that human beings, by due and proper use of their natural ability to reason, may develop a series of truths which are universal and necessary. Rationalism often appeals to the notion of "innate ideas," meaning by this ideas which appear to be naturally implanted within the human mind.

The origins of rationalism are particularly linked with seventeenth-century debates in western Europe over the nature and authority of divine revelation. Traditional religious writers argued that theology was a rational discipline, which could be justified by an appeal to reason. This did not mean that it established its distinctive ideas by the use of reason alone; rather, it was understood that certain truths could only be acquired through divine revelation, but that these truths, once revealed, could be seen to be rational. This position, associated with writers such as Thomas Aquinas, works on the assumption that the Christian faith is fundamentally rational, and can thus be both supported and explored by reason. Aquinas' Five Ways (that is, his series of arguments for the existence of God) illustrate his belief that reason is capable of lending support to the ideas of faith.

As we noted, Aquinas did not believe that Christianity was limited to what could be ascertained by reason. Faith goes beyond reason, having access to truths and insights of revelation, which reason could not hope to fathom or discover unaided. Reason has the role of building upon what is known by revelation, exploring what its implications might be.

In this sense, theology is a rational discipline, using rational methods to build upon and extend what is known by revelation.

This position was challenged during the seventeenth century, although traces of the criticisms which are associated with this period can be discerned at earlier stages. By the middle of the seventeenth century, especially in England and Germany, it was increasingly argued that faith must be capable of being deduced in its entirety by reason. Every aspect of faith, every item of Christian belief, must be shown to derive from human reason, without being dependent upon supernatural revelation. This supernatural revelation was increasingly held to compromise the autonomy of human reason. Such attitudes can be seen in the writings of Lord Herbert of Cherbury (1581–1648), particularly his works *De veritate* ("on truth") (1624) and *De religione gentilium* ("on the religion of the gentiles") (1645).

Cherbury argued for a rational Christianity based upon the innate sense of God and human moral obligation. This had two major consequences. First, Christianity was in effect reduced to those ideas which could be proven by reason. If Christianity was rational, then any parts of its system which could not be proved by reason could not be counted as "rational," and would therefore have to be abandoned as being "irrational." They would have to be discarded. Second, reason was understood to take priority over revelation. Reason thus came to be regarded as being capable of establishing what is right without needing any assistance from revelation; Christianity has to follow, being accepted where it endorses what reason has to say, and being disregarded where it went its own way. So why bother with the idea of revelation, when reason could tell us all we could possibly wish to know about God, the world, and ourselves?

The origins of this exclusive appeal to reason can thus be seen to lie in a desire to break free from any dependence upon divine revelation for reliable human knowledge of the truth. Many writers who were sympathetic to religion took to arguing that the existence of God could be defended on purely rational grounds. Perhaps the most important of these writers were Descartes and Leibniz, who are generally regarded as among the most significant rationalist philosophers. Descartes' argument for the existence of God, dating from 1642, takes the following form. God is a "supremely perfect being." As existence is a perfection, it follows that God must have the perfection of existence, as he would otherwise not be perfect. Descartes supplements this argument with two examples (triangles and mountains). To think of God is to think of his existence, in just the same way as to think of a triangle is to think of its three angles being equal to two right angles, or thinking of a mountain is to think of a valley.

Having given the matter careful attention, I am convinced that existence can no more be taken away from the divine essence than the magnitude of its three angles taken together being equal to two right angles can be taken away from the essence of a triangle, or than the idea of a valley can be taken away from the idea of a mountain. So it is no less absurd to think of God (that is, a supremely perfect being) lacking existence (that is, lacking a certain perfection), than to think of a mountain without a valley. . . . I am not free to think of God apart from existence (that is, of a supremely perfect being apart from supreme perfection) in the way that I am free to imagine a horse either with wings or without wings. . . . Whenever I choose to think of the First and Supreme Being, and as it were bring this idea out of the treasury of my mind, it is necessary that I ascribe all perfections to him . . . This necessity clearly ensures that, when I subsequently point out that existence is a perfection, I am correct in concluding that the First and Supreme Being exists.

Descartes' argument is not especially easy to follow. The important point to appreciate is that Descartes constructs an argument for the existence of God which makes no reference to either of the following:

1 the experience of the human senses;
2 any truth which is derived from supernatural revelation.

It will be clear that the general position outlined by Descartes has important implications for both science and religion. In the first place, Descartes' vigorous refusal to allow human experience or sense perception to have any decisive role in the formation of human knowledge means that an appeal to the investigation of the world (as, for example, in physics or biology) has no significance. In one sense, it may be argued that rationalism hindered the development of the empirical approach to knowledge by declaring in advance that such knowledge was of no genuine significance. It will also be clear that this approach has implications for religion, in that traditional religious understandings of how knowledge of God comes about (through revelation) are also discounted.

For Descartes and Leibniz, the science which had most to offer was pure mathematics. Like geometry, all knowledge could be stated in terms of axioms and principles. Euclid had demonstrated that, on the basis of a series of principles, an entire geometrical system could be devised. The basic principles were not derived form experience or sense-perception, nor from divine revelation, but from the process of reason itself. Descartes argued that a series of "universal concepts of reason" could be deduced in a similar manner, and set out in terms of certain fundamental mathematical and logical relationships. These could then be applied to human sense perception and experience. It is important to note that Descartes was denying the *priority*, not the *possibility*, of empirical data (that is, data derived from experience). Such data was to be interpreted in terms of the patterns and ideas generated by the human mind, independent of this experience.

Rationalism became of particular importance during the Enlightenment, the period of western culture which was dominated by the general acceptance of the priority and universality of human reason. Nevertheless, the growing successes of the natural sciences raised considerable difficulties for rationalism. We shall consider one specific example to illustrate this point, before turning to deal with empiricism in more detail.

In his *Dissertatio philosophica de orbitis planetarum* ("philosophical dissertation on the orbits of the planets"), published in 1801, the German philosopher Hegel had argued, on the basis of his philosophical presuppositions, that the number of planets was necessarily restricted to seven, and that no planet existed between Mars and Jupiter. This bold assertion of the astronomical competence of unaided human reason was rudely discredited, even as Hegel's book was in the course of its production. On January 1, 1801, as the new century dawned, the astronomer J. E. Bode (1746–1826) discovered the planetoid Ceres, and established that its orbit fell between that of Mars and Jupiter. Hegel's idealistic scheme thus lay in ruins.

The alternative to rationalism was an appeal to experience, generally known as "empiricism." The origins of empiricism can be argued to lie in the sixteenth century, or even earlier. However, its increasing acceptance and credibility dates from the late seventeenth century. One of the major contributions to the development of empiricism was John Locke (1632–1704), whose *Essay concerning Human Understanding* (1690) attacked the notion of "innate ideas" and principles on which Descartes would make so much. God does not implant ideas within our minds from birth, but provides us with the faculties which we need to acquire them. For Locke, the primary source of knowledge is human experience and sense perceptions; reason is brought into matters to reflect on those perceptions. It is not seen as a *primary* source of knowledge.

Locke criticizes those who appeal to mathematics as a means of interpreting the data of experience. For Locke, "the mathematician considers the truth and properties belonging to a rectangle or circle only as they are an idea in his mind." The "general principles" to which rationalism appealed are, in Locke's view, the conclusions rather than the foundations of science.

Locke himself was quite clear that there were religious implications to his empirical approach. The idea of God is not, he declared, innate. All human knowledge of God, including both God's existence and nature, derives from experience. The idea of "God" is constructed, according to Locke, by the human mind on the basis of its experience:

If we examine the idea that we have of the incomprehensible supreme Being, we shall find that we come by it the same way; and that the complex ideas we have both of God and separate spirits are made up of simple ideas we receive from reflection ... having from what we experiment in ourselves, got the ideas of existence and duration, of knowledge and power, of pleasure and happiness ... we enlarge every one of these with our idea of infinity, and so putting them together, make our complex idea of God.

The issue to emerge from this debate between rationalism and empiricism is whether certain truths are *a priori* or *a posteriori*. The former (literally, "from before") is typical of rationalism, and holds that truth arises within the human mind itself. The latter (literally, "from afterwards") holds that truth arises from reflection within the mind on what the human faculties experience through sense perception. That same debate arises within religion, in that the issue of whether knowledge of God is a *priori* (generated within the human mind, or implanted there by God) or a *posteriori* (generated by reflection on experience or divine revelation) remains debated.

A further philosophical debate which is significant within both science and religion concerns realism and idealism, and is the subject of what follows.

Realism and Idealism

Idealism does not deny that things such as physical objects exist in the world. Nevertheless, it argues that we can have knowledge only of *how things appear to us*, or are experienced by us, not things as they are in themselves. The form of idealism which stresses this point particularly forcefully is sometimes known as "phenomenalism," and we shall consider it in a little more detail presently. The most familiar version of this approach is that associated with the great German idealist philosopher Immanuel Kant, who argues that we have to deal with appearances or representations, rather than things in themselves. Kant thus draws a distinction between the world of phenomena and "things in themselves," holding that the latter can never be known directly. The idealist will thus hold that we can have knowledge of the manner in which things appear to us through the ordering activity of the human mind. We cannot, however, have knowledge of mind-independent realities.

This view is expressed particularly forcefully in the approach often referred to as "phenomenalism." This argues that we cannot know extra-mental realities directly, but only through their "appearances" or "representations." Although this view is relatively uncommon within the natural sciences, it has been defended by a number of significant figures, including Ernst Mach (1838–1916). For Mach, the natural sciences concern that which is immediately given by the senses. Science concerns nothing more and other than the investigation of the "dependence of phenomena on one another." The world consists only of our sensations. This led Mach to take a strongly negative view of the atomic hypothesis, in which he argued that atoms were merely theoretical constructs which cannot be perceived. Atoms were not "real"; they were simply useful fictitious notions which helped observers to understand the relationship between various observed phenomena.

To use the Kantian framework which seems to lie behind Mach's statements, he argued that it is impossible to move from the world of phenomena to the world of "things in themselves." It is simply not possible to move beyond the world of experience. Nevertheless, Mach allows the use of "auxiliary concepts" which serve as bridges linking one observation with another, provided that it is understood that they have no real existence, and must not be thought of as actual or existing entities. They are thus "products of thought" which "exist only in our imagination and understanding."

To understand the importance of this point, let us return to Mach's insistence that atoms were simply theoretical constructions which helped understand the relationship between phenomena. On the basis of this view, Mach argued that atoms could not be held to exist. It must be recalled that Mach was writing to this effect in the 1870s, at a time when experimental evidence for the atomic hypothesis was still at a relatively undeveloped stage. Although both Ludwig Boltzmannn and

Max Planck had argued that atoms were not simply "useful fictions," but were entities with a genuine independence of their own, Mach countered their arguments with the suggestion that the atoms were "things which can never be seen or touched." Indeed, one of Mach's most pointed questions when debating this matter addressed this issue. When anyone talked about "atoms," Mach would ask them whether they had ever seen one. In many ways, this approach resembles that associated with the philosopher George Berkeley in his *Principles* (1701), who argued that existence depended upon perception. A chair might exist in a room in which I am present – but does it continue to exist when I leave that room, and no longer perceive it?

The point at issue in Mach's discussion is of considerable importance, and is often discussed in terms of the technical phrase "hypothetical entities," "theoretical terms," or "unobservables." The basic issue is whether something has to be seen before it can be held to exist. Mach, who argued that the natural sciences were concerned only with reporting experimental observations, held that science was not committed to defending the real and independent existence of "unobserved" or "theoretical" entities which those observations might suggest.

A similar approach is adopted by the more recent philosopher of science Bas van Fraassen. Where Mach denies the real and independent existence of atoms, van Fraassen concedes their existence, but holds that electrons do not really exist. He draws a distinction between a realist, who holds that science aims to give a literally true description of what the world is like, and what he calls a "constructive empiricist," who argues that acceptance of a theory does not involve commitment to the *truth* of that theory, but to the belief that it adequately preserves the phenomena to which it relates:

To be an empiricist is to withhold belief in anything that goes beyond the actual, observable phenomena, and to recognize no objective modality in nature. To develop an empiricist account of science is to depict it as involving a search for truth only about the empirical world, about what is actual and observable . . . it must invoke throughout a resolute rejection of the demand for an explanation of the regularities in the observable course of nature, by means of truths concerning a reality beyond what is actual and observable, as a demand which plays no role in the scientific enterprise.

To speak of "laws of nature" or theoretical entities such as electrons is to introduce an unwarranted and unnecessary metaphysical element into scientific discourse.

It will be clear that one of the problems facing this position is the relentless advance of scientific knowledge and technological advance. Mach denied the existence of atoms, because he could not see them. But with the advent of the electron microscope, atoms could be "seen." Van Fraassen holds that electrons, which currently cannot be "seen," are thus not real. But what happens if technology advances to the point at which they can be? Entities may begin by being regarded as explicitly "theoretical," in that they are postulated as a means of explaining certain observations, even though the entities in question themselves could not be observed. With the advance of technology, at least some of these entities have themselves become observable. As Newton-Smith comments:

Consider the following typical development in the history of science. At one stage genes were posited in order to explain observed phenomena. At that time no one had in any sense observed or detected the existences of genes. However, with the development of sophisticated microscopes scientists came to describe themselves as seeing genes.

Against this approach, we must set the position which is generally known as "realism." Given the wide variety of "realisms" which can be found within both the philosophical and scientific communities, it may be helpful to try and identify its basic features. Realism holds that, as W. H. Newton-Smith expresses this point, "at least some of the theoretical terms of a theory denote real theoretical entities which are causally responsible for the observable phenomenon that prompts us to posit their existence."

Three ways of stating the central realist belief may be noted, each differing in the way in which the commitment to realism is stated.

1 Entities in the world exist independently of the human mind (against Berkeley's view that such existence is dependent upon perception);
2 The only entities that can really be said to exist are "extra-mental" – that is, those which have an independent and real existence.
3 Both mental and nonmental entities exist.

Each of these statements embodies a realist thesis, although it will be clear that there is a significant difference in the level of commitment and manner of formulation which they adopt. Nevertheless, the basic theme which unites the three different formulations of realism will be clear: entities exist in the world independent of human perception or any human mental process.

Some such approach is typical of the natural sciences. Despite difficulties in representing or detecting them, "theoretical" or "unobservable entities" may be held to genuinely exist. The fact that they cannot be observed cannot be taken to imply that they do not exist. There are excellent reasons for supposing that electrons, quarks and neutrons exist, even though they cannot be "perceived" or observed directly. As John Polkinghorne has further pointed out, difficulties in depiction cannot be taken as an indication that something does not exist:

It is our ability to understand the physical world which convinces us of its reality, even when, in the elusive world of quantum theory, that reality is not picturable. This gives physics a good deal in common with theology as the latter pursues its search for an understanding of the Unpicturable.

An excellent illustration of this point can be seen from the search for the "top quark," which reached its climax at the Fermi National Accelerator Laboratory in March 1995. The existence of this particle had been inferred from the discovery in 1977 of the "bottom quark," with a mass of 4.5 GeV. Though unobservable, the quark was widely agreed to exist; it was just a matter of detecting it through the creation of appropriate experimental conditions. In the event, the mass of the missing quark was much higher than expected (175 GeV), necessitating the concentration of immense amounts of energy to cause the production of the particle from a collision. Yet the top quark has never been "seen" or "observed" What actually have been observed are a series of events, some of which are interpreted (with good reason) as the creation of a top–antitop pair, allowing the mass of the top quark to be calculated. Yet the existence of the "top quark" is widely accepted, despite lack of direct observation – and the absence of any expectation that it will ever be "seen."

One form of realism which is of particular significance to the theme of science and religion is what is usually referred to as "critical realism." What is often referred to as a "naïve realism" holds that there is a direct relationship between the external world and human perception, so that "reality" can be perceived directly. Critical realism holds that this perception, although real, is indirect, and is mediated through models or analogies. For example, we will never know exactly what an electron looks like, and can never expect to see one. But that does not stop us from believing that electrons really exist, nor from developing models of electrons which help us understand their behavior.

The relevance of this debate to religion will be obvious. One of the most significant questions to be debated, particularly within the discipline of the philosophy of religion, is whether God is simply a construct of the human mind, or exists independently of human thought. In many areas of religious thinking, there is growing interest in "critical realism," which can be summarized in terms of two propositions.

1 God exists independently of human thought;
2 Humans are obliged to use models or analogies to depict God, who cannot be known directly.

For this reason, the use of models and analogies in both science and religion is a subject of considerable interest, and an entire chapter will be devoted to this subject (see pp. 144–76).

Our attention is now claimed by a specific issue which originally arose within the philosophy of science, but which has since become more widely discussed within philosophy as a whole. This is what is usually referred to as the "Duhem–Quine" thesis.

The Duhem–Quine Thesis

How do we know when a theory is wrong? The simple answer which might be offered, from a scientific perspective, is to carry out an experiment. A "crucial experiment" can be devised, which will allow the central features of a theory to be tested out. The experiment, providing that it is properly designed, will soon establish whether the theory is right or wrong.

Or will it? The issues which we shall be discussing in the present section concern the criticisms made of the idea of a "crucial experiment" by the noted French physicist and philosopher Pierre Duhem (1861–1916). Duhem notes that a theory is made up of a number of hypotheses, some of which may be of central importance, others of which are subsidiary. Duhem's point is that a theory consists of a complex network of crucial and auxiliary hypotheses. So, if something

which is predicted by the theory does not correspond with experimentation, which of the assumptions is wrong? A crucial hypothesis? If so, the
theory would have to be abandoned. Or one of the auxiliary assumptions? If so, the theory simply needs modification.

According to Duhem, the physicist simply is not in a position to
submit an isolated hypothesis to experimental test. "An experiment in
physics can never condemn an isolated hypothesis but only a whole
theoretical group." The physicist cannot subject an individual hypothesis to an experimental test, in that the experiment can only indicate that
one hypothesis within a larger group of hypotheses requires revision.
The experiment does not itself indicate which of the hypotheses requires
modification. Even when a strict deductive consequence of a theory is
shown to be false (assuming, of course, that a "crucial experiment" can
be devised which allows such an unequivocal conclusion to be drawn),
that falsity cannot be attributed to any specific site in the theory itself or
its auxiliary assumptions.

Yet can such a "crucial experiment" be devised? Duhem's argument
needs closer examination at this point. In the section of his *Aim and
Structure of Physical Theory* entitled "A 'Crucial Experiment' is Impossible in Physics," Duhem argues that we do not have access to the full list
of hypotheses which underlie our thinking. It might at first seem that we
could enumerate all the hypotheses than can be made to account for a
phenomenon, and then eliminate all of these hypotheses except one by
experimental contradiction. However, according to Duhem, the physicist is simply never going to be in a position to be sure that all the
hypotheses have been identified and checked.

In his seminal essay "Two Dogmas of Empiricism," the Harvard
philosopher Willard Van Orman Quine set out a development of
Duhem's argument which has come to be known as the "Duhem–Quine
thesis." This asserts that, if incompatible data and theory are seen to be
in conflict, one cannot draw the conclusion that any particular theoretical statement is responsible, and is therefore to be rejected. Quine
develops this point by noting the complex way in which belief systems
or worldviews relate to experience and experimentation:

The totality of our so-called knowledge or beliefs, from the most casual matters
of geography and history to the profoundest laws of atomic physics . . . is a man-
made fabric which impinges on experience only along the edges . . . A conflict
with experience at the periphery occasions adjustments in the interior of the
field . . . But the total field is so underdetermined by its boundary conditions,

experience, that there is much latitude of choice as to what statements to reevaluate in the light of any single contrary experience.

In other words, experience often has relatively little impact upon worldviews. Where experience or experiment seems to contradict a worldview or system of beliefs, the most likely outcome is an internal readjustment of the system, rather than its rejection. Quine thus points to some of the difficulties in refuting a theory on the basis of experience, which must be addressed by any empirical approach.

It needs to be noted that Duhem was quite specific that his concerns related specifically to the natural sciences, and particularly physics. Quine extended Duhem's approach far beyond its original application. Duhem saw his remarks as applying to physics. Quine extended them to any inquiry which involved the relation of theory and experience.

Quine's analysis has given rise to what is often referred to as the "underdetermination thesis" – the view, especially associated with sociological approaches to the natural sciences, which holds that there are, in principle, an indefinite number of theories that are capable of fitting observed facts more or less adequately. The choice of theory can thus be explained on the basis of sociological factors, such as interests. According to this view, experimental evidence plays a considerably smaller role in theory generation and confirmation than might be thought. The strongest form of this approach (usually referred to as "maximal underdetermination") would take the following form:

For any theoretical statement S and acceptable theory T essentially containing S, there is an acceptable theory T' with the same testable consequences but which contains, essentially, the negation of S.

Two implications of the underdetermination these should be noted:

1 That there are a number of possible theories which are consistent with any given experimental result. All are to be regarded as equally valid.
2 That theories cannot be explained purely on the basis of experimental evidence. Additional factors, generally of a sociological nature, need to be taklen into account.

It will be clear that the underdetermination thesis has been particularly attractive to sociologists of knowledge, who wish to stress the importance of social conditioning on scientific theory.

Nevertheless, it needs to be noted that underdetermination is a disputed notion. Duhem himself noted that physicists had a pretty good idea as to which theories were workable and which were not. He referred to the idea of "good sense," meaning by this an intuitive perception, based on experience of a laboratory-based scientific culture, as to what constituted a viable theory.

So what is the religious relevance of the Duhem–Quine thesis? One of the more significant areas in which it can be relevant concerns the problem of suffering, traditionally one of the most difficult aspects of belief in God. How, it is asked, can belief in God be justified in the face of suffering? If God is good and loving, how can the existence of suffering be understood? It seems that there is a radical contradiction between religious theory and experience at this point. But what are the implications of this apparent contradiction? Does the existence of suffering in the world cause us to abandon faith in God? Or merely to modify some small aspect of that belief – or perhaps an auxiliary assumption which is not really part of the Christian faith at all?

To understand the importance of the Duhem-Quine thesis, we may state the religious issues in language more reminiscent of the natural sciences. We may set out the basics of a theistic theory, which can be held to consist of a number of hypotheses, of which we shall note two, as follows:

Theory: that there exists a God

Main Hypotheses:
1 That this God is good and loving;
2 That this God is all-powerful

Auxiliary hypotheses:
1 That an all-powerful God can do anything (except logically inconsistent things, such as drawing square triangles);
2 That we are in a position to know enough about God to be able to make statements about God.

We must now introduce an observation statement, which parallels the results of an experiment – for example, the Michelson–Morley observation that there is no discernible ether drift.

Observation: there is suffering in the world.

The critical question is whether this observation statement causes us to abandon the theory as a whole, or one or more of its hypothesis, or one of the auxilliary hypotheses (which may not be specifically Christian in nature in any case). Duhem and Quine both affirm that it is not theoretically possible to identify the site of the tension between theory and experience.

It will be clear that this is a significant point, especially given the simplistic lines of argument which are often encountered on this subject. It is often suggested that the mere existence of suffering is sufficient to cause abandonment of faith in God. Duhem and Quine alike make the point that this is simply not the case. The issues at stake are considerably more complex, as recent discussions from within the philosophy of religion make clear.

Logical Positivism: The Vienna Circle

One of the most significant philosophical movements to arise in the twentieth century had its origins in the Austrian capital city of Vienna. The "Vienna Circle" is generally regarded as the group of philosophers, physicists, mathematicians, sociologists, and economists who gathered around Moritz Schlick during the period 1924–36. The group fell apart after Schlick was shot dead by a student in 1936, and dispersed as a result of the rise of National Socialism in Austria prior to the Second World War. As a result, the ideas of the "Vienna Circle" were widely propagated, particularly in the United States. So what were these ideas?

It must be stressed that there was considerable divergence between many of the thinkers of the Circle, and that the views of some of its leading members would change as time progressed. This makes generalizations concerning the leading themes of the group a little hazardous. However, in very general terms, it may be stated that one of the most fundamental themes of the group was that *beliefs must be justified on the basis of experience*. This belief can be seen to be grounded in the writings of David Hume, and is clearly empirical in tone. For this reason, the members of the group tended to place a particularly high estimation on the methods and norms of the natural sciences (which were seen as the most empirical of human disciplines) and a correspondingly low estimation of metaphysics (which was seen as an attempt to disengage with experience). Indeed, one of the more significant achievements of the

Vienna Circle was to cause the word "metaphysics" to have strongly negative connotations.

For the Vienna Circle, statements which did not directly connect up with or relate to the real world were of no value, and simply served to perpetuate fruitless conflicts of the past. The terms in statements or propositions had to be directly related to what we experience. Every proposition must therefore be capable of being stated in a manner which relates directly to the real world of experience.

The Vienna Circle developed this approach by making use of the forms of symbolic logic which had begun to appear in the late nineteenth century, and had been used very effectively by Bertrand Russell in the early twentieth century. The manner in which terms and sentences relate to each other can be clarified by an appropriate use of logic. As Schlick himself pointed out, the rigorous use of such logical principles could prevent absurd lapses in philosophical rigor. Schlick offered the following as elementary examples of such lapses which would be eliminated by this logical rigor:

1 My friend died the day after tomorrow.
2 The tower is both 100 and 150 meters high.

The overall program which was thus proposed can be seen to fall into two parts, as follows.

1 All meaningful statements can be reduced to, or are explicitly defined by, statements which contain only observational terms;
2 All such reductive statements must be capable of being stated in logical terms.

The most significant attempt to carry this program through is to be seen in the works of Rudolph Carnap, particularly his 1928 work *The Logical Construction of the World*. In this work, Carnap set out to show how the world could be derived from experience by logical construction. It was, as he put it, an attempt at the "reduction of 'reality' to the 'given'" by using the methods of logic on statements derived from experience. The only two sources of knowledge are thus sense perception and the analytical principles of logic. Statements are derived from and justified with reference to the former, and related to each other and their constituent terms by the latter.

It was clear from a very early stage that mathematical and logical statements were going to be a problem for the Vienna Circle. In what way was the statement "2 + 2 = 4" related to experience? Some argued that this was a meaningless statement; others (perhaps the majority) held that these were to be regarded as "analytic statements," whose truth was established by definition or convention, so that their validation required no empirical evidence. In what follows, we shall limit our comments to non-analytic statements, to avoid this difficulty in generalization.

For the Vienna Circle, a statement is meaningless unless it can be shown to be capable of being reduced to a statement which directly relates to observation. A statement which cannot be reduced in this way may make grammatical sense, but is meaningless in that it does not express anything. A statement may appear to say something; on closer examination, it proves to be little more than "verbal clutter" (Otto Neurath). Carnap himself illustrated this point by inventing the word "teavy," and indulging in a philosophically playful analysis:

Let us suppose by way of illustration that someone invented the new word "teavy", and maintained that there are things which are teavy and things which are not teavy ... How is one to ascertain in a concrete case whether a given thing is teavy or not? Let us suppose to begin with that we get no answer from him: there are no empirical signs of teavyness, he says. In that case, we would deny the legitimacy of using this word. If the person who uses the word says that all the same there are things which are teavy and things which are not teavy, only that it remains for the weak finite intellect of man an eternal secret which things are teavy and which are not, we shall regard this as empty verbiage.

In other words, there is nothing that we could possibly experience which allows us to determine the meaning of the word "teavy."

What Carnap is setting out is what is now generally known as the "verification principle." In its generally accepted form, this states that only statements which are capable of being verified are meaningful. It will therefore be clear that the natural sciences are being given a position of priority in terms of the theory of knowledge, with philosophy being seen as a tool for clarifying what has been established by empirical analysis. Philosophy, according to Carnap, "consists in the logical analysis of the statements and concepts of empirical science."

These views were popularized in the English language world through the publication of A. J. Ayer's book Language, *Truth and Logic* in 1936. Although the Second World War interfered with the process of its reception and evaluation, this single work is widely regarded as setting the philosophical agenda for at least the two decades which followed that war. Its vigorous and radical application of the verification principle eliminated as "meaningless" virtually everything which had tended to be thought of as metaphysical or religious.

Logical positivism is a philosophical approach which takes its lead from the methods of the natural sciences, and therefore has a particularly important place in this study. It is therefore important to consider its implications for religion. As might be expected from the above analysis, logical positivism has little time for religious statements, which are dismissed as meaningless due to an inability to verify them. Carnap asserted that religious statements were unscientific:

Systematic theology claims to represent knowledge concerning alleged beings of a supernatural order. A claim of this kind must be examined according to the same rigorous standards as any other claim of knowledge. Now in my considered opinion this examination has clearly shown that traditional theology is a remnant of earlier times, entirely out of line with the scientific way of thinking in the present century.

Sentences which make statements about "God," "the transcendent" or "the Absolute" are meaningless, in that there is nothing in experience which can verify them. Ayer allowed that religious statements might provide indirect information concerning the state of mind of the person making such a statement. They could not, however, be considered as making meaningful statements concerning the external world.

The theme of "eschatological verification" enjoyed a degree of popularity during the period 1955–65, and can be regarded as a direct response to the issues raised by the demand for verification as a condition for meaningfulness. (The term "eschatological" derives from the Greek phrase *ta eschata*, "the last things"). The idea can be discerned in I. M. Crombie's contribution to the debate at the Oxford University Socratic Club concerning whether the existence of God could be falsified, to which we shall return in the next section of this chapter. Commenting on the issues raised by the problem of suffering, Crombie remarked that the experience on the basis of which religious statements could be verified was simply not accessible *at present* – but that it would be available after death.

Since our experience is limited in the way it is, we cannot get into a position to decide it . . . For the Christian the operation of getting into position to decide it is called dying; and though we can all do that, we cannot return to report what we find.

This approach was developed more fully by John Hick, who offers an analogy of two people, traveling the same road and having the same experiences. One believes that it leads to the Celestial City; the other does not.

During the course of the journey the issue between them is not an experimental one. They do not entertain different expectations about the coming details of the road, but only about its ultimate destination. And yet when they do turn the last corner it will be apparent that one of them has been right all the time and the other wrong. Thus although the issue between them has been experimental, it has nevertheless from the start been a real issue. They have not merely felt differently about the road; for one was feeling appropriately and the other inappropriately in relation to the actual state of affairs. Their opposed inter-pretations of the road constituted genuinely rival assertions, though assertions whose assertion-status has the peculiar characteristic of being guaranteed retrospectively by a future crux.

However, the issue has since receded in importance, not least on account of an awareness of the severe limitations placed upon the verification principle proposed by logical positivism. To illustrate some of these difficulties, we may consider the following statement: "there were six geese sitting on the front lawn of Buckingham Palace at 5.15 p.m. on June 18, 1865". This statement is clearly meaningful, in that it asserts something which could have been verified. But we are not in a position to confirm them. A similar difficulty arises in relation to other statements concerning the past. For someone such as Ayer, these statements must be considered to be neither true nor false, in that they do not relate to the external world. Yet this clearly runs contrary to our basic intuition that such statements do make meaningful affirmations.

A further issue concerned unobservable theoretical entities – such as subatomic particles. As we noted earlier in this section, these cannot strictly be "observed." This raised significant difficulties for logical positivism, and led some of its leading advocates to modify their position on the matter. Thus in a 1938 paper entitled "Procedures of Empirical Science," V. F. Lenzen argued that certain entities had to be inferred from experimental observation. For example, the behavior of oil droplets in an electric field leads one to infer the existence of electrons as negatively charged particles of a certain mass. They cannot be seen (and hence cannot be "verified") – yet their existence is a reasonable inference from the observational evidence. This represented a very significant dilution of the original verification principle. What is of especial significance here is that this dilution is partly due to theoretical developments within the natural sciences, so highly esteemed by logical positivism.

Verificationism, then, has serious limits. It is therefore instructive to note a rival approach which developed in response to some of the perceived difficulties with the approach. This rival approach is generally known as "falsificationism," and will be considered in the following section.

Falsification: Karl Popper

Karl Popper felt that the verification principle associated with the Vienna Circle was too rigid, and ended up excluding many valid scientific statements.

My criticism of the verifiability criterion has always been this: against the intention of its defenders, it did not exclude obvious metaphysical statements; but it did exclude the most important and interesting of all scientific statements, that is to say, the scientific theories, the universal laws of nature.

But he was also convinced that the emphasis on verification was misplaced for another reason. It ended up by allowing a number of "pseudo-sciences" such as Freudianism and Marxism to pass themselves off as being "scientific" when they were, in reality, nothing of the sort.

Although Popper's original concerns appears to have been the elimination of metaphysics from "meaningful" statements, his attention appears to have shifted to a critique of what he termed "pseudosciences" soon afterwards. For Popper, pseudo-scientists such as Marxists and Freudians were capable of interpreting virtually anything as supportive of their theories:

What I found so striking about these theories, and so dangerous, was the claim that they were "verified" or "confirmed" by an incessant stream of observational evidence. And indeed, once your eyes were opened, you could see verifying instances everywhere. A Marxist could not look at a newspaper without finding verifying evidence of the class struggle on every page ... A psycho-analyst, whether Freudian or Adlerian, assuredly would tell you that he finds his theories daily, even hourly, verified by his clinical observations ... It was precisely this fact – that they always fitted, that they were always "verified" – which impressed their adherents. It began to dawn on me that this apparent strength was in fact a weakness, and that all these "verifications" were too cheap to count as arguments.

At some point around 1920, Popper recalls reading a popular scientific account of Einstein's theory of relativity. What impressed him was Einstein's precise statement of what would be required to demonstrate that his theory was incorrect. Einstein declared that "if the red shift of the spectral lines due to the gravitational potential should not exist, then the general theory of relativity will be untenable."

For Popper, this represented a totally different attitude and outlook from that he associated with Marxists and Freudians. Those committed to these ideologies simply looked for evidence which could confirm their ideas. Einstein was looking for something which might *falsify* his theory! If such evidence was found, he would abandon his theory.

In practice, this was something of an overstatement. What would happen if the predicted redshift was too small to be observed by the technology then available? Or if it was obscured by ineliminable interference from another effect? In the case of light emitted from the sun, general relativity predicted that there should be a gravitational redshift due to the reduction of the velocity of light by a very small amount – 2.12 parts in a million. No such redshift was, in fact, observed at the time – a fact which weighed heavily in the deliberations of the Nobel Prize committees in 1917 and 1919. Yet it is now known that the techniques available in the 1920s simply were not good enough to allow the predicted effect to be observed; it was not until the 1960s that final confirmation was forthcoming. By the criterion which Einstein himself had set out, his own theory could not be confirmed.

Yet Popper felt that the principle involved was important. Theories had to be tested against experience, which would lead to their being verified or falsified.

I shall certainly admit a system as empirical or scientific only if it is capable of being tested by experience. These considerations suggest that not the *verifiability* but the *falsifiability* of a system is to be taken as the criterion of demarcation ... It must be possible for an empirical scientific system to be refuted by experience.

From this discussion, it will be clear that Popper has accepted some of the most fundamental themes of logical positivism, above all the foundational role of experience of the real world. A theoretical system must be capable of being tested against observation of the world. But where logical positivism stressed the need for stating the conditions under which a theoretical statement could be verified, Popper held that the emphasis must fall upon being able to state the conditions under which the system could be falsified.

Popper thus placed emphasis upon experiments which could falsify a theory. However, as we noted earlier, Duhem had argued that it was, as a matter of fact, impossible to devise a "critical experiment," in that there would always be a significant degree of uncertainty as to whether the experiment required a theory to be abandoned in its totality, or whether the difficulty lay in only one of its hypotheses, or even an auxiliary hypothesis, which was not of fundamental importance to the theory itself. Popper's approach appeared to ignore the strongly theory-laden nature of experimental observation, which rendered his critique considerably less potent that he might have hoped.

Popper's approach had considerable influence within the philosophy of religion during the 1950s and 1960s, and is especially linked with what has come to be known as the "falsification" debate. In his study "Theology and Falsification," Anthony Flew argues that religious statements cannot be regarded as meaningful, in that nothing drawn from experience can be regarded as falsifying them. In effect, Flew is following Popper's criticisms of Marxism and Freudianism, which he held to be capable of interpreting observational or experiential evidence in whatever manner they pleased.

Flew sets out his concerns by way of what he calls a parable. Two explorers come across a clearing in the jungle. One of the explorers states his belief that there is an invisible gardener who looks after the clearing. The second explorer denies this, and suggests that they try to confirm this by means of various sensory tests – such as watching for the gardener to visit the clearing, and using bloodhounds and electric fences to detect his presence. None of the tests detects the gardener. The second explorer argues that this demonstrates that there is no gardener. The first, however, meets all these objections with qualifications. "There is a gardener," he argues, "who has no scent and makes no sound." In the end, Flew argues that the idea of the gardener meets the "death of a thousand qualifications." The gardener cannot be seen, heard, smelled, or touched. So might one not be forgiven for concluding that there really is no gardener? That, certainly, was Flew's conclusion. It rested upon the fact that religious statements cannot be formulated in a manner in which they can be falsified.

However, the demand for falsification – like the earlier demand for verification – proves to be much more complex than might at first have been thought. For example, Flew's absolute demands cannot be met by the natural sciences, which introduce precisely the modifications or "qualifications" to which Flew objects so strongly in the process of theory development. Anomalous data is generally accommodated within theories by a subtle and complex process of adjustment, modification, and qualification. The absolute demand for something which incontestably falsifies a theory – often stated in terms of a "crucial experiment" – is actually unrealistic in the natural sciences, on account of the issues explored by Duhem, and noted earlier (pp. 67–71).

Popper's particular concern lay with eliminating metaphysics from science, and he thought that he had found a way of excluding metaphysical statements by demanding that they be falsifiable. Yet Popper's attempt to set up a meaningful falsification criterion turns out to be rather more difficult than he had hoped. An excellent example is provided by what is known as the "tacking paradox." Let us define T as a falsifiable theory – for example, "all swans are white." Since T is falsifiable, there must be an observation statement O which follows from it. On the basis of the example we have given, such an observation statement might take the form "all swans are observed to be white". If we find that this observation does not correspond to the way things really are, then it follows that T itself is false.

So far, so good. But the "tacking paradox" now makes this simple scheme rather more complicated. Stated in its simplest form, the paradox involves the "tacking on" of an additional metaphysical statement M – for example, "Zeus is hungry" or "The Absolute is blue". Now define theory T' as follows:

$$T' = T \, \& \, M$$

In other words, the new theory is an amalgam of the original and a new metaphysical statement. Since T is falsifiable, it also follows that T' is falsifiable, in that the observation of a black swan would show the theory to be false. The fact that a totally arbitrary (and, one assumes, unverifiable and unfalsifiable) metaphysical statement has been tacked on makes no difference at this point.

To state this a little more clearly. Suppose that we have a theory which consists of two parts:

1 All swans are white;
2 The Absolute is blue.

If a black swan were to be observed, the theory which consists of both of these parts would be shown to be incorrect, in that one of its parts would be incorrect. The "tacking paradox" refers to the disconcerting fact that any arbitrary metaphysical hypothesis can be incorporated into a falsifiable theory – which seriously weakens the appeal of Popper's approach.

So how do scientific theories develop? In what follows, we shall explore the approach adopted by Thomas S. Kuhn, which is often stated in terms of "paradigm shifts."

Paradigm Shifts in Science: Thomas S. Kuhn

One of the most widely-discussed accounts of the development of the scientific method focused on the idea of "scientific revolutions." In his *Structure of Scientific Revolutions*, Thomas S. Kuhn argued that the prevailing view of the nature of scientific progress was that radically new theories arise gradually through verification or falsification. The transition from one paradigm to another is not gradual, but takes the form of a rapid transition, with major shifts in understanding. Kuhn here takes issue with the "gradual progress" model which can be found in Karl Popper's *Logic of Scientific Discovery*.

Kuhn's use of the term "paradigm" is confused, and has led to serious misunderstandings of what he intended. In general terms, he uses the term in two senses:

1 The word is used in a general sense, to refer to the broad group of common assumptions which unites particular group of scientists. It is an accepted cluster of generalizations, methods, and models.
2 The term is also used in a more specific and restricted sense to refer to a past scientific explanatory success, which seems to offer a framework which can be treated as normative, and is hence treated as exemplary thereafter – until something finally causes that paradigm to be abandoned.

For our purposes in this section, we shall use the term to refer to "a strong network of commitments – conceptual, theoretical, instrumental, and methodological."

On the basis of his studies of the development of the natural sciences, Kuhn argued that a given paradigm is accepted as normative on account of its past explanatory success. Once a given paradigm has been accepted, a period of what Kuhn terms "normal science" follows. During this period, the paradigm which resulted from this earlier success is accepted. Experimental evidence which appears to contradict is treated as anomalous – that is, as items which pose difficulties for the paradigm, but which do not require the paradigm to be abandoned. In effect, the anomaly is regarded as something for which a solution is anticipated within the context of that paradigm, even if at present the precise nature of that solution remains unclear. *Ad hoc* modifications are proposed to the existing paradigm – as in the case of Ptolemaic astronomy, in which disparity between theory and observation could be accounted for through the addition of additional epicyles to the system.

But what happens if a series of anomalies build up, and achieve a cumulative force which calls the paradigm into question? Or if a single anomaly becomes of such significance that the challenge which it poses cannot be overlooked? Kuhn argues that, in such situations, a crisis arises within the paradigm which is to be seen as a prelude to a "scientific revolution." Kuhn contrasts this *revolutionary* approach with an essentially *evolutionary* model which sees a steady progression in scientific understanding through a gradual accumulation of data and understanding. Where other historians of science spoke of "scientific progress," Kuhn preferred the imagery of a revolution, in which a major change in assumptions took place over a short period of time.

The transition between competing paradigms cannot be made one step at a time, forced by logic and neutral experience ... It must occur all at once (though not necessarily in an instant) or not at all ... In these matters neither proof nor error is at issue. The transfer of allegiance from paradigm to paradigm is a conversion experience that cannot be forced.

An essential point in Kuhn's argument is that established and future paradigms are incommensurable, so that the old must give way to the new. There is no way in which part of the older paradigm can be retained; it is displaced by the new. This paradigm shift leads to things being seen, understood, and investigated in a new way:

Led by a new paradigm, scientists adopt new instruments and look in new places. Even more important, during revolutions scientists see new and different things when looking with familiar instruments in places they have looked before. It is rather as if the professional communtity had been suddenly transported to another planet where familiar objects are seen in a different light and are joined by unfamiliar ones as well. Of course, nothing of quite that sort does occur: there is no geographical transplantation; outside the laboratory everyday affairs usually continue as before. Nevertheless, paradigm changes do cause scientists to see the world of their research-engagement differently. In so far as their only recourse to that world is through what they see and do, we may want to say that after a revolution, scientists are responding to a different world.

The critical point to note is that the factors which precipitate this revolution are not necessarily rational in character. Kuhn argues that a complex network of issues lie behind the decision to abandon one paradigm and accept another, and that these cannot be explained solely on the basis of scientific considerations. Highly subjective issues are involved. Kuhn compares a "paradigm shift" to a "conversion." His emphasis on the subjective reasons for paradigm shifts has led some of his critics to suggest that his account of scientific development seems to rest too much on "mob psychology."

Kuhn's analysis of the development of scientific understanding has been subjected to considerable criticism on other grounds. In part, this has related to the notion that successive paradigms are "incommensurable." For some of his critics, this is simply inaccurate. Stephen Toulmin argues that there is far more continuity across a revolution than Kuhn allows, and that he fails to observe that frequent small changes are far more typical of scientific progress than the more radical "revolutions" which Kuhn proposed. The changeover from, for example, Newtonian to Einsteinian physics does not require to be described as a "paradigm shift."

Kuhn's work has importance for religious belief, and two of his central themes may be explored to illustrate his relevance. First, Kuhn's concept of "paradigm shifts" is helpful in attempting to understand the major intellectual shifts which have taken place in the history of religious thought. As we have noted, religious thinking is influenced, at least to some extent, by the cultural and philosophical presuppositions of the day. Radical shifts in these background assumptions can thus be of major importance, as the development of Christian theology has demonstrated. For example, consider the following epochs in modern western Christian thought: The Reformation; The Enlightenment; Postmodernism. Each of these can be seen as representing a "paradigm shift", with radical changes in our understanding of how theology should be done. Existing understandings of background presuppositions, norms, and methods are often radically altered – and occasionally abandoned altogether – in the transition from one paradigm to another.

Our second point of interest concerns the issue of realism. Kuhn rejects realism as an explanation of the successes of scientific research, and thus does not see an increasing convergence between "theory" and "reality" as an explanation of scientific progress. Nothing, he argues is lost in rejecting the realist account of scientific development. Yet how can one meaningfully talk of "progress," unless there is some means of knowing that science is proceeding in the right direction, rather than taking a false turn which will need to be corrected in future?

Kuhn's work has inspired a substantial amount of writing in the field of the sociology of knowledge, arguing that, since theories are always underdetermined by evidence, theory-choice takes place on the basis of sociological considerations. In other words, the decision to accept one theory rather than another rests not so much on experimental evidence, as on various social values, vested interests, and institutional concerns. This has raised the very significant question of whether religious doctrines correspond to anything that is "real," or whether they can be seen as determined by social factors. For example, it might be argued that the traditional Christian doctrine of the "two natures" of Christ is not determined by the phenomena this doctrine is required to explain, but by some aspects of the political agenda of the Roman Empire.

This debate is of considerable importance, and cannot be gone into in any detail at this point. However, it is important to realize that Kuhn's understanding of how paradigms shift places considerable emphasis on non-scientific factors, and that this understanding of how paradigms are adopted and abandoned has wider implications for religious belief.

Knowledge and Commitment: Michael Polanyi

One of the most intriguing writers in the field of the philosophy of science is the Hungarian chemist Michael Polanyi (1890–1976). Polanyi's work has been extensively cited by religious writers, and it is arguable that he has had far greater impact on religious writers than his fellow scientists. Polanyi was born into a Jewish family in Budapest. In his early years, Polanyi belonged to "the Galileo Circle," a small group of students who held that science held the key to the solution of the world's problems. This somewhat ambitious and optimistic attitude toward what Mary Midgely has termed "science as salvation" gradually gave way to a growing interest in the spiritual side of life, inspired and nourished by Russian writers of the nineteenth century, such as Tolstoy and Dostoyevski. At the age of 28, he was received into the Roman Catholic church.

In the following year, Polanyi secured an academic teaching position at the Kaiser Wilhelm Institute for Physical Chemistry. This position became insecure through the rise of Nazism in the 1930s. The Nazis disliked having people of Jewish descent in significant academic positions, and Polanyi recognized that he would be wise to leave Germany. He obtained a position as Professor of Physical Chemistry in Manchester, in the north-west of England, in 1933. As his research interests shifted, so did his teaching responsibilities: in 1948, he was appointed to a chair in social science.

Polanyi's most significant work to deal with the philosophy of science is widely agreed to be *Personal Knowledge: Towards a Post-Critical Philosophy* (1958). This work has had considerable influence on many religious thinkers, particularly within the Christian tradition. Thomas F. Torrance (see pp. 225–8) is a particularly luminous example of a major Christian writer whose ideas have been developed in dialogue with Polanyi. This wide interest in Polanyi on the part of religious writers must not be seen as a distortion of Polanyi's intentions or interests. Polanyi himself was a religious man (although it is widely agreed that the precise nature of his own religious views will probably remain unclear) and frequently addresses religious issues in his published writings.

So what are the main areas in which Polanyi is significant in relation to the science and religion discussion? It is generally agreed that the insight of Polanyi which has been most extensively cited by religious writers relates to the nature of knowledge itself. This idea is developed with particular force in *Personal Knowledge*, although it can also be seen in the earlier work *Science, Faith and Society*. Polanyi's fundamental assertion here is that all knowledge – whether it relates to the natural sciences, religion, or philosophy – is *personal* in nature. Polanyi's post-critical approach to the nature of knowledge argues that knowledge must involve personal commitment. Although knowledge involves concepts or ideas, it also involves something more profound – a personal involvement with that which is known, which Polanyi refers to as "the fiduciary rootedness of all rationality."

The point at issue is not easy to appreciate, and may need further illustration and explanation. Polanyi uses the image of a blind man feeling his way by means of a white stick. He does not "see" anything, but gains an awareness of the obstacles in his path by interpreting the sensations which he derives from the stick into an awareness of the things which are being touched by its point. The blind man is dependent upon the stick for his knowledge of what lies around him. However, he cannot discern this information directly. He experiences or observes the world through his stick. Once he has become accustomed to using the stick, it becomes transparent to him, in that he does not *consciously* use the stick. He has become so used to it that it acts, so to speak, as an extension of himself. Polanyi thus speaks of the blind man *indwelling* the stick.

The significance of the analogy is not easily understood, and is perhaps best appreciated by comparing it with the theories of perception which are associated with the Enlightenment, and particularly the tradition associated with Descartes. This view tended to offer a dualism of *passive sense and active reason*. In other words, the senses (such as sight) passively provided data, which the mind actively interpreted. For Polanyi, the senses are active in the process of perception. Just as the blind man learns to trust his white stick and depend upon it, so we are obliged to trust our perceptions. Occasionally, they may mislead us. Knowledge is thus not disembodied ideas, as the Enlightenment suggested, but involves the personal element of commitment both to what is known, and the means which must be used to know it. The natural sciences can be understood in terms of personal knowledge, intellectual commitment, and a passionate and committed search for patterns in nature. Whereas the Enlightenment tended to regard personal commitment as incompatible with objectivity, Polanyi argues that it is integral to the process of knowing.

The religious significance of this line of thought will be clear. Polanyi liberates theology from several significant straitjackets of Enlightenment rationalism, most significantly the demand that theology should be devoid of any commitment to its object or methods. For the Enlightenment, commitment was detrimental to objectivity. This posed problems for religious writers, who were often deeply committed to the ideas which they were exploring. Polanyi's declaration of "the fiduciary rootedness of all rationality" eliminates this difficulty by asserting that all valid knowledge involves commitment on the part of the knower.

The present chapter has aimed to explore the way in which the philosophy of science has had an impact on religious thought. But what of the way in which the philosophy of religion has drawn upon scientific insights? We shall consider this in the following chapter.

For further reading

Achtemeier, P. M. "The Truth of Tradition: Critical Realism in the Thought of Alasdair MacIntyre and T. F. Torrance." *Scottish Journal of Theology* 47 (1994): 355–74.

Ariew, R. "The Duhem Thesis." *British Journal for the Philosophy of Science* 35 (1984): 313–25.

Aune, B. *Rationalism, Empiricism and Pragmatism: An Introduction*. New York: Random House, 1970.

Balashov, Y. "Duhem, Quine, and the Multiplicity of Scientific Tests." *Philosophy of Science* 61 (1994): 608–28.

Bloor, D. "Popper's Mystification of Objective Knowledge." *Science Studies* 4 (1974): 65–76.

Boyd, R. "Scientific Realism and Naturalistic Epistemology." *Proceedings of the Philosophy of Science Association*. Ed. Peter D. Asquith and Ronald N. Giere. Vol. 2. East Lansing, MI: Philosophy of Science Association, 1980, pp. 613–62.

Byrne, P. A. "Berkeley, Scientific Realism and Creation." *Religious Studies* 20 (1984): 453–64.

Devitt, M. *Realism and Truth*. Oxford: Blackwell, 1984.

Gellman, J. "Theological Realism." *International Journal for Philosophy of Religion* 12 (1981): 17–27.

Grünbaum, A. "The Duhemian Argument." *Philosophy of Science* 27 (1960): 75–87.

Harré, R. *Varieties of Realism: A Rationale for the Natural Sciences*. Oxford: Basil Blackwell, 1986.

Jeffrey, R. C. "Probability and Falsification: Critique of the Popper Program." *Synthese* 30 (1975): 95–117.

Kroger, J. "Theology and Notions of Reason and Science: A Note on a Point of Comparison in Lonergan and Polanyi." *Journal of Religion* 56 (1976): 157–61.

Kukla, A. "Scientific Realism, Scientific Practice and the Natural Ontological Attitude." *British Journal for the Philosophy of Science* 45 (1994): 955–75.

Polanyi, M. *Personal Knowledge*. New York: Harper & Row, 1964.

Polikarov, A. "On the Nature of Einstein's Realism." *Epistemologia* 12 (1989): 277–304.

Putnam, H. "Three Kinds of Scientific Realism." *The Philosophical Quarterly* 32 (1982): 195–200.

Schouls, P. A. *The Imposition of Method: A Study of Descartes and Locke*. Oxford: Clarendon Press, 1980.

Schrader, D. E. "Karl Popper as a Point of Departure for a Philosophy of Theology." *International Journal for Philosophy of Religion* 14 (1983): 193–201.

Smart, J. J. C. *Philosophy and Scientific Realism*. London: Routledge and Kegan Paul, 1963.

Soskice, J. "Theological Realism." *The Rationality of Religious Belief*. Ed. W. J. Abraham and S. Holtzer. Oxford and New York: Clarendon Press, 1987, pp. 105–19.

Torrance, T. F. "Realism and Openness in Scientific Inquiry." *Zygon* 23 (1988): 159–69.

Trigg, R. *Reality at Risk: a Defence of Realism in Philosophy and the Sciences*. 2nd edn. London: Harvester Press/Simon and Schuster, 1989.

Weightman, C. *Theology in a Polanyian Universe: The Theology of Thomas F. Torrance*. New York/Berne: Peter Lang, 1994.

4

Science and the Philosophy of Religion

In the previous chapter, we explored the way in which some of the leading themes of the philosophy of science were of interest and potential importance to religious issues. The present chapter develops this approach further, by examining the way in which the insights of the natural sciences have implications for the philosophy of religion. The philosophy of religion is a very broad subject, and for our purposes we shall focus on one of its most important themes – philosophical arguments for the existence of God. In what way do the insights of the natural sciences affect such arguments?

It is not our intention to provide an exhaustive discussion of these questions, but simply to indicate the way in which there is significant interaction between the natural sciences and the philosophy of religion. It is clear that the modern discussion of arguments for God's existence make extensive reference to scientific (especially astronomical) understandings of the world.

The most helpful way of examining this question is to explore some of the types of argument that have been developed within the philosophy of religion, and then focus specifically on the arguments which are particularly affected by the natural sciences. We shall therefore begin our analysis by turning to deal with some of the classic arguments for the existence of God, to allow the reader to gain something of an understanding of the types of approach which are widely discussed within this field of study.

Philosophical Arguments for the Existence of God

The most widely discussed philosophical arguments for the existence of God were developed by Anselm of Canterbury and Thomas Aquinas during the Middle Ages. We shall consider the "ontological argument" and the "Five Ways" in what follows.

Anselm of Canterbury's ontological argument

Anselm of Canterbury (*c.*1033–1109) was born in Italy He migrated to Normandy in 1059, entering the famous monastery of Bec, becoming its prior in 1063, and abbot in 1078. In 1093 he was appointed archbishop of Canterbury. He is chiefly noted for his strong defense of the intellectual foundations of Christianity, and is especially associated with the "ontological argument" for the existence of God. This "ontological argment" is first set out in his *Proslogion*, a work which dates from 1079. (The term "ontological" refers to the branch of philosophy which deals with the notion of "being".) Anselm himself does not refer to his discussion as an "ontological" argument. The *Proslogion* is really a work of meditation, not of logical argument. In the course of this work, Anselm reflects on how self-evident the idea of God has become to him, and what the implications of this might be.

In his *Proslogion*, Anselm offers a definition of God as "that than which no greater thing can be thought" (*aliquid quo maius cogitari non potest*). He argues that, if this definition of God is correct, it necessarily implies the existence of God. The reason for this is as follows. If God does not exist, the idea of God remains, yet the reality of God is absent. Yet the reality of God is greater than the idea of God. Therefore, if God is "that than which no greater thing can be thought," the idea of God must lead to accepting the reality of God, in that otherwise the mere idea of God is the greatest thing which can be thought. And this contradicts the definition of God on which the argument is based. Therefore, given the existence of the idea of God, and the acceptance of the definition of God as "that than which no greater thing can be thought," the reality of God necessarily follows. Note that the Latin verb *cogitare* is sometimes translated as "conceive," leading to the definition of God as "that than which no greater thing can be conceived." Both translations are acceptable.

God is thus defined as "that than which nothing greater can be conceived." Now the idea of such a being is one thing; the reality is another. Thinking of a hundred dollar bill is quite different from having a hundred dollar bill in your hands – and much less satisfying, as well. Anselm's point is this: the idea of something is inferior to the reality. So the idea of God as "that than which nothing greater can be conceived" contains a contradiction – because the reality of God would be superior to this idea. In other words, if this definition of God is correct, and exists in the human mind, then the corresponding reality must also exist. Anselm espresses this point as follows:

This [definition of God] is indeed so true that it cannot be thought of as not being true. For it is quite possible to think of something whose non-existence cannot be thought of. This must be greater than something whose non-existence can be thought of. So if this thing (than which no greater thing can thought) can be thought of as not existing, then, that very thing than which a greater thing cannot be thought is not that than which a greater cannot be thought. This is a contradiction. So it is true that there exists something than which nothing greater can be thought, that it cannot be thought of as not existing. And you are this thing, O Lord our God! So truly therefore do you exist, O Lord my God, that you cannot be thought of as not existing, and with good reason; for if a human mind could think of anything greater than you, the creature would rise above the Creator and judge you; which is obviously absurd. And in truth whatever else there be beside you may be thought of as not existing. So you alone, most truly of all, and therefore most of all, have existence: because whatever else exists, does not exist as truly as you, and therefore exists to a lesser degree.

This is an important argument, but it did not persuade one of his earliest critics, a Benedictine monk named Gaunilo who made a response known as "A Reply on Behalf of the Fool" (the reference being to Psalm 14: 1, cited by Anselm, "The fool says in his heart that there is no God"). There is, according to Gaunilo, an obvious logical weakness in Anselm's "argument" (although it must be stressed than Anselm does not really regard it as an argument in the first place). Imagine, Gaunilo suggests, an island, so lovely that a more perfect island cannot be conceived. By the same argument, Gaunilo suggested, that island must exist, in that the reality of the island is necessarily more perfect that the mere idea. In much the same way, we might argue that the idea of a hundred dollar bill seems, according to Anselm, to imply that we have such a bill in our hands. The mere idea of something – whether a perfect island or God – thus does not guarantee its existence. Gaunilo sets out his objections as follows:

People say that somewhere in the ocean there is an island which, because of the difficulty (or rather the impossibility) of finding that which does not exist, some have called the "Lost Island". And we are told that it is blessed with all manner of priceless riches and delights in abundance, far more than the Happy Isles, and, having no owner or inhabitant, it is superior in every respect in the abundance of its riches to all those other lands that are inhabited by people. Now, if someone were to tell me about this, I shall easily understand what is said, since there is nothing difficult about it. But if I am then told, as though it were a direct consequence of this: "You cannot any more doubt that this island that is more excellent than all other lands truly exists somewhere in reality than you can doubt that it is in your mind; and since it is more excellent to exist not just in your mind but in reality as well, therefore it must exist. For if it did not exist, any other land existing in reality would be more excellent than it, and so this island, already conceived by you to be more excellent than others, will not be more excellent." I say that if anyone wanted to persuade me in this way that this island really exists beyond all doubt, I should either think that they were joking, or I should find it hard to decide which of us I ought to think of as the bigger fool: I myself, if I agreed with them, or they, if they thought that they they had proved the existence of this island with any certainty, unless they had first persuaded me that its very excellence exists in my mind precisely as a thing existing truly and indubitably and not just as something unreal or doubtfully real.

The response offered by Gaunilo is widely regarded as exposing a serious weakness in Anselm's argument. The text itself is so clear that no comment is needed. It may, however, be pointed out that Anselm is not so easily dismissed. Part of his argument is that it is an essential part of the definition of God that he is "that than which nothing greater can be conceived." God therefore belongs to a totally different category than islands or dollar bills. It is part of the nature of God to transcend everything else. Once the believer has come to understand what the word "God" means, then God really does exist for him or her. This is the intention of Anselm's meditation in the *Proslogion*: to reflect on how the Christian understanding of the nature of God reinforces belief in his reality. The "argument" does not really have force outside this context of faith, and Anselm never intended it to be used in this general philosophical manner.

Furthermore, Anselm argued that Gaunilo had not entirely under-stood him. The argument which he set out in the *Proslogion* did not involve the idea that there is a being that is, as a matter of fact, greater than any other being; rather, Anselm had argued for a being so great that a greater one could not even be conceived. The argument continues, and it remains a disputed question to this day as to whether Anselm's argument has a genuine basis.

Thomas Aquinas' Five Ways

Thomas Aquinas (*c.*1225–74) is probably the most famous and influential theologian of the Middle Ages. Born in Italy, he achieved his fame through his teaching and writing at the university of Paris and other northern universities. His fame rests chiefly on his *Summa Theologica*, composed toward the end of his life and not totally finished at the time of his death. However, he also wrote many other significant works, particuarly the *Summa contra Gentiles*, which represents a major statement of the rationality of the Christian faith, and especially the existence of God. Aquinas believed that it was entirely proper to identify pointers toward the existence of God, drawn from general human experience of the world. His "Five Ways" represent five lines of argument in support of the existence of God, each of which draws on some aspect of the world which "points" to the existence of its creator.

So what kind of pointers does Aquinas identify? The basic line of thought guiding Aquinas is that the world mirrors God, as its creator – an idea which is given more formal expression in his doctrine of the "analogy of being." Just as an artist might sign a painting to identify it as his handiwork, so God has stamped a divine "signature" upon the creation. What we observe in the world – for example, its signs of ordering – can be explained on the basis of the existence of God as its creator. God is both its first cause and its designer. God both brought the world into existence, and impressed the divine image and likeness upon it.

So where might we look in creation to find evidence for the existence of God? Aquinas argues that the ordering of the world is the most convincing evidence of God's existence and wisdom. This basic assumption underlies each of the "Five Ways," although it is of particular importance in the case of the argument often referred to as the "argument from design" or the "teleological argument." We shall consider each of these "ways" individually, before focusing on two in a subsequent part of this chapter.

The first way begins from the observation that things in the world are in motion or change. The world is not static, but is dynamic. Examples of this are easy to list. Rain falls from the sky. Stones roll down valleys. The earth revolves around the sun (a fact, incidentally, unknown to

Aquinas). This, the first of Aquinas' arguments, is normally referred to as the "argument from motion"; however, it is clear that the "movement" in question is actually understood in more general terms, so that the term "change" is more appropriate as a translation at points.

So how did nature come to be in motion? Why is it changing? Why isn't it static? Aquinas argues that everything which moves is moved by something else. For every motion, there is a cause. Things don't just move – they are moved by something else. Now each cause of motion must itself have a cause. And that cause must have a cause as well. And so Aquinas argues that there are a whole series of causes of motion lying behind the world as we know it. Now unless there are an infinite number of these causes, Aquinas argues, there must be a single cause right at the origin of the series. From this original cause of motion, all other motion is ultimately derived. This is the origin of the great chain of causality which we see reflected in the way the world behaves. From the fact that things are in motion, Aquinas thus argues for the existence of a single original cause of all this motion – and this, he concludes, is none other than God.

The second way begins from the idea of causation. In other words, Aquinas notes the existence of causes and effects in the world. One event (the effect) is explained by the influence of another (the cause). The idea of motion, which we looked at briefly above, is a good example of this cause-and-effect sequence. Using a line of reasoning similar to that used above, Aquinas thus argues that all effects may be traced back to a single original cause – which is God.

The third way concerns the existence of contingent beings. In other words, the world contains beings (such as human beings) which are not there as a matter of necessity. Aquinas contrasts this type of being with a necessary being (one who is there as a matter of necessity). Whilst God is a necessary being, Aquinas argues that humans are contingent beings. The fact that we *are* here needs explanation. Why are we here? What happened to bring us into existence? Aquinas argues that a being comes into existence because something which already exists brought it into being. In other words, our existence is caused by another being. We are the effects of a series of causation. Tracing this series back to its origin, Aquinas declares that this original cause of being can only be someone whose existence is necessary – in other words, God.

The fourth way begins from human values, such as truth, goodness and nobility. Where do these values come from? What causes them? Aquinas argues that there must be something which is in itself true, good and noble, and that this brings into being our ideas of truth, goodness, and nobility. The origin of these ideas, Aquinas suggests, is God, who is their original cause.

The fifth and final way is the teleological argument itself. Aquinas notes that the world shows obvious traces of intelligent design. Natural processes and objects seem to be adapted with certain definite objectives in mind. They seem to have a purpose. They seem to have been designed. But things don't design themselves: they are caused and designed by someone or something else. Arguing from this observation, Aquinas concludes that the source of this natural ordering must be conceded to be God.

It will be obvious that most of Aquinas' arguments are rather similar in terms of their structure. Each depends on tracing a causal sequence back to its single origin, and identifying this with God. A number of criticisms of the "Five Ways" were made by Aquinas' critics during the Middle Ages, such as Duns Scotus and William of Ockham. The following are especially important.

1 Why is the idea of an infinite regression of causes impossible? For example, the argument from motion only really works if it can be shown that the sequence of cause and effect stops somewhere. There has to be, according to Aquinas, a Prime Unmoved Mover. But he fails to demonstrate this point.

2 Why do these arguments lead to belief in only one God? The argument from motion, for example, could lead to belief in a number of Prime Unmoved Movers. There seems to be no especially pressing reason for insisting that there can only be one such cause, except for the fundamental Christian insistence that, as a matter of fact, there is only one such God.

3 These arguments do not demonstrate that God continues to exist. Having caused things to happen, God might cease to exist. The continuing existence of events does not necessarily imply the continuing existence of their originator. Aquinas' arguments, Ockham suggests, might lead to a belief that God existed once upon a time – but not necessarily now. Ockham developed a somewhat complex argument, based on the idea of God continuing to sustain the universe, which attempts to get round this difficulty.

These, then, are some of the traditional arguments which have been used and developed within the philosophy of religion. But how are they affected by the kind of insights which are associated with the natural sciences? We shall consider this question in what follows.

Science and Arguments for the Existence of God

It is generally agreed that there are three general categories of arguments for the existence of God which are of particular importance in relation to the natural sciences. These are generally referred to as the "cosmological", "teleological" and "kalam" arguments, although there is some debate about whether the third is to be regarded as a distinct category or argument in its own right, or a category of the more general cosmological argument. For our purposes, we shall assume that it requires separate discussion as an argument in its own right.

The cosmological argument

In considering Aquinas' "Five Ways," we noted the importance of the argument from motion (often referred to by the Latin phrase *ex motu*), which argues from the observation of change or motion in the world to the existence of a first cause which is responsible for these events. The "first cause" argument is often referred to simply as "the cosmological argument," although it should be noted that it could be treated simply as one of several possible cosmological arguments (including the "kalam" argument, to be considered below). It will be helpful if we set out Aquinas' own presentation of this argument of this argument, which constitutes the first of his "Five Ways":

The existence of God can be proved in five ways. The first and most obvious proof is the argument from change (*ex parte motus*). It is clearly the case that some things in this world are in the process of changing. Now everything that is in the process of being changed is changed by something else, since nothing is changed unless it is potentially that towards which it being changed, whereas that which changes is actual. To change something is nothing else than to bring it from potentiality to actuality, and a thing can be brought from potentiality to actuality only by something which is actual. Thus a fire, which is actually hot, makes wood, which is potentially hot, to be actually hot, thus changing and altering it. Now it is impossible for the same thing to be both actual and potential in the same respect, although it may be so in different respects. What is actually hot cannot at the same time be potentially hot, although it is potentially cold. It is therefore impossible that, in the same manner and in the same way, anything should be both the one which effects and change and the one that is changed, so that it should change itself. Whatever is changed must therefore be changed by something else. If, then, whatever is changing it is itself changed, this also must be changed by something else, and this in turn by something else again. But this cannot go on forever, since there would then be no first cause to this process of change, and consequently no other agent of change, because secondary things which change cannot change unless they are changed by a first cause, in the same way as a stick cannot move unless it is moved by the hand. We are therefore bound to arrive at a first cause of change which is not changed by anything, and everyone understands that this is God.

As will be clear from this citation, Aquinas excludes the possibility that there exists an infinite series of causes for a given event. At some point, the chain of causality terminates in the first cause. For Aquinas, there can be no doubt that this is God.

In more recent times, this argument has been restated in more explicitly cosmological terms (hence the title now widely used to refer to it). The most commonly encountered statement of the argument runs along the following lines:

1 Everything within the universe depends on something else for its existence;
2 What is true of its individual parts is also true of the universe itself;
3 The universe thus depends on something else for its existence for as long as it has existed or will exist;
4 The universe thus depends on God for its existence.

The argument basically assumes that the existence of the universe is something that requires explanation. It will be clear that this type of argument relates directly to modern cosmological research, particularly the "big bang" theory of the origins of the cosmos. This is also true of the "kalam" version of the cosmological argument, to which we now turn.

The kalam argument

The argument which we shall refer to as the "kalam" argument derives its name from an Arabic school of philosophy which flourished in the early Middle Ages. A. E. Sabra has defined *kalam* as "an inquiry into God, and into the world as God's creation, and into man as the special creature placed by God in the world under obligation to his creator". The *mutakallimun* (as the practitioners of the *kalam* approach were known) saw themselves as reconciling revealed truth and human wisdom.

As part of that task, the *mutakallimun* developed an argument for the existence of God which stressed the importance of causality. Some scholars regard this as a variant of the cosmological argument, already set out above. However, others regard it has having distinct features, meriting its treatment in its own right. The basic structure of the argument can be set out as four propositions:

1 Everything which has a beginning must have a cause;
2 The universe began to exist;
3 Therefore the beginning of the existence of the universe must have been caused by something;
4 The only such cause can be God.

It will be clear that the basic contours of this argument can be discerned within Aquinas' "Five Ways," discussed earlier.

The structure of the argument is clear, and its implications need little in the way of further development. If the existence of something can be said to have begun, it follows – so it is argued – that it must have a cause. If this type of argument is linked with the idea of a "Big Bang" (see p. 180), its relevance for our discussion will be clear. Modern cosmology strongly suggests that the universe had a beginning. If the universe began to exist at a certain time, it must have had a cause. And what cause could there be other than God?

This form of the "kalam" argument has been widely debated in recent years. One of its most significant defenders has been William Lane Craig, who sets out its main features as follows:

Since everything that begins to exist has a cause of its existence, and since the universe began to exist, we conclude, therefore, the universe has a cause of its existence ... Transcending the entire universe there exists a cause which has brought the universe into being.

Debate over the argument has centred on three questions, one of which could be described as "scientific" and the other two philosophical.

1 Can something have a beginning without being caused? In one of his dialogues, David Hume argues that it is possible to conceive of something that comes into being, without necessarily pointing to

some definite cause of that existence. Nevertheless, this suggestion raises considerable difficulties.

2   Can one speak of the universe having a beginning? At one level, this is a profoundly philosophical question. At another, however, it is a scientific question, which can be considered on the basis of known observations concerning the rate of expansion of the universe, and the background radiation evidence for the "big bang."

3   If the universe can be considered to have been "caused," can this cause be directly identified with God? One line of argument of note here takes the following form. A cause must be prior to the event which it causes. To speak of a cause for the beginning of the existence of the universe is thus to speak of something which existed before the universe. And if this is not God, what is it?

It will be clear that the traditional "kalam" argument has been given a new lease of life by the "big bang" theory of the origins of the universe. The philosophical issues which are raised are likely to remain disputed. For example, consider Elizabeth Anscombe's criticism of the view that things are not caused, but just happen:

If I say I can imagine a rabbit coming into being without a parent rabbit, well and good: I imagine a rabbit coming into being, and our observing that there is no parent rabbit about. But what am I to imagine if I just imagine a rabbit coming into being without a cause? Well, I just imagine a rabbit coming into being. That this is the imagination of a rabbit coming into being without a cause is nothing but, as it were, *the title* of that picture. Indeed, I can form an image and give my picture that title. But from my being able to do *that*, nothing whatever follows about what it is possible to suppose "without contradiction or absurdity" as holding in reality.

Anscombe's point is that it is one thing to form a mental picture of something (such as a rabbit) coming into being without a cause. But that is no indication that this situation exists in reality.

A similar debate focuses on the question of whether the universe can be said to be "designed," and we shall consider this issue in what follows.

The teleological argument

The "teleological" argument is more widely known as the "argument from design," and is among the most widely discussed of the philosophical arguments for the existence of God. As stated by Thomas Aquinas, the argument (which is the fifth of his "Five Ways") takes the following form:

The fifth way is based on the governance of things. We see how some things, like natural bodies, work for an end even though they have no knowledge. The fact that they nearly always operate in the same way, and so as to achieve the maximum good, makes this obvious, and shows that they attain their end by design, not by chance. Now things which have no knowledge tend towards an end only through the agency of something which knows and also understands, as in the case of an arrow which requires an archer. There is therefore an intelligent being by whom all natural things are directed to their end. This we call "God."

Aquinas argues that there exist clear signs of design within the natural order. Things do not simply exist; they appear to have been designed with some form of purpose in mind. The term "teleological" (meaning "directed towards some goal") is widely used to indicate this apparently goal-directed aspect of nature.

It is this aspect of nature which has often been discussed in relation to the natural sciences. The orderliness of nature – evident, for example, in the laws of nature – seem to be a sign that nature has been "designed" for some purpose.

It is widely agreed that the most significant contribution to the "argument from design" is due to William Paley. His *Natural Theology; or Evidences of the Existence and Attributes of the Deity, Collected from the Appearances of Nature* (1802) had a profound influence on popular English religious thought in the first half of the nineteenth century, and is known to have been read by Charles Darwin. Paley was deeply impressed by Newton's discovery of the regularity of nature, especially in relation to the area usually known as "celestial mechanics." It was clear that the entire universe could be thought of as a complex mechanism, operating according to regular and understandable principles.

For some Deist writers, this suggested that God was no longer necessary. A mechanism could operate perfectly well without the need for its creator to be present all the time. One of Paley's significant achievements, which has not been fully recognized in the literature, was to rehabilitate the idea of the "world as a mechanism" within a Christian perspective. Paley managed to transform the "clockwork" metaphor from an image associated with scepticism and atheism to one associated with a clear affirmation of the existence of God.

For Paley, the Newtonian image of the world as a mechanism immediately suggested the metaphor of a clock or watch, raising the question of who constructed the intricate mechanism which was so evidently displayed in the functioning of the world. One of Paley's most significant arguments is that mechanism implies "contrivance." Writing against the backdrop of the emerging Industrial Revolution, Paley sought to exploit the apologetic potential of the growing interest in machinery – such as "watches, telescopes, stocking-mills, and steam engines" – within England's literate classes.

The general lines of Paley's approach are well known. At the time, England was experiencing the Industrial Revolution, in which machinery was coming to play an increasingly important role in industry. Paley argues that only someone who is mad would suggest that such complex mechanical technology came into being by purposeless chance. Mechanism presupposes contrivance – that is to say, a sense of purpose and an ability to design and fabricate. Both the human body in particular, and the world in general, could be seen as mechanisms which had been designed and constructed in such a manner as to achieve harmony of both means and ends. It must be stressed that Paley is not suggesting that there exists an analogy between human mechanical devices and nature. The force of his argument rests on an identity: nature is a mechanism, and hence was intelligently designed.

The opening paragraphs of Paley's *Natural Theology* have become so widely known that it will be helpful to cite them, and offer some comments.

In crossing a heath, suppose I pitched my foot against a *stone*, and were asked how the stone came to be there. I might possibly answer, that for any thing I knew to the contrary it had lain there for ever; nor would it, perhaps, be very easy to show the absurdity of this answer. But suppose I had found a *watch* upon the ground, and it should be inquired how the watch happened to be in that place. I should hardly think of the answer which I had before given, that for any thing I knew the watch might have always been there. Yet why should this answer not serve for the watch as well as for the stone; why is it not admissible in the second case as in the first? For this reason, and for no other, namely, that when we come to inspect the watch, we perceive – what we could not discover in the stone – that its several parts are framed and put together for a purpose, e.g., that they are so formed and adjusted as to produce motion, and that motion so regulated as to point out the hour of the day; that if the different parts had been differently shaped from what they are, or placed after any other manner or in any other order than that in which they are placed, either no motion at all would have been carried on in the machine, or none which would have answered the use that is now served by it.

Paley then offers a detailed description of the watch, noting in particular its container, coiled cylindrical spring, many interlocking wheels, and glass face. Having carried his readers along with this careful analysis, Paley turns to draw his critically important conclusion:

This mechanism being observed – it requires indeed an examination of the instrument, and perhaps some previous knowledge of the subject, to perceive and understand it; but being once, as we have said, observed and understood, the inference we think is inevitable, that the watch must have had a maker – that there must have existed, at some time and at some place or other, an artificer or artificers who formed it for the purpose which we find it actually to answer, who comprehended its construction and designed its use.

Paley's English prose is a little florid, reflecting the taste of the period. Nevertheless, the points which he is concerned to establish are clear.

The essential point is that nature bears witness to a series of biological structures which are "contrived" – that is, constructed with a clear purpose in mind. "Every indication of contrivance, every manifestation of design, which existed in the watch, exists in the works of nature." Indeed, Paley argues, the difference is that nature shows an even greater degree of contrivance than the watch. Perhaps it is fair to say that Paley is at his best when he deals with the description of mechanical systems within nature, such as the immensely complex structure of the human eye, or the heart. In this second instance, Paley is able to treat the heart as a machine with valves, and draw the conclusion that it has been designed with a purpose in mind:

It is evident that it must require the interposition of *valves* – that the success indeed of its action must depend upon these; for when any one of its cavities contracts, the necessary tendency of the force will be to drive the enclosed blood not only into the mouth of the artery where it ought to go, but also back again into the mouth of the vein from which it flowed.

The influence of Paley upon English attitudes to natural theology was immense. The celebrated *Bridgewater Treatises* show his influence at many points, even if they develop an independent approach at others. Richard Dawkins pays him a somewhat backhanded compliment in the title of one of his best-known anti-teleological works, *The Blind Watchmaker*. For Dawkins, the "watchmaker" who Paley identified with God was none other than the blind and purposeless process of natural selection.

The "argument from design" was subjected to criticism on a number of grounds by the Scottish philosopher David Hume. The most significant of Hume's main criticisms can be summarized as follows.

1   The direct extrapolation from the observation of design in the world to a God who created that world is not possible. It is one thing to suggest that the observation of design leads to the inference that there is a design-producing being; it is quite another to insist that this being is none other than God. There is thus a logical weak link in the chain of argument.

2   To suggest that there is a designer of the universe could lead to an infinite regression. Who designed the designer? We noted that Aquinas explicitly rejected the idea of an infinite regression of causes; however, he fails to offer a rigorous justification of this point, apparently assuming that his readers will regard his rejection of this series as being self-evidently correct. Hume's point is that this is not the case.

3   The argument from design works by analogy with machines. The argment gains its plausibility by a comparison with something that has clearly been designed and constructed – such as a watch. But is this analogy valid? Why could the universe not be compared to a plant, or some other living organism? Plants are not designed; they just grow. The importance of this point in relation to Paley's argument will be obvious.

God's Action in the World

One of the interfaces between scientific and religious thought concerns the manner in which God can be said to act in the world. In what follows, we shall explore three broad approaches to this important question.

Deism: God acts through the laws of nature

In an earlier section, we noted how the Newtonian emphasis upon the mechanical regularity of the universe was closely linked with the rise of the movement known as "Deism." The Deist position could be summarized very succinctly as follows. God created the world in a rational and ordered manner, which reflected God's own rational nature. The ordering of the world is open to human investigation. On being discovered, this ordering demonstrates the wisdom of God. The laws of nature have been set in place by God; it merely remained for a brilliant human being to discover them. Alexander Pope's celebrated epitaph for Newton brings out the popular understanding of the scientist's importance.

> Nature and Nature's Law lay hid in Night
> God said, let Newton be, and all was light.

Deism defended the idea that God created the world, and endowed it with the ability to develop and function without the need for his continuing presence or interference. This viewpoint, which became especially influential in the eighteenth century, regarded the world as a watch, and God as the watchmaker. God endowed the world with a certain self-sustaining design, such that it could subsequently function without the need for continual intervention. It is thus no accident that William Paley chose to use the image of a watch and watchmaker as part of his celebrated defense of the existence of a creator God.

So how does God act in the world, according to Deism? The simple answer to this question is that God does not act in the world. Like a watchmaker, God endowed the universe with its regularity (seen in the "laws of nature"), and set its mechanism in motion. Having provided the impetus to set the system in motion, and establishing the principles which govern that motion, there is nothing left for God to do. The world is to be seen as a large-scale watch, which is completely autonomous and self-sufficient. No action by God is necessary.

Inevitably, this led to the question of whether God could be eliminated completely from the Newtonian world-view. If there was nothing left for God to do, what conceivable need was there for any kind of divine being? If it can be shown that there self-sustaining principles within the world, there is no need for the traditional idea of "providence" – that is, for the sustaining and regulating hand of God to be present and active throughout the entire existence of the world. The Newtonian worldview thus encouraged the view that, although God may well have created the world, there was no further need for divine involvement. The discovery of the laws of conservation (for example, the laws of conservation of momentum) seemed to imply either that God had endowed the creation with all the mechanisms which it required in order to continue. It is this point which is encapsulated in Laplace's famous comment, made in relation to the idea of God as a sustainer of planetary motion: "I have no need of that hypothesis."

A more activist understanding of the manner in which God acts in the world is due to Thomas Aquinas and modern writers influenced by him, which focuses on the use of secondary causes.

Thomism: God acts through secondary causes

A somewhat different approach to the issue of God's action in the world can be based on the writings of the leading medieval theologian Thomas Aquinas. Aquinas' conception of divine action focusses on the distinction between primary and secondary causes. According to Aquinas, God does not work directly in the world, but through secondary causes.

The idea is best explained in terms of an analogy. Suppose we imagine a pianist, who is remarkably gifted. She possesses the ability to play the piano beautifully. Yet the quality of her playing is dependent upon the quality of the piano with which she is provided. An out of tune piano will prove disastrous, no matter how expert the player. In our analogy the pianist is the primary cause, and the piano secondary cause, for a performance of, for example, a Chopin nocturne. Both are required; each has a significantly different role to play. The ability of the primary cause to achieve the desired effect is dependent upon the secondary cause which has to be used.

Aquinas uses this appeal to secondary causes to deal with some of the issues relating to the presence of evil in the world. Suffering and pain are not to be ascribed to the direct action of God, but to the fragility and frailty of the secondary causes through which God works. God, in other words, is to be seen as the primary cause, and various agencies within the world as the associated secondary causes.

For Aristotle (from whom Aquinas draws many of his ideas), secondary causes are able to act in their own right. Natural objects are able to act as secondary causes by virtue of their own nature. This view was unacceptable to theistic philosophers of the Middle Ages, whether Christian or Islamic. For example, the noted Islamic writer al-Ghazali (1058–1111) held that nature is completely subject to God, and it is therefore improper to speak of secondary causes having any independence. God is to be seen as the primary cause who alone is able to move other causes. A similar idea is found in Aquinas, who argues that God is the "unmoved mover," the prime cause of every action, without whom nothing could happen at all. (Earlier, we noted the importance of this point in relation to the argument *ex motu*: see p. 95).

The theistic interpretation of secondary causes thus offers the following account of God's action in the world. God acts indirectly in the world through secondary causes. A great chain of causality can be discerned, leading back to God as the originator and prime mover of all that happens in the world. Yet God does not act *directly* in the world, but through the chain of events which God initiates and guides.

It will thus be clear that Aquinas' approach leads to the idea of God initiating a process which develops under divine guidance. God, so to speak, *delegates* divine action to secondary causes within the natural order. For example, God might move a human will from within so that someone who is ill receives assistance. Here an action which is God's will is carried out *indirectly* by God – yet, according to Aquinas, we can still speak of this action being "caused" by God in some meaningful way.

An approach which is clearly related to this, but differing radically at points of significance, can be found in the movement known as "process thought," to which we now turn.

Process theology: God acts through persuasion

The origins of process thought are generally agreed to lie in the writings of the Anglo-American philosopher Alfred North Whitehead (1861–1947), especially his important work *Process and Reality* (1929). Reacting against the rather static view of the world associated with traditional metaphysics (expressed in ideas such as "substance" and "essence"), Whitehead conceived reality as a process. The world, as an organic whole, is something dynamic, not static; something which *happens*. Reality is made up of building blocks of "actual entities" or "actual occasions," and is thus characterized by becoming, change, and event.

All these "entities" or "occasions" (to use Whitehead's original terms) possess a degree of freedom to develop, and be influenced by their surroundings. It is perhaps at this point that the influence of biological evolutionary theories can be discerned: like the later writer Pierre Teilhard de Chardin (see pp. 221–5), Whitehead is concerned to allow for development within creation, subject to some overall direction and guidance. This process of development is thus set against a permanent background of order, which is seen as an organizing principle essential to growth. Whitehead argues that God may be identified with this background of order within the process. Whitehead treats God as an "entity," but distinguishes God from other entities on the grounds of imperishability. Other entities exist for a finite period; God exists permanently. Each entity thus receives influence from two main sources: previous entities and God.

Causation is thus not a matter of an entity being coerced to act in a given manner: it is a matter of *influence* and *persuasion*. Entities influence each other in a "dipolar" manner – mentally and physically. Precisely the same is true of God, as for other entities. God can only act in a persuasive manner, within the limits of the process itself. God "keeps the rules" of the process. Just as God influences other entities, so God is also influenced by them. God, to use Whitehead's famous phrase, is "a fellow-sufferer who understands." God is thus affected and influenced by the world. This aspect of Whitehead's thought has been developed in the context of the science–religion interaction by Ian R. Barbour, and we shall note the particular use which he makes of it presently (pp. 207–10).

Process thought thus redefines God's omnipotence in terms of persuasion or influence within the overall world-process. This is an important development, as it explains the attraction of this way of understanding God's relation to the world in relation to the problem of evil. Where the traditional free-will defense of moral evil argues that human beings are free to disobey or ignore God, process theology argues that the individual components of the world are likewise free to ignore divine attempts to influence or persuade them. They are not bound to respond to God. God is thus absolved of responsibility for both moral and natural evil.

The traditional free-will defense of God in the face of evil is persuasive (although the extent of that persuasion is contested) in the case of moral evil – in other words, evil resulting from human decisions and actions. But what of natural evil? What of earthquakes, famines and other natural disasters? Process thought argues that God cannot force nature to obey the divine will or purpose for it. God can only attempt to influence the process from within, by persuasion and attraction. Each entity enjoys a degree of freedom and creativity, which God cannot override.

While this understanding of the persuasive nature of God's activity has obvious merits, not least in the way in which it offers a response to the problem of evil (as God is not in control, God cannot be blamed for the way things have turned out) critics of process thought have suggested that too high a price is paid. The traditional idea of the transcendence of God appears to have been abandoned, or radically reinterpreted in terms of the primacy and permanency of God as an entity within the process. In other words, the divine transcendence is understood to mean little more than that God outlives and surpasses other entities.

Whitehead's basic ideas have been developed by a number of writers, most notably Charles Hartshorne (1897–), Schubert Ogden (1928–) and John B. Cobb (1925–). Hartshorne modified Whitehead's notion of God in a number of directions, perhaps most significantly by suggesting that the God of process thought should be thought of more as a person than an entity. This allows him to meet one of the more significant criticisms of process thought: that it compromises the idea of divine perfection. If God is perfect, how can he change? Is not change tantamount to an admission of imperfection? Hartshorne redefines perfection in terms of a receptivity to change which does not compromise God's superiority. In other words, God's ability to be influenced by other entities does not mean that God is reduced to their level. God surpasses other entities, even though he is affected by them.

One of the most influential early statements of process theology is to be found in Charles Hartshorne's *Man's Vision of God* (1941), which includes a detailed comparison of "classical" and "neoclassical" understandings of God. The former term is used to refer to the understanding of the nature and attributes of God found in the writings of Thomas Aquinas, and the latter to refer to the ideas developed by Hartshorne. Given the importance of Hartshorne to the formulation of process theology, his ideas on the attributes of God will be set out in tabular form, to allow easy comparison with the classical views which he criticizes.

While Hartshorne does not use the fully developed vocabulary of process thought, as this would emerge after the Second World War, it will be clear that the basic ideas are firmly in place in this early work.

It will be clear that process theology has no difficulty in speaking of "God's action within the world", and that it offers a framework within which this action can be described in terms of "influence within the process". Nevertheless, the specific approach adopted causes anxiety to traditional theism, which is critical of the notion of God associated with

Process and Classical Views

The classical view (e.g., Thomas Aquinas)	Charles Hartshorne
Creation takes place *ex nihilo* by a free act of will. There is no necessary reason for anything other than God existing. Creation depends on God's decision to create; God could have decided not to create anything.	Both God and the creation exist necessarily. The world does not depend on any action of God for its existence, although the fine details of the nature of its existence are a matter of contingency.
God has the power to do anything that God wills to do, provided that a logical contradiction is not involved (e.g., God cannot create a square triangle).	God is one agent among many within the world, and has as much power as any such agent. This power is not absolute, but is limited.
God is incorporeal, and is radically distinct from the created order.	The world is to be seen as the body of God.
God stands outside time, and is not involved in the temporal order. It is therefore inappropriate to think of God "changing" or being affected by any involvement in or experience of the world.	God is involved in the temporal order. God is continually achieving richer syntheses of experience through this involvement.
God exists in a state of absolute perfection, and cannot be conceived to exist in a state of higher perfection.	At any point in time, God is more perfect than any other agent in the world. However, God is capable of achieving higher levels of perfection at a later stage of development on account of God's involvement in the world.

process theology. For traditional theists, the God of process thought seems to bear little relation to the God described in the Old or New Testaments.

For further reading

Behrens, G. "Peirce's 'Third Argument' for the Reality of God and Its Relation to Scientific Inquiry." *Journal of Religion* 75 (1995): 200–18.

Bowler, P. J. "Darwinism and the Argument from Design: Suggestions for a Reevaluation." *Journal of the History of Biology* 10 (1977): 29–43.

Craig, W. L. *The Kalam Cosmological Argument*. London: Macmillan, 1979.

——. "The Kalam Cosmological Argument and the Hypothesis of a Quiescent Universe." Faith and Philosophy 8 (1991): 104–8.

Donnell, J. J. O. *Trinity and Temporality: The Christian Doctrine of God in the Light of Process Thought and the Theology of Hope*. Oxford: Oxford University Press, 1983.

Doore, G. "The Argument from Design: Some Better Reasons for Agreeing with Hume." *Religious Studies* 16 (1980): 145–61.

Fiddes, P. "Process Theology." *The Blackwell Encyclopaedia of Modern Christian Thought*. Ed. A. E. McGrath. Oxford: Blackwell, 1993, pp. 472–6.

Gale, R. "The Overall Argument of Alston's Perceiving God." *Religious Studies* 30 (1994): 135–49.

Gaskin, J. C. A. "The Design Argument: Hume's Critique of Poor Reason." *Religious Studies* 12 (1976): 331–45.

Gay, P. *Deism*. Princeton, NJ: van Nostrand, 1968.

Gleick, J. *Chaos: Making a New Science*. New York: Penguin Books, 1987.

Goetz, S. C. "Craig's Kalam Cosmological Argument." *Faith and Philosophy* 6 (1989): 99–102.

Nelson, K. V. "Evolution and the Argument from Design." *Religious Studies* 14 (1978): 423–43.

Niditch, S. *Chaos to Cosmos: Studies in Biblical Patterns of Creation*. Chico, CA: Scholars Press, 1985.

O'Higgins, J. "Hume and the Deists." *Journal of Theological Studies* 22 (1971): 479–501.

Olding, A. "The Argument from Design: A Reply to R. G. Swinburne." *Religious Studies* 7 (1971): 361–73.

Oppy, G. "Craig, Mackie and the Kalam Cosmological Argument." *Religious Studies* 27 (1991): 189–97.

Platt, J. *Reformed Thought and Scholasticism: The Arguments for the Existence of God in Dutch Theology*. Leiden: Brill, 1982.

Prigogine, I., and I. Stengers. *Order out of Chaos: Man's New Dialogue with Nature*. New York: Bantam Books, 1984.

Rowe, W. L. *The Cosmological Argument*. Princeton, NJ: Princeton University Press, 1975.

Stewart, I. *Does God Play Dice: The Mathematics of Chaos*. Oxford: Blackwell, 1989.

Sullivan, R. E. *John Toland and the Deist Controversy*. Cambridge, MA: Harvard University Press, 1982.

Swinburne, R. "The Argument from the Fine-Tuning of the Universe." *Physical Cosmology and Philosophy*. Ed. John Leslie. New York: Macmillan, 1990, pp. 154–73.

Swinburne, R. G. "The Argument from Design: A Defence." *Religious Studies* 8 (1972): 193–205.

Wykstra, S. J. "The Humean Objection to Evidential Arguments from Suffering: On Avoiding the Evils of 'Appearance'." *International Journal for Philosophy of Religion* 16 (1984): 73–93.

Wynn, M. "Some Reflections on Richard Swinburne's Argument from Design." *Religious Studies* 29 (1993): 325–35.

5

Creation and the Sciences

The idea that the world is created is of fundamental importance to many religions, especially Christianity and Judaism. In an earlier chapter, we noted the importance of this theme in relation to arguments for the existence of God (see pp. 95–102). It is thus clearly of some interest to explore something more of the concept of creation, and its potential relevance to our theme. The present chapter aims to explore the basic contours of the religious idea of "creation," focusing especially on its Christian statements, which are known to have been of major importance to the development of the natural sciences in western culture.

The idea that the world was created is one of the most widely encountered and fundamental religious ideas, and finds different expressions in the various religions of the world. Religions of the Ancient Near East often take the form of a conflict between a creator deity and the forces of chaos. The dominant form of the doctrine of creation is that associated with Judaism, Christianity and Islam. In what follows, I shall set out the basic features of this doctrine from a Christian perspective, and explore its implications for the theme of "science and religion."

Some Themes of the Concept of Creation

The theme of "God as creator" is of major importance within the Old Testament. Perhaps one of the most significant affirmations which the Old Testament makes is that nature is *not divine*. The Genesis creation account stresses that God created the moon, sun, and stars. The significance of this point is too easily overlooked. Each of these celestial entities was worshipped as divine in the ancient world. By asserting that they were created by God, the Old Testament is insisting that they are subordinate to God, and have no intrinsic divine nature.

Attention has often focused on the creation narratives found in the first two chapters of the book of Genesis, with which the Old Testament canon opens. However, it must be appreciated that the theme is deeply embedded in the wisdom and prophetic literature in the Old Testament. For example, Job 38: 1 – 42: 6 sets out what is unquestionably the most comprehensive understanding of God as creator to be found in the Old Testament, stressing the role of God as creator and sustainer of the world. It is possible to discern two distinct, though related, contexts in which the notion of "God as creator" is encountered: first, in contexts which reflect the praise of God within Israel's worship, both individual and corporate; and second, in contexts which stress that the God who created the world is also the God who liberated Israel from bondage, and continues to sustain her in the present.

Of particular interest for our purposes is the Old Testament theme of "creation as ordering," and the manner in which the critically important theme of "order" is established on and justified with reference to cosmological foundations. It has often been pointed out how the Old Testament portrays creation in terms of an engagement with and victory over forces of chaos. This "establishment of order" is generally represented in two different ways:

1 Creation is an imposition of order on a formless chaos. This model is especially associated with the image of a potter working clay into a recognizably ordered structure (e.g., Genesis 2: 7; Isaiah 29: 16; 44: 8; Jeremiah 18: 1–6).

2 Creation concerns conflict with a series of chaotic forces, often depicted as a dragon or another monster (variously named "Behemoth," "Leviathan," "Nahar," "Rahab," "Tannim," or "Yam") who must be subdued (Job 3: 8; 7: 12; 9: 13; 40: 15–32; Psalm 74: 13–15; 139: 10–11; Isaiah 27: 1; 41: 9–10; Zechariah 10: 11).

It is clear that there are parallels between the Old Testament account of God engaging with the forces of chaos and Ugaritic and Canaanite mythology. Nevertheless, there are significant differences at points of importance, not least in the Old Testament's insistence that the forces of chaos are not to be seen as divine. Creation is not be to understood in terms of different gods warring against each other for mastery of a (future) universe, but in terms of God's mastery of chaos and ordering of the world.

The concept of "world-order" is closely linked with two concepts which play a major role in the Old Testament, and in the thought of the Ancient Near East in general – "righteousness" and "truth." While generalizations are dangerous, it seems that "righteousness" can be thought of as ethical conformity to the world-ordering established by God, while "truth" can be considered to be its metaphysical counterpart. The theme of "conforming to the order of the world" can be seen as underlying both.

This theme is developed subsequently within the tradition of theological reflection on the Old Testament, and is perhaps seen at its clearest in the writings of the eleventh-century theologian Anselm of Canterbury. For Anselm, the concept of "rectitude" corresponds to the fundamental ordering of the world, as intended by God. "Truth" may then be considered to be metaphysical, and righteousness to be moral, rectitude. The theme of "natural order" is also particularly significant in the writings of the leading Reformed theologian John Calvin, and is widely thought to have been of importance in stimulating Calvin's positive attitude towards the close study of nature as a means of learning more about God.

Having briefly introduced some aspects of the concept of creation, particularly within a Jewish or Christian context, we may now pass on to consider some of its aspects in a more theological manner.

Creation: A Brief Theological Analysis

As we have seen, the doctrine of God as creator has its foundations firmly laid in the Old Testament (e.g., Genesis 1, 2). In the history of theology, the doctrine of God the creator has often been linked with the authority of the Old Testament. The continuing importance of the Old Testament for Christianity is often held to be grounded in the fact that the god of which it speaks is the same god to be revealed in the New Testament. The creator and redeemer god are one and the same. In the case of Gnosticism, which became especially influential during the second century, a vigorous attack was mounted on both the authority of the Old Testament, and the idea that God was creator of the world. We shall explore the importance of this in what follows.

For Gnosticism, in most of its significant forms, a sharp distinction was to be drawn between the God who redeemed humanity from the world, and a somewhat inferior deity (often termed "the demiurge") who created that world in the first place. The Old Testament was regarded by the Gnostics as dealing with this lesser deity, whereas the New Testament was concerned with the redeemer God. As such, belief in God as creator and in the authority of the Old Testament came to be interlinked at an early stage. Of the early writers to deal with this theme, Irenaeus of Lyons is of particular importance.

A distinct debate centred on the question of whether creation was to be regarded as *ex nihilo* – that is to say, out of nothing. In one of his dialogues (*Timaeus*), Plato developed the idea that the world was made out of pre-existent matter, which was fashioned into the present form of the world. This ides was taken up by most Gnostic writers, who were here followed by individual Christian theologians such as Theophilus of Antioch and Justin Martyr, professed a belief in pre-existent matter, which was shaped into the world in the act of creation. In other words, creation was not *ex nihilo*; rather, it was to be seen as an act of construction, on the basis of material which was already to hand, as one might construct an igloo out of snow, or a house from stone. The existence of evil in the world was thus to be explained on the basis of the intractability of this pre-existent matter. God's options in creating the world were limited by the poor quality of the material available. The presence of evil or defects within the world are thus not to be ascribed to God, but to deficiencies in the material from which the world was constructed.

However, the conflict with Gnosticism forced reconsideration of this issue. In part, the idea of creation from pre-existent matter was discredited by its Gnostic associations; in part, it was called into question by an increasingly sophisticated reading of the Old Testament creation narratives. Writers such as Theophilus of Antioch insisted upon the doctrine of creation *ex nihilo*, which may be regarded as gaining the ascendency from the end of the second century onwards. From that point onwards, it became the received doctrine within the church.

The importance of the decisive rejection of Gnosticism by the early church for the development of the natural sciences has been explored by Thomas F. Torrance, who points out that the affirmation of the fundamental goodness of creation "established the reality of the empirical, contingent world, and thus destroyed the age-old Hellenistic and Oriental assumption that the real is reached only by transcending the contingent." Against any idea that the natural order was chaotic, irrational or inherently evil (three concepts which were often regarded as interlocking), the early Christian tradition affirmed that the natural order possessed a goodness, rationality and orderedness which derived directly from its creation by God.

A radical dualism between God and creation was thus eliminated, in favour of the view that the truth, goodness and beauty of God (to use the Platonic triad which so influenced many writers of the period) could be discerned within the natural order, in consequence of that order having been established by God. For example, Origen argued that it was God's creation of the world which structured the natural order in such a manner that it could be comprehended by the human mind, by conferring upon that order an intrinsic rationality and order which derived from and reflected the divine nature itself.

Three Models of Creation

Three main ways of conceiving the creative action of God became widely established within Christian circles by the end of the fifth century. We shall note them briefly, and identify their relevance to our theme.

Emanation

This term was widely used by early Christian writers to clarify the relation between God and the world. Although the term is not used by either Plato or Plotinus, many patristic writers sympathetic to the various forms of Platonism saw it as a convenient and appropriate way of articulating Platonic insights. The image that dominates this approach is that of light or heat radiating from the sun, or a human source such as a fire. This image of creation (hinted at in the Nicene Creed's phrase "light from light") suggests that the creation of the world can be regarded as an overflowing of the creative energy of God. Just as light derives from the sun and reflects its nature, so the created order derives from God, and expresses the divine nature. There is, on the basis of this model, a *natural* or *organic* connection between God and the creation.

However, the model has weaknesses, of which two may be noted. First, the image of a sun radiating light, or a fire radiating heat, implies an involuntary emanation, rather than a conscious decision to create. The Christian tradition has consistently emphasized that the act of creation rests upon a prior decision on the part of God to create, which this model cannot adequately express. This naturally leads on to the second weakness, which relates to the impersonal nature of the model in question. The idea of a personal God, expressing a personality both in the very act of creation and the subsequent creation itself, is difficult to convey by this image. Nevertheless, the model clearly articulates a close connection between creator and creation, leading us to expect that something of the identity and nature of the creator is to be found in the creation. Thus the beauty of God – a theme which was of particular importance in early medieval theology, and has emerged as significant again in the later writings of Hans Urs von Balthasar – would be expected to be reflected in the nature of the creation.

Construction

Many biblical passages portray God as a master builder, deliberately constructing the world (for example, Psalm 127: 1). The imagery is powerful, conveying the ideas of purpose, planning and a deliberate intention to create. The image is important, in that it draws attention to both the creator and the creation. In addition to bringing out the skill of the creator, it also allows the beauty and ordering of the resulting creation to be appreciated, both for what it is in itself, and for its testimony to the creativity and care of its creator.

However, the image has a deficiency, which relates to a point we noted made in connection with Plato's dialogue *Timaeus*. This portrays creation as involving pre-existent matter. Here, creation is understood as giving shape and form to something which is already there – an idea which, we have seen, causes at least a degree of tension with the doctrine of creation *ex nihilo*. The image of God as a builder would seem to imply the assembly of the world from material which is already to hand, which is clearly deficient. Nevertheless, despite this slight difficulty, it can be seen that the model expresses the insight that the character of the creator is, in some manner, expressed in the natural world, just as that of an artist is communicated or embodied in her work. In particular, the notion of "ordering" – that is, the imparting or imposing of a coherence or structure to the material in question – is clearly affirmed by this model. Whatever else the complex notion of "creation" may mean within a Christian context, it certainly includes the fundamental theme of ordering – a notion which is especially significant in the creation narratives of the Old Testament.

Artistic expression

Many Christian writers, from various periods in the history of the church, speak of creation as the "handiwork of God," comparing it to a work of art which is both beautiful in itself, as well as expressing the personality of its creator. This model of creation as the "artistic expression" of God as creator is particularly well expressed in the writings of the eighteenth-century North American theologian Jonathan Edwards, as we shall see presently.

The image is profoundly helpful, in that it supplements a deficiency of both the two models noted above – namely, their impersonal character. The image of God as artist conveys the idea of personal expression in the creation of something beautiful. Once more, the potential weaknesses need to be noted: for example, the model could easily lead to the idea of creation from pre-existent matter, as in the case of a sculptor with a statue carved from an already existing block of stone. However, the model offers us at least the possibility of thinking about creation from nothing, as with the author who writes a novel, or the composer who creates a melody and harmony. It also encourages us to seek for the self-expression of God in the creation, and gives added theological credibility to a natural theology (see pp. 134–42). There is also a natural link between the concept of creation as "artistic expression" and the highly significant concept of "beauty."

Creation and Time

One of the most significant debates within Christian theology for the purposes of our discussion focuses on the complex issue of the relation of creation and time. We have already noted the use of the image of "emanation" in early Christian thinking on the nature of creation, and its background in Platonic thought. One of the most significant critics of this view was Augustine of Hippo, who held that the view presupposed or implied a change in the divine substance itself. In order to uphold what he believed to be integral to the doctrine of creation, Augustine argued that God could not be considered to have brought the creation into being at a certain definite moment in time, as if "time" itself existed prior to creation. For Augustine, "time" itself must be seen as an aspect of the created order, to be contrasted with the "timelessness" which he held to be the essential feature of "eternity." This has important implications for his understanding of the nature of history, and especially his interest in the idea of "memory."

This notion of "time as created" can probably be seen at its most clearest in Augustine's musings in the *Confessions*, an extended soliloquy which takes the form of a prayer to God:

> You have made time itself. Time could not elapse before you made time. But if time did not exist before heaven and earth, why do people ask what you were then doing? There was no "then" when there was no time. . . . It is not in time that you precede times. Otherwise you would not precede all times. In the sublimity of an eternity which is always in the present, you are before all things past and transcend all things future, because they are still to come, and then they have come they are past . . . You created all times and you exist before all times. Nor was there any time when time did not exist. There was therefore no time when you had not made something, because you made time itself.

Augustine thus speaks of the creation of time (or "creation with time"), rather than creation in time. There is no concept of a period intervening before creation, nor an infinitely extended period which corresponds to "eternity". Eternity is timelessness. Time is an aspect of the created order. To speak of $t = 0$ is to speak of the origin, not merely of the creation, but of time as well.

Augustine's ideas have enjoyed a new surge of popularity and plausibility in the light of the new insights offered by modern cosmology. For example, consider the comments of Paul Davies on this point:

> People often ask: When did the big bang occur? The bang did not occur at a point in space at all. Space itself came into existence with the big bang. There is a similar difficulty over the question: What happened before the big bang? The answer is, there was no "before". Time itself began at the big bang. As we have seen, Saint Augustine long ago proclaimed that the world was made with time and not in time, and that is precisely the modern scientific position.

My concern here is not to enter into the specifics of this cosmological debate. Rather, it is to note that the new directions in cosmological thinking can prompt a positive and critical re-reading of the Christian, leading to the discovery that it already possesses resources which are relevant and appropriate to the new scientific debates which are taking place.

Creation and Ecology

At this point, we may pause to consider an issue of some importance: the question of the relationship of the doctrine of creation to the exploitation of nature. In 1967, Lynn White published an influential article in which he asserted that Christianity was to blame for the emerging ecological crisius on account of its using the concept of the "image of God", found in the Genesis creation account (Genesis 1: 26–27), as a pretext for justifying human exploitation of the world's resources. The Book of Genesis, he argued, legitimated the notion of human domination over the creation, hence leading to its exploitation. Despite (or perhaps on account of?) its historical and theological superficiality, the paper had a profound impact on the shaping of popular scientific attitudes toward Christianity in particular, and religion in general.

With the passage of time, a more informed evaluation of White's argument has gained the ascendancy. The argument is now recognized to be seriously flawed. A closer reading of the Genesis text indicated that such themes as "humanity as the steward of creation" and "humanity as the partner of God" are indicated by the text, rather than that of "humanity as the lord of creation." Far from being the enemy of ecology, the doctrine of creation affirms the importance of human responsibility towards the environment. In a widely-read study, the noted Canadian writer Douglas John Hall stressed that the biblical concept of "domination" was to be understood specifically in terms of "stewardship," no matter what kind of interpretation might be placed on the word in a secular context. To put it simply: the Old Testament does see creation as the possession of humanity; it is something which is to be seen as entrusted to humanity, who are responsible for its safekeeping and tending. Similar lines of thought can be found in other religions, with discernible differences of emphasis and grounding; the Assisi Declaration (1986) on the ecological importance of religion may be seen as marking the recognition of this significant point.

A doctrine of creation can thus act as the basis for an ecologically sensitive ethic. In an important recent study, Calvin B. DeWitt has argued that four fundamental ecological principles can readily be discerned within the biblical narratives.

1 The "earth-keeping principle": just as the creator keeps and sustains

humanity, so humanity must keep and sustain the creator's creation;

2 the "sabbath principle": the creation must be allowed to recover from human use of its resources;

3 the "fruitfulness principle": the fecundity of the creation is to be enjoyed, not destroyed;

4 the "fulfilment and limits principle": there are limits set to humanity's role within creation, with boundaries set in place which must be respected.

A further contribution has been made by the noted German theologian Jürgen Moltmann (born 1926), noted for his concern to ensure the theologically rigorous application of Christian theology to social, political, and environmental issues. For example, in his 1985 work *God in Creation*, Moltmann argues that the exploitation of the world reflects the rise of technology, and seems to have little to do with specifically Christian teachings. Furthermore, he stresses the manner in which God can be said to indwell the creation through the Holy Spirit, so that the pillage of creation becomes an assault on God. On the basis of this analysis, Moltmann is able to offer a rigorously Trinitarian defense of a distinctively Christian ecological ethic. Such is the importance of this point that it merits further discussion.

A fundamental theme of modernism – a term which is usually taken to refer to the cultural mood which began to emerge towards the opening of the twentieth century – is its desire to control, perhaps seen at its clearest in the Nietzschean theme of "will-to-power." Humanity needs only the will to achieve autonomous self-definition; it need not accept what has been given to it, whether in nature or tradition. In principle, all can be mastered and controlled. The rise of technology was seen as a tool to allow humanity to control its environment, without the need to respect natural limitations.

This desire to master led to a reaction against traditional religious belief, which often stressed the need to respect the "givenness" of the created order. A major theme of direct relevance to this point can be seen emerging in the writings of Ludiwg Feuerbach and Karl Marx during the 1830s and 1840s: the deification of humanity. For Feuerbach, the notion of "God" arises through an error in the human analysis of experience, whereby experience of oneself is misinterpreted as experience of God. In the end, therefore, it is humanity itself which is "God," not some objective external reality. In the Marxian development of

Feuerbach's theme, the origins of the religious experience which is interpreted as "God" lie in socioeconomic alienation.

By changing the world, the human experience which is conceptualized as "God" will be removed. Socioeconomic transformation therefore allows the mastery of religion, which will be eliminated along with its causes. The mastery of religion therefore lies within the grasp of humanity, allowing the Promethean dream to be realized by revolutionary activity.

This vital theme of "the human right to mastery" is intimately connected with the rise of technology in the modern period. In a remarkably astute analysis of the social role of technology, written in 1923, the Roman Catholic theologian and philosopher Romano Guardini (1885–1968) argues that the fundamental link between nature and culture has been severed as a result of the rise of the "machine." Humanity was once prepared to regard nature as the expression of a will, intelligence and design that are "not of our own making." Yet the rise of technology has opened up the possibility of *changing* nature, of making it become something which it was not intended to be. Technology offers humanity the ability to impose its own authority upon nature, redirecting it for its own ends. Where once humanity was prepared to contemplate nature, its desire now "is to achieve power so as to bring force to bear on things, a law that can be formulated rationally. Here we have the basis and character of its dominion: arbitrary compulsion devoid of all respect." No longer does humanity have to respect nature; it can dominate and direct it through the rise of technology.

Materials and forces are harnessed, unleashed, burst open, altered, and directed at will. There is no feeling for what is organically possible or tolerable in any living sense. No sense of natural proportions determines the approach. A rationally constructed and arbitrarily fixed goal reigns supreme. On the basis of a known formula, materials and forces are put into the required condition: machines. Machines are an iron formula that direct the material to the desired end.

This ability to dominate and control nature will inevitably, according to at least some cultural analysts, lead to the deification of technology, resulting in a culture which "seeks its authorization in technology, finds its satisfaction in technology, and takes its orders from technology" (Postman). As Moltmann correctly observes, blame for this development can hardly be laid at the door of Christianity, or any other religion.

The ecological debate is one clear example of a modern discussion in which science and religion interact which demands a thorough and clear understanding of the history of religious traditions and their implications. Lynn White's article has probably had an influence which is inversely proportional to its accuracy and reliability; there is a clear need for an informed contribution to this debate which avoids the rhetoric, inaccuracy, and simplistic assertions of the past.

Having explored some classical models of creation within the Christian tradition, we may now turn to considering their potential relevance to the theme of religion and science. We shall do so under the aegis of two general themes – creation and order, and creation and beauty.

Creation and the Laws of Nature

The theme of "regularity within nature" is widely regarded as an essential theme of the natural sciences. Indeed, one modern physicist has suggested that "the God of the physicists is cosmic order" (Pagels). It could be argued that the natural sciences are founded on the *perception of explicable regularity to the world*. In other words, there is something about the world – and the nature of the human mind – which allows us to discern patterns within nature, for which explanations may be advanced and evaluated. One of the most significant parallels between the natural sciences and religion is this fundamental conviction that the world is characterized by regularity and intelligibility. This perception of ordering and intelligibility is of immense significance, both at the scientific and religious levels. As Paul Davies points out, "in Renaissance Europe, the justification for what we today call the scientific approach to inquiry was the belief in a rational God whose created order could be discerned from a careful study of nature."

This insight is directly derived from the Christian doctrine of creation, and reflects the deeply religious worldview of the medieval and Renaissance periods, which ensured that even the most "secular" of activities – whether economic, political, or scientific – were saturated with the themes of Christian theology. This foundational assumption of the natural sciences – that God has created an ordered world, whose ordering could be discerned by humanity, which had in turn been created "in the image and likeness of God" – permeates the writings of the period, whether it is implicitly assumed or explicitly stated.

We have already noted how the theme of "order" is of major

importance within the Old Testament, and noted briefly how it was incorporated into subsequent theological reflection. In view of its importance to our theme, we shall consider it in more detail. One of the most sophisticated explorations of the centrality of the concept of ordering for Christian theology and moral reasoning is to be found in Oliver O'Donovan's *Resurrection and Moral Order* (1986), now firmly established as a classic work in the field. In this work, O'Donovan – Regius Professor of Moral and Pastoral Theology at Oxford University – establishes the close connection between the theological notions of "creation" and "order":

We must understand "creation" not merely as the raw material out of which the world as we know it is composed, but as the order and coherence *in* which it is composed. ... To speak of this world as "created" is already to speak of an order. In the first words of the creed, before we have tried to sketch an outline of created order with the phrase "heaven and earth", simply as we say "I believe in God the Creator", we are stating that the world is an ordered totality. By virtue of the fact that there is a Creator, there is also a creation that is ordered to its Creator, a world which exists as his creation and in no other way, so that by its existence it points to God.

Three highly significant themes of major relevance to our theme can be discerned as emerging from O'Donovan's analysis.

1   The concept of creation is understood to be focused on the establishment of ordering and coherence within the world.
2   The ordering or coherence within the world can be regarded as expressing or reflecting the nature of God himself.
3   The creation can thus be seen as pointing to God, in that the exploration of its ordering or coherence leads to an understanding of the one who ordered it in this manner.

O'Donovan rejects the idea, which is especially associated with the Scottish philosopher David Hume, that such "ordering" as can be discerned is, in fact, a creation of the human mind, rather than an objective reality in itself. For Hume, "ordering" was the creation of an order-loving human mind, and was not itself objectively present in nature. It was a human construct, rather than an intrinsic feature of the natural world itself.

In speaking of the order which God the Creator and Redeemer has established in the universe, we are not speaking merely of our own capacities to impose order upon what we see there. Of course, we can and do impose order on what we see, for we are free agents and capable of creative interpretation of the world we confront. But our ordering depends upon God's to provide the condition for its freedom. It is free because it has a given order to respond to in attention or disregard, in conformity or disconformity, with obedience or rebellion.

A Christian understanding of the concept of creation is, as we have seen, closely linked with the concept of ordering. We have already drawn attention to the notion of the explicable regularity of the world, and linked this with the concept of "creation as ordering" (pp. 112–13). As Stephen Hawking, among many others, has pointed out, the existence of God is easily and naturally correlated with the regularity and ordering of the world. "It would be completely consistent with all we know to say that there was a Being who is responsible for the laws of physics." The noted theoretical physicist Charles A. Coulson pointed out the importance of "religious conviction" in explaining the "unprovable assumption that there is an order and constancy in Nature." In what follows, we shall explore the idea of the "laws of nature," a highly significant way of depicting (and interpreting) the order found within the world.

The theme of cosmic order is of major importance within the writings of Isaac Newton, who argued that the regularity and predictability of the world were a direct consequence of its created origins. Pope's celebrated epitaph for Newton, which we noted earlier, captures aspects of this point well:

> Nature and Nature's Law lay hid in Night
> God said, let Newton be, and all was Light.

The universe is not "random," but behaves in a regular manner which is capable of observation and explanation. This led to the widespread belief that systems which satisfied Newton's laws of motion behaved in manners which were predetermined, and which could therefore be predicted with considerable accuracy – a view which is often represented at a popular level in terms of the image of a "clockwork universe."

The phrase "law of nature" appears to have begun to be used systematically during the early eighteenth century. It is generally agreed that the phrase reflects the widely-held notion, prevalent within both orthodox Christianity and Deism, that the world was ordered by a divine law-giver, who laid down the manner in which the creation should behave. A "law of nature" was thus held to be more than a description or summary of observable features of the world; it reflected a divine decision that the world was intended to behave in this manner. With the widespread secularization of western culture, this general belief has been eroded, both inside and outside the scientific community. The phrase "laws of nature" remained, nevertheless, although it has acquired something of the status of a dead metaphor. It remains, however, a concept with profound religious implications.

We may begin by attempting to clarify what a "law of nature" might be. The general consensus on the nature and scope of the "laws of nature" within the scientific community has been set out by Paul Davies. In general terms, the "laws of nature" can be considered to have the following features.

1 They are *universal*. The laws of physics are assumed to be valid at every place and every time. They are held "to apply unfailingly everywhere in the universe and at all epochs of cosmic history."

2 They are *absolute* – that is to say, they do not depend on the nature of the observer (for example, his or her social status, gender or sexual orientation). The state of a system may change over time, and be related to a series of contingent and circumstantial considerations; the laws, which provide correlation between those states at various moments, do not change with time.

3 They are *eternal*, in that they are held to be grounded in the mathematical structures which are used to represent the physical world. The remarkable correlation between what we shall loosely term "mathematical reality" and the observed physical world is of considerable significance, and we shall return to this matter later. It is of considerable importance in this context to note that all known fundamental laws are mathematical in form.

4 They are *omnipotent*, in that nothing can be held to be outside their scope.

It will be clear that these attributes show remarkable affinities with those which are traditionally applied to God in theistic religious systems, such as Christianity.

The Humean suggestion that "laws of nature" are imposed on nature is widely regarded as implausible within the scientific community. Regularity, according to this viewpoint, is not to be seen as a feature of the "real world," but as a construct of an order-imposing human mind.

It is widely held within the scientific community that regularity (including statistical regularity) is an intrinsic feature of the world, uncovered (not imposed) by human investigation. For example, consider the comments of Paul Davies, which would be widely endorsed by natural scientists:

It is important to understand that the regularities of nature are real. . . . I believe any suggestion that the laws of nature are similar projections of the human mind is absurd. The existence of regularities in nature is an objective mathematical fact. On the other hand, the statements called laws that are found in textbooks clearly are human inventions, but inventions designed to reflect, albeit imperfectly, actually existing properties of nature. Without this assumption that regularities are real, science is reduced to an absurdity. Another reason why I don"t think the laws of nature are simply made up by us is that they help us to uncover new things about the world, sometimes things we never suspected. The mark of a powerful law is that it goes beyond a faithful description of the original phenomenon it was invoked to explain, and links up with other phenomena too. . . . The history of science shows that, once a new law is accepted, its consequences are rapidly worked out, and the law is tested in many novel contexts, often leading to the discovery of new, unexpected and important phenomena. This leads me to believe that in conducting science we are uncovering real regularities and linkages out of nature, not writing them into nature.

It will be clear that a religious (and especially a Christian) approach to the debate will focus on the idea of the ordering of the world as something which exists in that world, independent of whether the human mind recognizes it or not, and that this ordering can be understood to be related to the doctrine of creation. While many natural scientists have discarded the original theological framework which led their predecessors of the seventeenth and eighteenth centuries to speak of "laws of nature," there is no reason why such an insight should not be reappropriated by those natural scientists sensitive to the religious aspects of their work.

This brief survey of the relation of the doctrine of creation and the "laws of nature" brings out the remarkable manner in which the sciences and religion converge on the issue of regularity and ordering within nature. What the sciences uncover, religion is able to account for. This leads us on to consider the extent to which something can be known about God from the natural order – an aspect of religious thought which is generally referred to as "natural theology."

For further reading

Armstrong, D. M. *What is a Law of Nature?* Cambridge: Cambridge University Press, 1983.

Attfield, R. "Science and Creation." *Journal of Religion* 58 (1978): 37–47.

Ayer, A. J. "What is a Law of Nature?" *The Concept of a Person*. Ed. A. J. Ayer. London: Macmillan, 1956, pp. 209–34.

Brooke, G. J. "Creation in the Biblical Tradition." *Zygon* 22 (1987): 227–48.

Brun, R. B. "Integrating Evolution: A Contribution to the Christian Doctrine of Creation." *Zygon* 29 (1994): 275–96.

Craig, W. L. "Creation and Big Bang Cosmology." *Philosophia Naturalis* 31 (1994): 217–24.

Davies, P. *The Mind of God: Science and the Search for Ultimate Meaning*. Harmondsworth: Penguin, 1992.

DeWitt, C. B. "Ecology and Ethics: Relation of Religious Belief to Ecological Practice in the Biblical Tradition." *Biodiversity and Conservation* 4 (1995): 838–48.

Ford, L. S. "Contrasting Conceptions of Creation." *Review of Metaphysics* 45 (1991): 89–109.

Foster, M. B. "The Christian doctrine of Creation and the Rise of Modern Science." *Mind* 43 (1934): 446–68.

Gilkey, L. *Maker of Heaven and Earth: the Christian Doctrine of Creation in the Light of Modern Knowledge*. Garden City: Doubleday, 1959.

Larson, E. J. *Trial and Error: The American Controversy over Creation and Evolution*. New York: Oxford University Press, 1989.

O'Donovan, O. *Resurrection and Moral Order*. Grand Rapids, MI: Eerdmans, 1986.

Pannenberg, W. "The Doctrine of Creation and Modern Science." *Zygon* 23 (1988): 3–21.

Peacocke, A. *Creation and the World of Science*. Oxford and New York: Oxford University Press, 1979.

Peters, T. *Cosmos as Creation*. Nashville: Abingdon, 1989.

Quinn, P. L. "Creation, Conservation and the Big Bang." *Philosophical Problems of the Internal and External Worlds*. Ed. John Earman et al. Pittsburg, PA: University of Pittsburg Press, 1993, pp. 589–612.

van Bavel, T. "The Creator and the Integrity of Creation in the Fathers of the Church." *Augustinian Studies* 21 (1990): 1–33.

van Cangh, J.-M. "Creation and Origin of the World in the Bible." *Epistemologia* 14 (1991): 139–52.

6

Natural Theology: Finding God in Nature

Can God be known from nature? If anything of God can be known from a study of the natural world, it will be clear that the religions and the natural sciences will have some significant common features. One of the most important issues here concerns "nature" itself, and whether it is to be regarded as something which has, in some way, been fashioned by God (and thus reflects the nature of God, however indirectly). We explored this theme in the previous chapter, noting in particular the way in which doctrine of creation forges a link between God and nature.

In the present chapter, we shall explore some aspects of what is known as "natural theology" – that is, the religious belief, grounded in a doctrine of creation, which affirms that at least something of God can be known from the study of nature. We may begin, however, by noting two significant objections to natural theology which have been influential in the twentieth century.

Objections to Natural Theology

Yet if this positive approach to a natural knowledge of God represents the majority report within the Christian tradition, it is important to acknowledge that there have been other views. In what follows, we shall explore two significant (although ultimately not decisive) objections to natural theology, reflecting theological and philosophical concerns respectively.

Theological objections

Perhaps the most negative attitude to have been adopted in recent Christian theology is that of the leading Swiss Reformed theologian Karl Barth, whose controversy with Emil Brunner over this matter illustrates some of the serious concerns associated with it within the Protestant theological community. Barth's stringent and strident criticisms of natural theology can be answered effectively, and are often regarded as lying on an extreme end of the theological spectrum. Nevertheless, they merit consideration, not least on account of the fact that they have become "landmarks" in the discussion of the matter.

In 1934, the Swiss theologian Emil Brunner published a work entitled *Nature and Grace*, in which he argued that "the task of our theological generation is to find a way back to a legitimate natural theology." Brunner located this approach in the doctrine of creation, specifically the idea that human beings are created in the *imago Dei*, "the image of God." Human nature is constituted in such a way that there is an analogy with the being of God. Despite the sinfulness of human nature, the ability to discern God in nature remains. Sinful human beings remain able to recognize God in nature and the events of history, and to be aware of their guilt before God. There is thus a what Brunner termed "a point of contact (*Anknüpfungspunkt*)" for divine revelation within human nature.

In effect, Brunner was arguing that human nature is constituted in such a way that there is a ready-made point of contact for divine revelation. Revelation addresses a human nature which already has some idea of what that revelation is about. For example, take the New Testament demand to "repent of sin." Brunner argues that this makes little sense, unless human beings already have some idea of what "sin" is. The gospel demand to repent is thus addressed to an audience which already has at least something of an idea of what "sin" and "repentance" mean. Revelation brings with it a fuller understanding of what sin means – but in doing so, it builds upon an existing human awareness of sin.

Barth reacted with anger to this suggestion. His published reply to Brunner – which brought their long-standing friendship to an abrupt end – has one of the shortest titles in the history of religious publishing: *Nein!*. Barth was determined to say "no!" to Brunner's positive evaluation of natural theology. It seemed to imply that God needed help to become known, or that human beings somehow cooperated with God in the act of revelation. "The Holy Spirit . . . needs no point of contact other than that which that same Spirit establishes," was his angry retort. For Barth, there was no "point of contact" inherent within human nature. Any such "point of contact" was itself the result of divine revelation. It is something that is evoked by the Word of God, rather than something which is a permanent feature of human nature.

Underlying this debate is another matter, which is too easily over-looked. The Barth–Brunner debate took place in 1934, the year in which Hitler gained power in Germany. Underlying Brunner's appeal to nature is an idea, which can be traced back to Luther, known as "the orders of creation." According to Luther, God providentially estab-lished certain "orders" within creation, in order to prevent it collapsing into chaos. Those orders included the family, the church, and the state. (The close alliance between church and state in German Lutheran thought reflects this idea.) Nineteenth-century German Liberal Protes-tantism had absorbed this idea, and developed a theology which allowed German culture, including a positive assessment of the state, to become of major importance theologically. Part of Barth's concern is that Brunner, perhaps unwittingly, has laid a theological foundation for allowing the state to become a model for God. And who wanted to model God on Adolf Hitler?

An equally critical approach to natural theology has been developed on other grounds by the noted Scottish theologian Thomas F. Tor-rance. There are clear parallels between Torrance and Barth. Thus Torrance sets out what he understands to be Barth's fundamental objection to natural theology – the radical separation which some writers assert between "revealed theology" and a totally autonomous and unconnected "natural theology":

Epistemologically, then, what Barth objects to in traditional natural theology is not any invalidity in its argumentation, nor even its rational structure, as such, but its *independent character* – i.e., the autonomous rational structure that natural theology develops on the ground of "nature alone," in abstraction from the active self-disclosure of the living and Triune God – for that can only split the knowledge of God into two parts, natural knowledge of the One God and revealed knowledge of the triune God, which is scientifically as well as theo-logically intolerable. This is not to reject the place of a proper rational structure in knowledge of God, such as natural theology strives for, but to insist that unless that rational structure is intrinsically bound up with the actual content of knowledge of God, it is a distorting abstraction. That is why Barth claims that, properly understood, natural theology is included within revealed theology.

Torrance also stresses that Barth's criticism of natural theology does not rest on any form of dualism – for example, some kind of deistic dualism between God and the world which implies that there is no active relation between God and the world, or with some form of Marcionite dualism between redemption and creation implying a depreciation of the creature. It is clear that Torrance himself sympathizes with Barth at these junctures.

Torrance also notes a fundamental philosophical difficulty which seems to him to lie behind the forms of natural theology rejected by Barth. This kind of autonomous natural theology is, he argues, a "desperate attempt to find a *logical bridge* between concepts and experience in order to cross the fatal separation between God and the world which it had posited in its initial assumptions, but it had to collapse along with the notion that science proceeds by way of abstraction from observational data." It attempted, by means of establishing a logical bridge between ideas and being, to reach out inferentially toward God, and thus to produce a logical formalization of empirical and theoretical components of the knowledge of God. For Torrance, this development was assisted considerably by the medieval assumption that "to think scientifically was to think more geometrico, that is, on the model of Euclidean geometry, and it was reinforced in later thought as it allowed itself to be restricted within the logico-causal connections of a mechanistic universe." It will thus be clear that Torrance sees the "traditional abstractive form" of natural theology as resting on a "deistic disjunction between God and the world" – a disjunction to which we shall return presently.

What is of especial interest is the manner in which Torrance identifies a parallel between the theological status and significance of natural theology and the empirical challenge to the unique status of Euclidian geometry, which was challenged through the rise of non-Euclidian geometry in the nineteenth century, and Einstein's argument for the Riemannian geometry of space–time.

If in the relation of geometry to physics, as Einstein pointed out, it was forgetfulness that the axiomatic construction of Euclidean geometry has an empirical foundation that was responsible for the fatal error that Euclidean geometry is a necessity of thought which is prior to all experience, theological science ought to be warned against the possibility of regarding natural theology in the heart of dogmatic theology as a formal system which can be shown to have validity on its own, for that would only serve to tranpose it back into an a priori system that was merely an empty scheme of thought.

It will be clear that Torrance accepts that a natural theology has a significant place within Christian theology, in the light of an understanding of the nature of God and the world which rests on divine revelation, and which cannot itself be ascertained by human inquiry.

Torrance can therefore be thought of as moving natural theology into the domain of systematic theology, in much the same manner as Einstein moved geometry into the formal content of physics. The proper locus for the discussion of natural theology is not debate about the possibility of a hypothetical knowledge of God, but within the context of the positive and revealed knowledge of creator God. A proper theological perspective on nature allows it to be seen in its proper light:

So it is with natural theology: brought within the embrace of positive theology and developed as a complex of rational structures arising in our actual knowledge of God it becomes "natural" in a new way, natural to its proper object, God in self-revealing interaction with us in space and time. Natural theology then constitutes the epistemological geometry, as it were, within the fabric of revealed theology.

The Barthian challenge can thus be met, in a manner which Torrance believed had Barth's support.

Other objections, however, have been raised against the idea of a "natural theology" from within Protestantism, particularly those found in the writings of the leading Reformed philosopher of religion Alvin Plantinga. We may turn to consider these before proceeding further.

Philosophical objections

In recent years, philosophers of religion working within a Reformed theological perspective have risen to considerable prominence. Alvin Plantinga and Nicholas Wolterstorff are examples of writers belonging to this category of thinkers, who have made highly significant contributions to the philosophy of religion in recent decades. Plantinga understands "natural theology" to be an attempt to prove or demonstrate the existence of God, and vigorously rejects it on the basis of his belief that it depends on a fallacious understanding of the nature of religious belief. The roots of this objection are complex, and can be summarized in terms of two foundational considerations:

1 Natural theology supposes that belief in God must rest upon an evidential basis. Belief in God is thus not, strictly speaking, a basic belief – that is, something which is self-evident, incorrigible or evident to the senses. It is therefore a belief which requires to be itself grounded in some more basic belief. However, to ground a belief in God upon some other belief is, in effect, to depict that latter belief as endowed with a greater epistemic status than belief in God. For Plantinga, a properly Christian approach is to affirm that belief in God is itself basic, and does not require justification with reference to other beliefs.
2 Natural theology is not justified with reference to the Reformed tradition, including Calvin and his later followers.

The latter point is inaccurate historically, and need not detain us. However, the first line of argument has met with growing interest.

Plantinga clearly regards Aquinas as the "natural theologian *par excellence*," and directs considerable attention to his methods. For Plantinga, Aquinas is a foundationalist in matters of theology and philosophy, in that "*scientia*, properly speaking, consists in a body of propositions deduced syllogistically from self-evident first principles." The *Summa contra Gentiles* shows, according to Plantinga, that Aquinas proceeds from evidential foundations to argue for a belief in God, which clearly makes such belief dependent upon appropriate evidential foundations. (The importance of the growing criticism of classic foundationalism in modern philosophy and theology should be noted at this point.) Our concern here is to note that Plantinga's conception of natural theology involves his belief that it intends to *prove* the existence of God.

It is clearly not necessary that a natural theology should make any such assumption; indeed, there are excellent reasons for suggesting that, as a matter of historical fact, natural theology is to be understood as a demonstration, from the standpoint of faith, of the consonance between that faith and the structures of the world. In other words, natural theology is not intended to prove the existence of God, but presupposes that existence; it then asks "what should we expect the natural world to be like if it has indeed been created by such a God?" The search for order in nature is therefore not intended to demonstrate that God exists, but to reinforce the plausibility of an already existing belief. This kind of approach can be found in the writings of William P. Alston, who can be seen as sharing at least some of Plantinga's commitments to a Reformed epistemology, while tending to take a considerably more positive attitude to natural theology.

In his major study *Perceiving God*, Alston sets out what he regards as a responsible and realistic approach. Alston defines natural theology as "the enterprise of providing support for religious beliefs by starting from premises that neither are nor presuppose any religious beliefs." Conceding that it is impossible to construct a demonstrative proof of the existence of God from extra-religious premises, Alston argues that this is not, in any case, a proper approach to natural theology.

Properly speaking, natural theology begins from a starting point such as the existence of God or the ordering of the world, and show that this starting point leads us to recognize the existence of a being which would be accepted as God. There is thus, in Alston's view, a strong degree of convergence between natural theology and traditional arguments for the existence of God, particularly those deriving from Thomas Aquinas. Yet his conception of natural theology goes beyond such narrow proofs, and encourages the engagement with other areas of human life and concern, amongst which he explicitly includes science. Natural theology thus offers "metaphysical reasons for the truth of theism as a general world-view," and allows us to build bridges to other disciplines.

It will be clear from the above discussion that both Plantinga and Barth have raised significant concerns about the nature and scope of natural theology. Equally, many orthodox Christian theologians would express concern at the possible revitalization of a deist worldview resulting from an emphasis on the regularity of nature. Yet these are criticisms which seem to concern potential abuses of natural theology, rather than its actual use within responsible Christian thinking, whether Protestant or Roman Catholic. In what follows, we shall explore three positive approaches to the matter which can be regarded as typical of the Christian theological tradition.

Three Approaches to Natural Theology

Within Christianity, three general approaches to the question of whether – and to what extent – God may be known through nature have been given. In what follows, we shall give a brief account of three of the more significance, of which two have particular importance to the relation of science and religion.

The appeal to reason

One of the most widely encountered approaches to natural knowledge of God is an appeal to human reason. An excellent example of this approach can be found in the writings of Augustine of Hippo, particularly in his major work *De Trinitate*. The general line of argument developed by Augustine can be summed up as follows. If God is indeed to be discerned within his creation, we ought to expect to find him at the height of that creation. Now the height of God's creation, Augustine argues (basing himself on Genesis 1 and 2), is human nature. And, on the basis of the neo-Platonic presuppositions which he inherited from his cultural milieu, Augustine further argued that the height of human nature is the human capacity to reason. Therefore, he concluded, one should expect to find traces of God (or, more accurately, "vestiges of the Trinity") in human processes of reasoning. On the basis of this belief, Augustine develops what have come to be known as "psychological analogies of the Trinity."

The appeal to the ordering of the world

This is one of the most significant themes for our study, in the light of its close connection with the findings of the natural sciencies. Thomas Aquinas' arguments for the existence of God base themselves on the perception that there is an ordering within nature, which requires to be explained. Equally, the fact that the human mind can discern and investigate this ordering of nature is of considerable significance. There seems to be something about human nature which prompts it to ask questions about the world, just as there seems to be something about the world which allows answers to those questions to be given. The noted theoretical physicist and Christian apologist John Polkinghorne comments on this point as follows, in his *Science and Creation*:

We are so familiar with the fact that we can understand the world that most of the time we take it for granted. It is what makes science possible. Yet it could have been otherwise. The universe might have been a disorderly chaos rather than an orderly cosmos. Or it might have had a rationality which was inaccessible to us. ... There is a congruence between our minds and the universe, between the rationality experienced within and the rationality observed without.

There is a deep-seated congruence between the rationality present in our minds, and the *orderedness* which we observe as present in the world. One of the most remarkable aspects of this ordering concern the abstract structures of pure mathematics – a free creation of the human mind – which, as Polkinghorne stresses, nevertheless provide important clues to understanding the world.

An example of this congruence between rationality and the natural order can be seen in Paul Dirac's 1931 explanation of a puzzling aspect of an equation he had derived to explain the behavior of an electron. It had two types of solution, one with positive energy and the other with negative energy. The latter class could be interpreted as implying the existence of a particle which was identical to an electron in every respect, save that it was positively charged. This point was brought out clearly by Hermann Weyl's demonstration that such "negative energy solutions" had electron mass. In 1932, Carl Anderson observed real-life effects which led him to postulate the existence of the positive electron, corresponding to Dirac's postulated particle. The new particle was observed only in cloud chamber experiments; this was accounted for by Blackett's observation that Dirac's theory indicated that the particle would soon annihilate itself on collision with a (negatively-charged) electron, and was therefore not (as some had thought) a constituent element of stable matter. In a sense, the positron can thus be said to have been known to the mathematicians before the physicists discovered it.

So important is this appeal to the ordering of nature that we shall be exploring it in greater detail in a later chapter, as we deal with the concept of a "law of nature," and the relation of such laws to a doctrine of creation. The appeal to the beauty of nature is also of importance in this respect, and we shall consider it in what follows.

The appeal to the beauty of nature

A number of major Christian theologians have developed natural theologies, based on the sense of beauty which arises from contemplating the world. Hans Urs von Balthasar and Jonathan Edwards offered such an approach in the twentieth and eighteenth centuries respectively, the former from a Roman Catholic and the latter from a Reformed perspective. Robert Boyle developed the image of nature as a temple and the natural scientist as a priest, thus drawing attention to the sense of wonder evoked by the study of nature in all its beauty.

Augustine of Hippo argued that there was a natural progression from an admiration of the beautiful things of the world to the worship of the one who had created these things, and whose beauty was reflected in them. The great medieval theologian Thomas Aquinas set out "Five Ways" of inferring from the orderliness of the world to the reality of God; the fourth of those ways is based upon the observation of the existence of perfection in the world. Although Aquinas does not specifi- cally identity "beauty" as one of these perfections at this point, it is clear that this identification can be made without difficulty, and is made elsewhere in Aquinas' work. This general line of argument was devel- oped in the early twentieth century by the noted philosophical theologian F. R. Tennant, who argued that part of the cumulative case for the existence of God was the observation of beauty within the world.

Within the Reformed tradition, a recognition of the importance of "beauty" as a theological theme can be discerned in the writings of Calvin. However, its most powerful exposition within this tradition is generally agreed to be found in the writings of the leading eighteenth- century American theologian Jonathan Edwards. Edwards argues that the beauty of God is to be expected – and duly found – in the derived beauty of the created order.

It is very fit and becoming of God who is infinitely wise, so to order things that there should be a voice of His in His works, instructing those that behold him and painting forth and shewing divine mysteries and things more immediately appertaining to Himself and His spiritual kingdom. The works of God are but a kind of voice or language of God to instruct intelligent beings in things pertaining to Himself. And why should we not think that he would teach and instruct by His works in this way as well as in others, viz., by representing divine things by His works and so painting them forth, especially since we know that God hath so much delighted in this way of instruction. . . . If we look on these shadows of divine things as the voice of God purposely by them teaching us these and those spiritual and divine things, to show of what excellent advantage it will be, how agreeably and clearly it will tend to convey instruction to our minds, and to impress things on the mind and to affect the mind, by that we may, as it were, have God speaking to us. Wherever we are, and whatever we are about, we may see divine things excellently represented and held forth.

The most theologically sustained and sophisticated exploration of the significance of "beauty" of the present century can be found in the writings of the Swiss Roman Catholic theologian Hans Urs von Balthasar (1905–88). "The fundamental principle of a theological aesthetics . . . is the fact that, just as this Christian revelation is absolute truth and goodness, so also it is absolute beauty." Von Balthasar thus describes his own work as "an attempt to develop a Christian theology in the light of the third transcendental, that is to say: to complement the vision of the true and the good with that of the beautiful."

It will therefore be clear that the concept of beauty is of major importance to a religious understanding of the nature of the world. Its importance has long been appreciated in pure mathematics, although the new interest in fractals has opened up the issue in a new and highly exciting manner. In the present century, that interest in beauty has also become significant for the natural sciences. While "beauty" can be understood to refer to the natural world itself, it is generally understood to refer to the manner in which that world is to be interpreted, especially at the theoretical level. The beauty of theories is often associated with their symmetry, as we noted when dealing with the elegance of Maxwell's equations. Steven Weinberg, who received the 1979 Nobel Prize for physics, comments as follows on the beauty of scientific theories:

The kind of beauty that we find in physical theories is of a very limited sort. It is, as far as I have been able to capture it in words, the beauty of simplicity and inevitability – the beauty of perfect structure, the beauty of everything fitting together, of nothing being changeable, of logical rigidity. It is a beauty that is spare and classic, the sort we find in the Greek tragedies.

This is especially clear from the writings of Paul Dirac, who managed to establish a connection between quantum theory and general relativity at a time when everyone else had failed to do so. Dirac's approach appears to have been based on the concept of "beauty," in that an explicitly aesthetic criterion is laid down as a possible means of evaluating scientific theories:

It is more important to have beauty in one's equations than to have them fit experiment. . . . It seems that it one is working from the point of view of getting beauty in one's equations, and if one has a really good insight, one is on a sure line of progress.

It will be clear that this offers a significant interface between religion and the natural sciences, which points to the importance of natural theology as a means of dialogue between these disciplines.

These, then, are merely some of the ways in which Christian theologians have attempted to describe the manner in which God can be known, however fleetingly, through nature. Within a specifically Christian perspective, these insights which may be obtained into the existence and nature of God are to be seen as pointers to the greater reality of God's self-revelation, rather than as complete in themselves. In view of the importance of this point, we shall explore it further in what follows.

Natural and Revealed Theology

In the writings of both Thomas Aquinas and John Calvin, a distinction is drawn between a valid yet partial knowledge of God available through the observation of the world and a fuller knowledge of God resulting from God's decision to reveal himself. As we considered Aquinas in some detail earlier in relation to the issue of ordering, it is appropriate to illustrate the point at issue in this later section of the work from Calvin.

Calvin draws a fundamental distinction between a general "knowledge of God the creator," which can be had through reflection on the created world, and a more specifically Christian "knowledge of God the redeemer," which can only be had through the Christian revelation. Calvin argues that the latter is consistent with the former, and extends its insights.

The first book of Calvin's *Institutes of the Christian Religion* (1559) opens with discussion of this fundamental problem of Christian theology: how do we know anything about God? Calvin affirms that a general knowledge of God may be discerned throughout the creation – in humanity, in the natural order, and in the historical process itself. Two main grounds of such knowledge are identified, one subjective, the other objective. The first ground is a "sense of divinity (*sensus divinitatis*)" or a "seed of religion (*semen religionis*)", implanted within every human being by God. God has thus endowed human beings with some inbuilt sense or presentiment of the divine existence. It is as if something about God has been engraved in the hearts of every human being. The second ground lies in experience of and reflection upon the ordering of the world. The fact that God is creator, together with an appreciation of the divine wisdom and justice, may be gained from an inspection of the created order, culminating in humanity itself.

It is important to stress that Calvin makes no suggestion whatsoever that this knowledge of God from the created order is peculiar to, or restricted to, Christian believers. Calvin is arguing that anyone, by intelligent and rational reflection upon the created order, should be able to arrive at the idea of God. The created order is a "theatre" or a "mirror" for the displaying of the divine presence, nature and attributes. Although God is invisible and incomprehensible, God wills to be known under the form of created and visible things, by donning the garment of creation. It is of the utmost significance to observe that Calvin therefore commends the natural sciences (such as astronomy), on account of their ability to illustrate further the wonderful ordering of creation, and the divine wisdom which this indicates. Significantly, however, Calvin makes no appeal to specifically Christian sources of revelation at this stage in his argument. His argument up to this point is based upon empirical observation and ratiocination. If Calvin introduces scriptural quotations, it is to consolidate a general natural knowledge of God, rather than to establish that knowledge in the first place. There is, he stresses, a way of discerning God which is common to those inside and outside the Christian community.

Having thus laid the foundations for a general knowledge of God, Calvin stresses its shortcomings; his dialogue partner here is the classical Roman writer Cicero, whose On the *Nature of the Gods* is perhaps one of the most influential classical expositions of a natural knowledge of God. Calvin argues that the gap between God and humanity, already of enormous magnitude, is increased still further on account of human sin. Our natural knowledge of God is imperfect and confused, even to the point of contradiction on occasion. A natural knowledge of God serves to deprive humanity of any excuse for ignoring the divine will; nevertheless, it is inadequate as the basis of a fully-fledged portrayal of the nature, character and purposes of God.

Having stressed this point, Calvin then introduces the notion of revelation; scripture reiterates what may be known of God through nature, while simultaneously clarifying this general revelation and enhancing it. "The knowledge of God, which is clearly shown in the ordering of the world and in all creatures, is still more clearly and familiarly explained in the Word." It is only through scripture that the believer has access to knowledge of the redeeming actions of God in history, culminating in the life, death and resurrection of Jesus Christ. For Calvin, revelation is focused upon the person of Jesus Christ; our knowledge of God is mediated through him. God may thus only be fully known through Jesus Christ, who may in turn only be known through Scripture; the created order, however, provides important points of contact for and partial resonances of this revelation. The basic idea here, then, is that a knowledge of God the creator may be had both through nature and through revelation, with the latter clarifying, confirming and extending what may be known through the former. Knowledge of God the redeemer – which for Calvin is a distinctively *Christian* knowledge of God – may only be had by the Christian revelation, in Christ and through Scripture.

This general approach was developed with particular rigor within the Reformed tradition. The importance attached to the notion of natural theology in the writings of Jean-Alphonse Turrettini (1671–1737), the leading Genevan theologian of the eighteenth century, illustrates this point particularly clearly. Thomas Chalmers, the leading Scottish nineteenth-century Presbyterian theologian, also adopted a strongly positive approach to the matter.

Particular attention should be paid to the "two books" tradition, which is known to have been of importance to English natural theology during the seventeenth and early eighteenth centuries. This approach can be argued to drawn on Calvin's theological approach, which we have just explored above. It was also influential in Protestant circles after Calvin. For example, the "Belgic Confession" (1561), a Reformed confession of faith which had its origins in the Lowlands, spoke of nature as being "before our eyes as a most beautiful book in which all created things, both great and small, are like characters leading us to contemplate the invisible things of God." This idea of the "book of nature" which complemented the "book of Scripture" rapidly gained popularity. Francis Bacon commended the study of "the book of God's word" and the "book of God's works" in his *Advancment of Learning* (1605). This latter work had considerable impact on English thinking on the relation of science and religion. Thus in his 1674 tract *The Excellency of Theology compared with Natural Theology*, Robert Boyle noted that "as the two great books, of nature and of scripture, have the same author, so the study of the latter does not at all hinder an inquisitive man's delight in the study of the former." Similar thoughts can be found expressed in Sir Thomas Browne's 1643 classic *Religio Medici*:

There are two books from whence I collect my divinity. Besides that written one of God, another of his servant, nature, that universal and publick manuscript, that lies expansed unto the eyes of all. Those that never saw him in the one have discovered him in the other.

Note especially the idea of the world as "God's epistle written to mankind" (Boyle). This metaphor of the "two books" with the one author was of considerable importance in holding together Christian theology and piety, and the emerging interest and knowledge of the natural world at this time.

From the material which has been presented in this chapter, it will be clear that natural theology represents one of the most significant areas of dialogue between the natural sciences and religion. While the writings of William Paley (see p. 99) are often regarded with a considerable degree of suspicion today, they nevertheless represent a major attempt to relate scientific observation and religious belief. Paley's specific approach may have been abandoned. Yet, as the writings of John Polkinghorne (see pp. 218–21) and others have shown, an appeal to the ordering of the natural world continues to be seen as of major importance to religious writers.

Our attention now turns to the language and imagery which is used to depict the world, whether in the sciences or religion.

For further reading

Barr, J. *Biblical Faith and Natural Theology*. Oxford: Clarendon Press, 1993.

Brooke, J. H. "Science and the Fortunes of Natural Theology: Some Historical Perspectives." *Zygon* 24 (1989): 3–22.

Brown, H. "Alvin Plantinga and Natural Theology." *International Journal for Philosophy of Religion* 30 (1991): 1–19.

Cairns, D. "Thomas Chalmer's Astronomical Discourses: A Study in Natural Theology." *Scottish Journal of Theology* 9 (1956): 410–21.

Clarke, M. L. *Paley: Evidences for the Man*. London: SPCK, 1974.

Fisch, H. "The Scientist as Priest: A Note on Robert Boyle's Natural Theology." *Isis* 44 (1953): 252–65.

Garcia, L. L. "Natural Theology and the Reformed Objection." *Christian Perspectives on Religious Knowledge*. Ed. C. Stephen Evans and Merold Westphal. Grand Rapids, MI: Eerdmans, 1993, pp. 112–33.

Gascoigne, J. "From Bentley to the Victorians: The Rise and Fall of British Newtonian Natural Theology." *Science in Context* 2 (1988): 219–56.

Gillespie, N. C. "Divine Design and the Industrial Revolution: William Paley's Abortive Reform of Natural Theology." *Isis* 81 (1990): 214–29.

Gillispie, C. C. *Genesis and Geology: A Study in the Relations of Scientific Thought,*

Natural Theology and Social Opinion in Great Britain, 1790–1850. Harvard Historical Studies 58. Cambridge, MA: Harvard University Press, 1996.

Gingerich, O. "Is there a Role for Natural Theology Today?" *Science and Theology: Questions at the Interface*. Ed. M. Rae, H. Regan and J. Stenhouse. Edinburgh: T. & T. Clark, 1994, pp. 29–48.

Kretzmann, N. *The Metaphysics of Theism: Aquinas's Natural Theology in Summa contra Gentiles I*. Oxford: Clarendon Press, 1997.

LeMahieu, D. L. *The Mind of William Paley: A Philosopher and His Age*. Lincoln: University of Nebraska Press, 1976.

Long, E. T. "Experience and Natural Theology." *Philosophy of Religion* 31 (1992): 119–32.

Robinson, N. H. G. "The Problem of Natural Theology." *Religious Studies* 8 (1972): 319–33.

Wilkinson, D. A. "The Revival of Natural Theology in Contemporary Cosmology." *Science and Christian Belief* 2 (1990): 95–115.

7

Models and Analogies in Science and Religion

One of the most intriguing aspects of the interface between science and religion is the use of "models" or "analogies" to depict complex entities – whether the entity in question is an atomic nucleus or God. In this chapter, we shall explore the different ways in which these "visual aids" are developed and deployed in science and religion. The theoretical physicist John Polkinghorne notes an important parallel between the two disciplines, which relates specifically to the need to represent in a visual manner entities which cannot presently be seen:

We habitually speak of entities which are not directly observable. No one has ever seen a gene (though there are X-ray photographs which, suitably interpreted, led Crick and Watson to the helical structure of DNA) or an electron (though there are tracks in bubble chambers which, suitably interpreted, indicate the existence of a particle of negative electric charge of about 4.8×10^{-10} esu and mass about 10^{-27} gm). No one has ever seen God (though there is the astonishing Christian claim that "the only Son, who is in the bosom of the Father, he has made him known" (John 1: 18)).

It is a matter of fact that most religions make statements which relate to a series of entities (such as "God," "forgiveness," or "eternal life") which are unobservable in themselves at present. The question of how such theoretical or unobservable entities are to be depicted, and their precise ontological status, is a matter of considerable interest and importance within both science and religion, and will occupy our attention throughout the present chapter. We begin by considering the use of models in the natural sciences.

Models in the Natural Sciences

One of the most distinctive features of the natural sciences is the tendency to use "models" to depict at least certain aspects of complex systems. A model is understood to be a simplified way of representing a complex system, which allows its users to gain an increased understanding on at least some of its many aspects. Once a model has been constructed and tested, it can be developed in such a way that it includes some more complicated features of the system which were initially ignored in constructing the model. To illustrate some aspects of the use of such models, we may consider one of the most familiar of such models – the kinetic theory of gases.

The behavior of gases was studied in some detail from the seventeenth century onwards, particular by Robert Boyle and Jacques Charles. A series of experiments examined the way in which gases behaved when their pressure, volume and temperature were changed. It was found that the behavior of gases could be described in terms of a series of laws, which applied to all gases at low pressures, irrespective of their chemical identity. The two most famous such laws are known as "Boyle's Law" and "Charles' Law", which can be formulated as follows:

Boyle's Law: $pV = $ constant
Charles' Law: $V = $ constant $\times T$

where p is the pressure of the gas, V its volume, and T its temperature, expressed in terms of the temperature scale devised by Lord Kelvin according to which $0°$ centigrade is $273.15°$. (This scale thus identifies the temperature of "absolute zero" as being $-273.15°$ centigrade.) The "perfect gas equation," which combines these two laws and other observations, can be summarized as

$$pV = nRT$$

where R is the gas constant ($8.31451 \, JK^{-1}mole^{-1}$) and n the number of moles of gas present. This equation holds universally, irrespective of the identity of the gas in question.

So how can this behaviour be explained? The kinetic theory of gases offers a model of an ideal gas which is based on three assumptions:

1   A gas consists of molecules in ceaseless random motion, which do not interact in any manner.
2   The size of the molecules is negligible, in that their diameter is assumed to be insignificant in comparison with the mean distance travelled by the molecule between collisions.
3   On striking the walls of their container, gas molecules make perfectly elastic collisions, in which the translational kinetic energy of the molecule remains unchanged.

In effect, the model suggests that we think of gas molecules as billiard balls, in constant collision with the walls of the container. It is quite easy to use this model to predict how pressure, volume, and temperature are related. For example, the pressure on the container can be calculated in terms of the rate of change of momentum of gas molecules. The gas laws noted above can be derived theoretically on the basis of this model of gases, suggesting that the kinetic theory is a good basic model for these systems.

Of course, the model is very simple, and does not take account of some more complex features of the behavior of gases. For example, it assumes that the volume occupied by gas molecules is negligible, so that the portion of the overall gas volume occupied by those molecules can be disregarded in calculations. While this is true at low pressures, it becomes a more serious complication at higher pressure. The model also ignores inter-molecular collisions and forces (which are insignificant at low pressure), and focuses on the interaction of those molecules with the walls of the container.

Yet it is important to appreciate that models can be made more sophisticated, to allow for the more complicated aspects of the system to be modelled. The basic idea is to establish a model which is able to explain the most important features of a system, and then develop the model further to incorporate more complex features of the behaviour of the system. For example, the model set out above does not take account of the fact that gas molecules have a definite volume. This fact can be ignored at low pressures; at high pressures, however, the volume occupied by the gas molecules begins to become significant. This can be incorporated into the mathematical modeling of the system as follows. Earlier, we saw how the behavior of gases could be predicted using the following formula:

$$pV = nRT$$

This formula assumes that the gas molecules are of negligible size. A small adjustment to the formula allows it to take account of the finite size of the molecules. If b is the volume occupied by a mole of gas molecules, then the behavior of that gas is given by the formula:

$$P(V - \text{nb}) = nRT$$

In this case, the value of b will depend upon the gas in question, in that the volume occupied by gas molecules is dependent on the identity of the gas.

This same pattern can be seen at work throughout the development of scientific models. It may be helpful to summarize the basic features of the pattern.

1 The behavior of a system is established, and certain patterns noted.
2 A model is developed, which aims to explain the most important aspects of the system.
3 The model is found to have weaknesses at a number of points, on account of its simplicity.
4 The model can then be made more complex, in order to take account of these weaknesses.

Other examples of models can easily be given. For example, in December 1910 Ernest Rutherford developed a simple model of the atom, based on the solar system. The atom consists of a central body (the nucleus), in which practically the entire mass of the atom is concentrated. Electrons orbit this nucleus, in much the same way as the planets orbit the sun. Whereas the orbits of the planets were determined by the gravitational attraction of the sun, Rutherford argued that the orbits of the electrons were determined by the electrostatic attraction between the negatively-charged electrons and the positively-charged nucleus. Interestingly, Rutherford argued that the way in which alpha-particles were scattered by atoms could be explained if the alpha-particles were assumed to behave like certain types of comets, whose orbits around the sun took the form of hyperbolae. The behavior of these alpha-particles, as recently observed by Hans Wilhelm Geiger, was thus analogous to that of other members of the solar system (non-periodic comets). The model was visually simple and easy to understand, and offered a theoretical framework which explained at least some of the known behavior of atoms at this time.

Two serious errors can arise in relation to the use of models in the natural sciences. First, it can be assumed that models are as identical with the systems with which they are associated. This is not correct. Gas molecules are not minute inelastic spheres; the kinetic theory of gases simply points out that we can understand at least some aspects of the behavior of gases under certain conditions if we picture them in this manner. The natural scientist will affirm that there really are such things as "gas molecules," and that certain aspects of their behaviour parallels that of billiard balls. Similarly, the atom is not a miniature solar system; the Rutherford model merely points out that we can understand some of their features if we think of them in this way. In each case, we are presented with a visualizible representation of a system, which assists explanation and interpretation. They are to be taken seriously (in that they clearly bear some relation to the system that is being modeled); they are not, however, to be taken literally.

The second error that can be made is to assume that some aspect of the model is necessarily present in the system being modelled. As we have stressed, models are like analogies: the model and system resemble each other in some ways, and not in others. The fact that there is a parallel in one area does not mean that the same parallel exists in all areas. An excellent example of this problem can be found in late nineteenth-century physics. By this stage, it was widely accepted that light consisted of waves. This had been established by a series of experiments earlier in the century, particularly through studying the phenomenon of diffraction. Light was widely regarded as a wave phenomenon, showing similar behavior to other wave phenomena – such as sound.

One of the most interesting aspects of sound is that it requires a medium through which to travel. If a source of sound is placed in a glass vessel, and the air is pumped out, the intensity of the sound will gradually decrease. Sound has to travel through something, and cannot travel in a vacuum. Noting the many similarities between the behavior of light and sound, many physicists drew the conclusion that an analogy existed at this point as well. If sound needed a medium to travel through, then so did light. The term "luminiferous ether" was used to refer to this medium (the term "luminiferous" literally means "light-bearing").

The Michelson–Morley experiment was designed to detect "ether drift" – that is, the motion of the ether with respect to the earth. It failed, although it took some time for the implication of the negative result to be fully understood. Either the ether was totally at rest with regard to the movement of the earth, or it did not exist. In the end, it had to be accepted that there was no experimental support for the existence of "luminiferous ether." At least in this respect, there was a fundamental distinction between light and sound.

From this brief discussion, it will be clear that models play a significant role in the natural sciences. The most important points to note are the following:

1 Models are often seen as significant ways of visualizing complex and abstract concepts. This is especially true in relation to aspects of quantum theory, to which we shall return presently.
2 Models are seen as "intermediates" between the complex entities and the human mind.
3 Models do not necessarily "exist," although what they attempt to represent has a real and independent existence.
4 Models are selected or constructed on the basis of the belief that there exist significant points of similarity between the model and what it is meant to represent.
5 Models are therefore not identical with what they model, and must not be treated as if they are.
6 In particular, it must not be assumed that every aspect of the model corresponds to the entity being modelled.

So what of the situation with regard to religion? At first sight, there might be expected to be significant similarities here between the sciences and religion. Both aim to talk about complex entities which cannot be seen in terms of familiar language and images. In what follows, we shall explore the role of analogies in religion.

Analogy, Metaphor and Religion

Theology can be usefully defined as "talk about God." But how can God ever be described or discussed using human language? The Austrian philosopher Ludwig Wittgenstein made this point forcefully: if human words are incapable of describing the distinctive aroma of coffee, how can they cope with something as subtle as God? One of the answers which is given to this question focuses on the idea of analogies and metaphors – ways of thinking and speaking about God which are based on images, such as the biblical images of "God as shepherd" and "God as king". We may begin by considering the way in which analogies and metaphors are used in theology.

Perhaps the most basic idea which underlies the theological reply to such questions is usually referred to as "the principle of analogy," and is particularly associated with the great scholastic theologian Thomas Aquinas. According to Aquinas, the fact that God created the world points to a fundamental "analogy of being" between God and the world. There is a continuity between God and the world on account of the expression of the being of God in the being of the world. For this reason, it is legitimate to use entities within the created order as analogies for God. In doing this, theology does not reduce God to the level of a created object or being; it merely affirms that there is a likeness of correspondence between God and that being, which allows the latter to act as a signpost to God. A created entity can thus be like God, without being identical to God.

The argument deployed by Aquinas can be summarized along the following lines. In that God created the natural order, some form of correspondence between that order and its creator is to be expected. This does not mean that God is to be considered to be identical to nature; there are areas of similarity and dissimilarity. In that the likeness between God and creatures is established by God in the act of creation, Aquinas argues that it is not proper to suggest that "God is like a creature." Rather, it is to be said that "the creature is like God," in that the act of creation established that relationship from the Godward side. Aquinas sets this out clearly in the section of his *Summa contra Gentiles* in which he deals with the issue of "the likeness of creatures to God":

Effects that fall short of their causes do not agree with them in name and nature. Yet some likeness must be found between them, since it belongs to the nature of action that an agent produce its like, since each thing acts according as it is in act. The form of an effect, therefore, is certainly found in some measure in a transcending cause ... God gave all things their perfection, and thereby is both like and unlike all of them. Hence it is that Sacred Scripture recalls the likeness between God and creatures, as when it is said in Genesis 1: 26: "Let us make man to our image and likeness". .... A creature receives from God that which makes it like him. The converse, however, does not hold. God, then, is not likened to a creature; rather, the converse is true.

For Aquinas, the use of analogies based on creatures to refer to God is thus not arbitrary, but is ultimately grounded in creation itself.

We should note here a severe difficulty encountered in arguments from analogy – the potentially arbitrary character of the analogies employed. The assumption that "A is an analogy for B" requires justification. On what basis is the analogy posited? Is the existence of some similarity a happy coincidence? Or does it rest on something more fundamental, perhaps reflecting something deeply embedded in the structure of the universe? It is important to pause here, and note the importance of the way in which the growth of "super-symmetry" theories have posited a fundamental relationship between various aspects of modern physics. The doctrine of creation places such relationships on a secure intellectual footing, suggesting that a correlation exists within the created order prior to its being discerned through human investigation.

Consider the statement "God is our Father." Aquinas argues that this should be understood to mean that God is like a human father. In other words, God is analogous to a father, being like a human father in some respects, and not in others. There are genuine points of similarity. For example, God cares for us, as human fathers care for their children (note Matthew 7: 9–11). God is the ultimate source of our existence, just as our fathers brought us into being. God exercises authority over us, as do human fathers. Equally, there are genuine points of dissimilarity. God is not a human being, for example. Nor does the necessity of a human mother point to the need for a divine mother.

The point that Aquinas is trying to make is that God is revealed in images and ideas which relate to our world of everyday existence – yet which do not reduce God to that everyday world. To say that "God is our father" is not to say that God is just yet another human father. Nor, as we shall explore presently, does it mean that God is to be thought of as male (see pp. 159–62). Rather, it is to say that thinking about human fathers helps us think about God. They are analogies. Like all analogies, they break down at points. However, they are still extremely useful and vivid ways of thinking about God, which allow us to use the vocabulary and images of our own world, to describe something which ultimately lies beyond that world.

Yet analogies and metaphors require interpretation. What aspects of the image are *intended* to be carried over? What aspects of the image might be appropiately carried over, and on the basis of what criteria should this decision be made? How does one know when an analogy has been pressed too far? Analogies break down. There comes a point when they cannot be pressed further. How do we know when they break down? To illustrate this point, we may consider an example from another area of theology, before moving on to consider its solution. The New Testament talks about Jesus giving his life as a "ransom" for sinners (Mark 10: 45; 1 Timothy 2: 6). What does this analogy mean? The everyday use of the word "ransom" suggests three ideas.

1 Liberation. A ransom is something which achieves freedom for a person who is held in captivity. When someone is kidnapped, and a ransom demanded, the payment of that ransom leads to liberation.
2 Payment. A ransom is a sum of money which is paid in order to achieve an individual's liberation.
3 Someone to whom the ransom is paid. A ransom is usually paid to an individual's captor, or an intermediate.

These three ideas thus seem to be implied by speaking of Jesus' death as a "ransom" for sinners.

But are they all intended to be implied? There is no doubt whatsoever that the New Testament proclaims that we have been liberated from captivity through the death and resurrection of Jesus. We have been set free from captivity to sin and the fear of death (Romans 8: 21; Hebrews 2: 15). It is also clear that the New Testament understands the death of Jesus as the price which had to be paid to achieve our liberation (1 Corinthians 6: 20; 7: 23). Our liberation is a costly and a precious matter. In these two respects, the scriptural use of "redemption" corresponds to the everyday use of the word. But what of the third aspect?

The New Testament is silent over any suggestion that Jesus' death was the price paid to someone (such as the devil) to achieve our liberation. Some of the writers of the first four centuries, however, assumed that they could press this analogy to its limits, and declared that God had delivered us from the power of the devil by offering Jesus as the price of our liberation. Origen, perhaps the most speculative of early patristic writers, developed this in some detail. If Christ's death was a ransom, Origen argued, it must have been paid to someone. But who? It could not have been paid to God, in that God was not holding sinners to ransom. In what can only be seen as a fateful theological move, Origen concluded that it had to be paid to the devil.

Rufinus of Aquileia and Gregory the Great developed this idea still further. The devil had acquired rights over fallen humanity, which God was obliged to respect. The only means by which humanity could be released from this satanic domination and oppression was through the devil exceeding the limits of his authority, and thus being obliged to forfeit his rights. So how could this be achieved? Gregory suggests that it could come about if a sinless person were to enter the world, yet in the form of a normal sinful person. The devil would not notice until it was too late: in claiming authority over this sinless person, the devil would have overstepped the limits of his authority, and thus be obliged to abandon his rights.

Rufinus suggests the image of a baited hook: Christ's humanity is the bait, and his divinity the hook. The devil, like a great sea-monster, snaps at the bait – and then discovers, too late, that he is trapped by the hook:

[The purpose of the Incarnation] was that the divine virtue of the Son of God might be like a kind of hook hidden beneath the form of human flesh . . . to lure on the prince of this world to a contest; that the Son might offer him his human flesh as a bait and that the divinity which lay underneath might catch him and hold him fast with its hook. . . . Then, just as a fish when it seizes a baited hook not only fails to drag off the bait but is itself dragged out of the water to serve as food for others; so he that had the power of death seized the body of Jesus in death, unaware of the hook of divinity which lay hidden inside. Having swallowed it, he was immediately caught. The gates of hell were broken, and he was, as it were, drawn up from the pit, to become food for others.

The aspect of this approach to the meaning of the cross that caused the most disquiet subsequently was the apparent implication that God was guilty of deception.

It can be argued that this thoroughly unsatisfactory theory resulted from an analogy being pressed far beyond its intended limits. But how do we know whether an analogy has been pressed too far? How can the limits of such analogues be tested? Such questions have been debated throughout Christian history. An important twentieth-century discussion of this point may be found in British philosopher of religion Ian T. Ramsey's *Christian Discourse: Some Logical Explorations* (1965), which puts forward the idea that models or analogies are not freestanding, but interact with and qualify each other.

Ramsey argues that Scripture does not give us one single analogy (or "model") for God or for salvation, but uses a range of analogies. Each of these analogies or models illuminates certain aspects of our understanding of God, or the nature of salvation. However, these analogies also interact with each other. They modify each other. They help us understand the limits of other analogies. No analogy or parable is exhaustive in itself; taken together, however, the range of analogies and parables builds up to give a comprehensive and consistent understanding of God and salvation.

An example of how images interact may make this point clearer. Take the analogies of king, father, and shepherd. Each of these three analogies conveys the idea of authority, suggesting that this is of fundamental importance to our understanding of God. Kings, however, often behave in arbitrary ways, and not always in the best interests of their subjects. The analogy of God as a king might thus be misunderstood to suggest that God is some sort of tyrant. However, the tender compassion of a father towards his children commended by scripture (Psalms 103: 13–18), and the total dedication of a good shepherd to the welfare of his flock (John 10: 11), show that this is not the intended meaning. Authority is to be exercised tenderly and wisely.

Aquinas' doctrine of analogy, then, is of fundamental importance to the way we think about God. It illuminates the manner in which God is revealed in and through Scriptural images and analogies, allowing us to understand how God can be above our world, and yet simultaneously be revealed in and through that world. God is not an object or a person in space and time; nevertheless, such persons and objects can help us deepen our appreciation of God's character and nature. God, who is infinite, is able to be revealed in and through human words and finite images.

Having explored the idea of an analogy in a little detail, we may now turn to consider metaphors. The precise nature of the differences between analogies and metaphors remains disputed. Aristotle defined a metaphor as involving "the transferred use of a term that properly belongs to something else." This definition is so broad that it embraces just about every figure of speech, including analogy. In modern use, the word "metaphor" would generally be taken to mean something rather different, with the following being a useful definition.

A metaphor is a way of speaking about one thing in terms which are suggestive of another. It is, to use Nelson Goodman's famous phrase, "a matter of teaching an old word new tricks," This definition clearly includes analogy; so what is the difference between them?

Once more, it is necessary to note that there is no general agreement on this matter. Perhaps a working solution to the problem could be stated as follows: analogies seem to be appropriate, where metaphors involve a sense of surprise or initial incredulity. For example, consider the two statements which follow:

1 God is wise.
2 God is a lion.

In the first case, it is being affirmed that there is an analogical connection between the nature of God and the human notion of "wisdom." It is being suggested, that at both the linguistic and ontological levels, there is a direct parallel between human and divine notions of wisdom. Human wisdom serves as a analogy of divine wisdom. The comparison does not cause us any surprise.

In the second case, the comparison can cause a slight degree of consternation. It does not seem to be appropriate to compare God to a lion. However many similarities there may be between God and a lion, there are obviously many differences. For some modern writers, a metaphor mingles similarity and dissimilarity, stressing that there are both parallels and divergences between the two objects being compared.

With these points in mind, we may explore three features of metaphors which have attracted theological attention in recent decades.

1 Metaphors imply both similarity and dissimilarity between the two things being compared. It is perhaps for this reason that some recent writings – particularly those of Sallie McFague – have stressed the metaphorical, rather than the analogical, nature of theological language. As McFague puts it:

A metaphor is seeing one thing as something else, pretending "this" is "that" because we do not know how to think or talk about "this", so we use "that" as a way of saying something about it. Thinking metaphorically means spotting a thread of similarity between two dissimilar objects, events, or whatever, and using the better-known as a way of speaking about the lesser-known.

To speak of "God as father" should thus be seen as a metaphor, rather than an analogy, implying significant differences between God and a father, rather than (as in the case of a analogy) a direct line of similarities.

2 Metaphors cannot be reduced to definitive statements. Perhaps the most attractive feature of metaphors for Christian theology is their

open-ended character. Although some literary critics have suggested that metaphors can be reduced to a set of equivalent literal expressions, others have insisted that no limits can be set to the extent of the comparison. Thus the metaphor "God as father" cannot be reduced to a set of precise statements about God, valid for every place and every time. It is meant to be suggestive, allowing future readers and interpreters to find new meanings within it. A metaphor is not simply an elegant description or memorable phrasing of something that we already know. It is an invitation to discover further levels of meaning, which others may have overlooked or forgotten.

3   Metaphors often have strongly emotional overtones. Theological metaphors are able to express the emotional dimensions of Christian faith in a way which makes them appropriate to worship. For example, the metaphor of "God as light" has enormously powerful overtones, including those of illumination, purity and glorification. Ian G. Barbour summarizes this aspect of metaphorical language as follows:

Where poetic metaphors are used only momentarily, in one context, for the sake of an immediate expression or insight, *religious symbols* become part of the language of a religious community in its scripture and liturgy and in its continuing life and thought. Religious symbols are expressive of human emotions and feelings, and are powerful in calling forth response and commitment.

The Ambivalence of Analogy: Case Studies in Science and Religion

It will be clear that the use of models or analogies in both science and religion has the potential to illuminate and to mislead. On the positive side, analogies and models can help us understand what was previously opaque and puzzling. On the other, it can lead us to make assumptions which are inaccurate or misleading, resulting in inappropriate nuances and emphases – and occasionally serious distortions – being developed. To indicate the manner in which this can happen, we may consider two case studies, one drawn from the natural sciences and the other from Christian theology.

The analogy of "natural selection"

The way in which Darwin developed the notion of "natural selection" is of particular interest, as it illustrates clearly some of the issues which arise through the use of analogies or metaphors in developing scientific theories. Darwin saw his task as being that of making sense of the bewildering diversity of plants and animals, both living and extinct, which had generally been a source of mystery to those who had gone before him. The first chapter of *The Origin of Species* examined the way in which domestic plants and animals are bred, the manner in which variations develop in successive generations through this breeding, and how these can be exploited to bring about inherited characteristics which are regarded as being of particular value by the breeder.

It is then argued that this process "artificial selection" constitutes an analogy which can be used as a framework for understanding that a related process of selection is taking place within nature itself. A known process, which would have been familiar to English stockbreeders and market gardeners, is argued to be an analogy for a similar process within nature. "As man can produce and certainly has produced a great result by his methodical and unconscious means of selection, what may not nature effect?" To emphasize this analogy, Darwin developed the term "natural selection" as a metaphorical or non-literal means of referring to a process which he believed to be the most convincing means of explaining the patterns of diversity be observed within nature.

Darwin himself claimed that the concept and the term were suggested by the methods of livestock breeders and pigeon-fanciers, who used artificial selection as a means of generating and preserving desirable characteristics within the animal world. The concept of "natural selection" was thus based on the perception of an analogy between the existing and familiar notion of "artificial selection." The term first appears in Darwin's writings after March 1840, when he is known to have read a standard manual of cattle management entitled *Cattle: Their Breeds, Management and Diseases*, which explained the methods and results of artificial selection.

Darwin was quite clear that the methods of domestic animal breeders were of major importance to his thinking, and that his idea of "natural selection" was derived from this analogy. "All my notions about how species changed derive from long-continued study of the works of agriculuralists and horticulturalists; and I believe I see my way pretty clearly on the means used by nature to change her species and *adapt* them to the wondrous and exquisitely beautiful contingencies to which every living being is exposed." This passage is significant for two reasons. First, it makes it clear that Darwin clearly saw an analogy between the familiar process of "artificial selection" and the inferred or proposed process of *natural* selection. Second, it also implies the notion of a *conscious process of selection*. Darwin speaks explicitly of nature changing her species and adapting them. The analogy is apparently being allowed to imply that the active selection of the animal or plant breeder is somehow paralleled within nature itself. This is certainly suggested by his frequent references to "nature" as an agent who actively "selects" variants which she approves as good.

But is this analogy being pressed too far? Can one speak of nature "selecting" anything, when "selection" would seem to imply purpose, choice, and intelligence? Darwin's colleague Alfred Russell Wallace was one of many who was alarmed at the implication of active choice and purposefulness on the part of nature. Did not the term "natural selection" imply an active process of selection on the part of a personified nature, which was thus understood to have the powers of rational analysis and an intended goal.

I think this arises almost entirely from your choice of the term "Natural Selection" and so constantly comparing it in its effects to Man's Selection, and also your so frequently personifying nature as "selecting", as "preferring", as "seeking only the good of the species", etc., etc. To the few, this is as clear as daylight, and beautifully suggestive, but to many it is evidently a stumbling block.

The analogy of natural selection developed by Darwin thus seems to transfer the developed notions of intention, active selection and ultimate purpose from the model (established procedures of artificial selection) to what the model is meant to explain or illuminate (the natural order). At both the verbal and conceptual level, the anthropomorphic concept of "purpose" is retained, despite Darwin's apparent intention to eliminate this (and Wallace's more explicit views on this matter). Darwin himself realized the dangers of his somewhat anthropomorphic manner of speaking about "nature." In a preface added to the third edition of *The Origin of Species* (1861), Darwin sought to correct possible misunderstandings along such lines:

Others have objected that the term selection implies conscious choice in the animals which become modified; and it has even been urged that, as plants have no volition, natural selection is not applicable to them! In the literal sense of the word, no doubt, natural selection is a false term; but who ever objected to chemists speaking of the elective affinities of the various elements? and yet an acid cannot strictly be said to elect the base with which it in preference combines. It has been said that I speak of natural selection as an active power or Deity; but who objects to an author speaking of the attraction of gravity as ruling the movement of the planets? Everyone knows what is meant and is implied by such metaphorical expressions; and they are almost necessary for brevity. So again it is difficult to avoid personifying the word Nature; but I mean by Nature, only the aggregate action and product of many natural laws, and by laws the sequence of events as ascertained by us.

This passage is of considerable importance, on account of its explicit affirmation of the analogical or metaphorical nature of the term "natural selection". It is a "false term" – that is, a term which cannot be pressed to its literal limits of meaning. In effect, the ideas of "active choice" and any personification of the selecting agent (which might be argued to be essential to the notion of "selection") have been suppressed or eliminated from the analogy.

It will therefore be clear that Darwin's use of the analogy of "natural selection" vividly illustrates both the positive and negative aspects of an argument from analogy. Positively, the analogy allows a complex situation to be illuminated or partly understood by an appeal to a known and understood event, process, or action. Yet negatively, it can lead to the transference of inappropriate aspects of the model to what the model is intended to explain. Darwin clearly did not intend his readers to understand that nature acted purposefully and rationally in "selecting" variants. Yet that is precisely what the analogy suggested to many of his readers.

Precisely the same problem can arise in relation to the religious use of analogies, as will become clear when we consider the analogy of "God as Father."

The analogy of "God as Father"

One of the interesting aspects of the analogical nature of theological language is the way in which persons or social roles, largely drawn from the rural world of the Ancient Near East, were seen to be suitable models for the divine activity or personality. One such analogy is that of a father. We have already noted the helpful way in which this image can be explored (see pp. 153–6). Yet the image is seen as profoundly unhelpful by some, particularly women, who interpret it as implying that God is a man, or that God is male. This nuance is not intended by the image, and it is worth exploring this issue in a little more detail to see how the misunderstanding arises, and how it can be countered.

It must be stressed that the statement that "a father in ancient Israel society is a suitable model for God" is not equivalent to saying that "God is male." When we suggest that a suitable model for God is a father, we are saying that, *in certain respects*, God may be thought of as being like a father – for example, in his disciplining of his children. And in certain respects, God is like a mother – for example, in his care and compassion for his children. But God is not male nor female. It must be recalled that a model is both like and unlike what is being modeled. The critically important issue is to determine what the points of likeness are. To model God on a human father is not to say that God is male, or that males are superior to females. The maleness of this language is to be seen as an accommodation to human speech and ways of thinking, not a literal representation of God.

Mary Hayter, reflecting on such issues in her work *New Eve in Christ*, writes:

It would appear that certain "motherly prerogatives" in ancient Hebrew society – such as carrying and comforting small children – became metaphors for Yahweh's activity *vis-à-vis* his children Israel. Likewise, various "fatherly pre-rogatives" – such as disciplining a son – became vehicles for divine imagery. Different cultures and ages have different ideas about which roles are proper to the mother and which to the father.

To speak of God as father is to say that the role of the father in ancient Israel allows us insights into the nature of God. It is not to say that God is a male human being. Neither male nor female sexuality is to be attributed to God. For sexuality is an attribute of the created order, which cannot be assumed to correspond directly to any such polarity within the creator God himself.

Indeed, the Old Testament avoids attributing sexual functions to God, on account of the strongly pagan overtones of such associations. The Canaanite fertility cults emphasized the sexual functions of both gods and goddesses; the Old Testament refuses to endorse the idea that the gender or the sexuality of God is a significant matter. As Mary Hayter puts it:

Today a growing number of feminists teach that the God/ess combines male and female characteristics. They, like those who assume that God is exclusively male, should remember that any attribution of sexuality to God is a reversion to paganism.

There is no need to revert to pagan ideas of gods and goddesses to recover the idea that God is neither masculine or feminine; those ideas are already potentially present, if neglected, in Christian theology. Wolfhart Pannenberg develops this point further in his *Systematic Theology*:

The aspect of fatherly care in particular is taken over in what the Old Testament has to say about God's fatherly care for Israel. The sexual definition of the father's role plays no part. . . . To bring sexular differentiation into the understanding of God would mean polytheism; it was thus ruled out for the God of Israel. . . . The fact that God's care for Israel can also be expressed in terms of a mother's love shows clearly enough how little there is any sense of sexual distinction in the understanding of God as Father.

In an attempt to bring out the fact that God is not male, a number of recent writers have explored the idea of God as "mother" (which brings out the female aspects of God), or as "friend" (which brings out the more gender-neutral aspects of God). An excellent example of this is provided by Sallie McFague, in her *Models of God*. Recognizing that speaking of "God as father" does not mean that God is male, she writes:

God as mother does not mean that God is mother (or father). We imagine God as both mother and father, but we realize how inadequate these and any other metaphors are to express the creative love of God. . . . Nevertheless, we speak of this love in language that is familiar and dear to us, the language of mothers and fathers who give us life, from whose bodies we come, and upon whose care we depend.

Of course, as some feminist writers point out, many male theologians do indeed think of God as being male. But this represents a criticism of their interpretation of scripture, not of scripture itself. As the noted biblical scholar George Caird has pointed out:

it is precisely when theologians have claimed biblical authority for their own beliefs and practices that they have been peculiarly exposed to the universal temptation . . . of jumping to the conclusion that the biblical writer is referring to what they would be referring to, were they speaking the words themselves.

It is only if God is understood to be a projection, a result, of human culture, that the objections raised by feminist writers have decisive force. Now it is true that many radical feminist writers subscribe to this theory of the origins of religion (associated with writers as diverse as Feuerbach, Marx, and Freud: see pp. 194–8; 201–5); but this remains a hypothesis, not a fact. Traditional Christian theology speaks and knows of a God who reveals himself through human culture, but is not bound by its categories. God is supra-cultural, just as he is supra-sexual. There is all the difference in the world between saying that God is the product of a culture, and that God reveals himself in and through a culture.

Interestingly, the new interest in the question of the "maleness" of God has led to a careful reading of the spiritual literature of earlier periods in Christian history, and a rediscovery of the extent to which female imagery has been used to describe God in the past. A good example is provided in the writings of the fourteenth-century mystic Julian of Norwich, which make reference to God in terms of both male and female models and analogies:

I saw that God rejoices to be our Father, and also that he rejoices to be our Mother; and yet again, that he rejoices to be our true Husband, with our soul as his beloved bride. And Christ rejoices to be both our Brother and our Saviour. . . . [God's] love never allows us to lag behind. All this is due to God's innate goodness, and comes to us by the operation of his grace. God is kind because it is his nature. Goodness-by-nature implies God. He is the foundation, substance and the thing itself, what it is by nature. He is the true Father and Mother of what things are by nature.

Models, Analogies and Metaphor: Science and Religion Compared

In his study of the interaction of science and religion, Ian G. Barbour identified three similarities and a corresponding number of differences between religious models and theoretical models in science. The similarities which he identifies are the following.

1 In both science and religion, models are analogical in their origins, can be extended to cope with new situations, and are comprehensible as individual units.
2 Models, whether scientific or religious, are not to be taken either as

literal depictions of reality, nor simply as "useful fictions." "They are symbolic representations, for particular purposes, of aspects of reality which are not directly accessible to us."

3 Models function as organizing images, allowing us to structure and interpret patterns of events in our personal lives and in the world. In the sciences, the models relate to observational data; in the religions, to the experience of individuals and communities.

Significantly, Barbour also identified three areas of difference between the use of models in scientific and religious contexts. At this point, a degree of generalization about the nature of religion may perhaps lead to some incautious conclusions, although there is no doubt that, at least in some cases, the points which Barbour makes are valid.

1 Religious models serve non-cognitive functions which have no parallel in science.
2 Religious models evoke more total personal involvement than their scientific counterparts.
3 Religious models appear to be more influential than the formal beliefs and doctrines which are derived from them, whereas scientific models are subservient to theories.

A further point of importance in this comparison concerns the way in which analogies or models are chosen. In the sciences, analogies or models are chosen and validated partly on the basis of whether they offer a good empirical fit. These two themes – selection and validation – are of considerable importance, not least in that they highlight a significant difference between the natural sciences and religion. Analogies are generated within the scientific community; if they prove to be unsatisfactory, they are discarded, and replaced by new ones.

For example, consider the Bohr model (1913) of the hydrogen atom, which postulates that a single electron orbits a central nucleus (a feature derived from the Rutherford model of 1910), with an angular momentum which is confined to certain limited values. On the basis of this model, Bohr was able to explain the spectral formula proposed by Johann Balmer and postulate certain "quantum numbers" corresponding to the state and energy of the system. Yet the model had serious weaknesses (for example, the assumption that the electron orbited the nucleus in a circle) which had to be modified as experimental data built up.

The point here is that a model was *devised*, partly as an analogue of a simple harmonic oscillator and partly as an analogue of the solar system, which was found to have explanatory potential. Bohr's genius lay in devising the model. It was not self-evident, but rested on Bohr's belief that the application of quantum concepts to statistical mechanics by Einstein and Planck could be paralleled in the field of dynamics. Subsequent to its being formulated, the model required validation, both in terms of its ability to explain what was already known, and to predict novel phenomena.

It will also be clear that scientific models may be dispensed with when a superior model has been devised. The Rutherford model of the hydrogen atom, although regularly used at the popular level, has been discarded within professional circles on account of its obvious deficiencies. There is no commitment within the scientific community to any one model; in principle, the advancement of understanding may – but does not necessarily – lead to the discarding of earlier models.

These key themes of *formulation* and *validation* have no direct parallel in classical Christian thought. For a religion such as Christianity, it has been traditionally understood that the analogies or models in question are "given," not chosen; the two tasks which confront the theologian are those of establishing the limits of the analogy, and correlating it with other such given analogies. Let me make it clear immediately that not all theologians would support this traditional view; some would argue that we are at liberty to develop new models which avoid certain features of traditional models which are deemed to be unsatisfactory. Nevertheless, the traditional view remains influential, as can be seen from works such as Thomas F. Torrance's exploration of "theological science."

There would be no question of abandoning a traditional Christian model of God within orthodox Christian circles – for example, the model of God as "shepherd." Such models are far too deeply embedded in the biblical material, and both theological reflection and liturgical practice, to be treated in this manner. They have assumed the status of "root metaphors," which are regarded as permanent and essential components of the truth of the Christian tradition. These models may prove to require reinterpretation, or the exploration of aspects which had, up to this point, been ignored – but the model itself remains fundamental for theological reflection.

Our attention now turns to the complex issue of "complementarity" in science and religion. This concerns the way in which certain complex systems require two apparently contradictory models or analogies to represent their behavior.

The Concept of Complementarity

In the previous sections, we have seen how models or analogies served an important role in both science and religion. The present section considers a particular situation which arises through the use of models. What happens if the behavior of a system is such that it appears to need more than one model to represent it? In religion, this situation is well known. The Old and New Testaments, for example, use a wide variety of models or analogies to refer to God, such as "father," "king," "shepherd," and "rock". Each of these is regarded as illustrating one aspect of the divine nature. Taken together, they provide a cumulative and more comprehensive depiction of the divine nature and character than any one such analogy might allow on its own.

But what happens if two apparently contradictory analogies seem to be required, on the basis of the evidence available? For example, let us define two models, A and A', which are linked by the logical condition that the two are mutually exclusive. This immediately raises the question of the ontological status of the thing which is being modelled. Can we say that it "is" A, when the associated suggestion that it is also A' would lead to a blatant logical contradiction?

In the present section, we shall explore the issue of complementarity in science and religion, focusing on the work of Niels Bohr (1885–1962) in quantum theory, and the identity of Jesus Christ in theology. We begin by exploring the way in which the issue of complementarity arose in quantum theory.

Complementarity in quantum theory

The origins of Bohr's theory of complementarity is to be found in the origins of quantum theory. To understand rhe point at issue, we need to consider the following question: is light composed of waves or particles? From the standpoint of classical physics, these are two completely different and mutually incompatible entities. Waves cannot be particles, nor can particles be waves. By the beginning of the final decade of the nineteenth century, it was widely agreed that light consisted of waves.

As we have already seen, one of the questions which this raised was whether light waves required a medium for their propagation. The nearest analogy seemed to be sound, which consisted of waves which required a medium if they were to be propagated. The analogy seemed to suggest that light also seemed to require a medium. This led many to postulate the existence of "luminiferous ether" – a light-bearing medium. The quest for this ether became of major importance during the final decade of the century. Particles, of course, did not require a medium in order to travel.

Yet evidence was beginning to accumulate which called the wave model of light into question. One of the most important pieces of evidence relates to black-body radiation – that is, the way in which a perfect body radiates energy. Classical physics found it impossible to explain why something known as the "ultraviolet catastrophe" did not occur – that is, why a black body did not emit radiation at an infinite density at very high frequencies. This phenomenon was explained by Max Planck in a publication of 1900 on the basis of hypothesis of the "quantization" of energy. This hypothesis stated that the energy of an oscillator is not infinitely continuous, but is made up of "packets" of fixed size. Planck introduced a fundamental constant h (now universally known as "Planck's constant") to refer to this basic unit of energy. For an oscillator of frequency v, the energy of the oscillator can be defined as hv.

An analogy may be helpful to explain this very difficult idea. The basic point is that energy turns out not to be continuous but is actually discrete. It is like looking at a great sand-dune in the African desert. From a distance, it seems smooth; on closer examination, it is made up of millions of small grains of sand. Energy may seem to be continuous; on closer examination, it is made up of tiny grains. At very high energy levels, these packets of energy are so small that they have little or no discernible impact on anything. But at very low energy levels, the effect was pronounced.

A further development of importance was Albert Einstein's explanation of the photo-electric effect in 1905. Einstein argued that the photoelectric effect could be conceived as a collision between an incoming particle-like bundle of energy and an electron close to the surface of the metal. The electron could only be ejected from the metal if the incoming packets of light (or particle-like bundles of energy) possessed sufficient energy to eject this electon. Einstein's theory (which need not be explored in greater detail for our purposes) allowed the following facts to be explained.

1   The critical factor which determines whether an electron is ejected is not the intensity of the light, but its frequency. Note that Planck had

argued that the energy of an oscillator was directly proportional to its frequency.

2   The observed features of the photoelectric effect can be accounted for by assuming that the collision between the incoming photon and the metallic electron obeys the principle of the conservation of energy. If the energy of the incoming photon is less than a certain quantity (the 'work function' of the metal in question) no electrons will be emitted, no matter how intense the bombardment with photons. Above this threshold, the kinetic energy of the emitted photons is directly proportional to the frequency of the radiation.

The incoming light can be treated as if it consists of particles (now referred to as "photons") with a definite energy or momentum.

Einstein's brilliant theoretical account for the photoelectric effect suggested that electromagnetic radiation had to be considered as behaving as particles under certain conditions. It met with intense opposition, not least because it appeared to involve the abandonment of the prevailing classical understanding of the total exclusivity of waves and particles: something could be one, or the other – but not both. Even those who subsequently verified Einstein's analysis of the photoelectric effect were intensely suspicious of his postulation of "photons." Einstein himself was careful to refer to the light-quantum hypothesis as a "heuristic point of view" – that is, as something which was helpful as a model to understanding, but without any necessary existence on its part.

By the 1920s, it was clear that the behavior of light was such that it required to be explained on the basis of a wave-model in some respects, and a particle-model in others. The work of Louis de Broglie suggested that even matter had to be regarded as behaving as a wave in some respect. These theories led Niels Bohr to develop his concept of "complementarity." For Bohr, the classical models of "waves" and "particles" were both required to explain the behavior of light and matter. This does not mean that electrons "are" particles or that they "are" waves; it means that, whatever they ultimately are, their behavior may be described on the basis of wave or particle models, and that a complete description of that behavior rests upon the bringing together of what are, in effect, mutually exclusive ways of representing them.

This is not an intellectually shallow and lazy expedient of affirming two mutually exclusive options, rather than attempting to determine which is the superior. As has been stressed, it was – for Bohr – the inevitable outcome of a series of critical theories and experiments which demonstrated the impossibility of representing the situation in any other manner. In other words, Bohr held that the experimental data at his disposal forced him to the conclusion that a complex situation (the behavior of light and matter) had to be represented by using two apparently contradictory and incompatible models.

It is this principle of holding together two apparently irreconcilable models of a complex phenomenon in order to account for the behavior of that phenomenon which is known as the "principle of complementarity." So what is the religious relevance of this point? We shall explore this issue by focusing on one specific area of Christian theology which is widely regarded as illustrating the religious significance of complementarity – Christology. Before this, however, it is appropriate to note some important general convergences in this field, focusing on the convergences between Niels Bohr on the scientific side, and Karl Barth and Thomas F. Torrance on the theological side.

Complementarity in theology

Some scholars have noted a clear parallel between Bohr's "principle of complementarity" and Karl Barth's "dialectical method." For example, James Loder and Jim Neidhardt suggested that a number of significant points of convergence can be noted between the two writers. In the case of Bohr, the "phenomenon" to be explained is the behaviour of quantum events; for Barth, it is the relation between time and eternity on the one hand, and humanity and divinity in the person of Jesus Christ on the other:

1 For both Bohr and Barth, classical forms of reason are pushed to their limits to explain the phenomena in question.
2 Both writers vigorously maintain the principle that the phenomenon should be allowed to disclose how it can be known, and avoid reducing the phenomenon to known forms.
3 In both cases, the phenomenon discloses itself as an irreducible bipolar relationship which imposes itself upon the knower, and thus requires representation in terms of either the complementarity or dialectic of classical forms. The relationality between these polarities is asymmetrical.
4 Both situations require that the influence of the observer be recognized, and incorporated into what is known.

5   The observation of the phenomena requires that the knower should be able to communicate those observations in language.

The general convergences between Barth and Bohr noted above can also be discerned within the works of Thomas F. Torrance, widely respected both as an interpreter of Barth and an advocate of dialogue between theology and the natural sciences. Torrance's insistence on God's self-revelation determining our understanding shows clear parallels with the approach adopted by Barth:

Christian theology arises out of the actual knowledge of God given in and with concrete happenings in space and time. It is knowledge of the God who actively meets us and gives Himself to be known in Jesus Christ – in Israel, in history, on earth. It is essentially positive knowledge, with articulated content, mediated in concrete experience. It is concerned with fact, the fact of God's self-revelation; it is concerned with God Himself who just because He really is God always comes first. We do not therefore begin with ourselves or our questions, nor indeed can we choose where to begin; we can only begin with the facts prescribed for us by the actuality of the subject positively known.

Torrance thus strongly affirms the need to interpret the "phenomenon" of revelation on its own terms.

As we noted earlier, it is widely agreed that the most obvious area of theology which is amenable to this kind of complementarist approach is Christology. Torrance illustrates this point well, in that he forges a link between the knowledge of God and Christology, which leads to an affirmation of the bipolarity of revelation. As several recent studies of Torrance's doctrine of the knowledge of God have stressed the incarnation plays a central role in his understanding of how God can be known and the substance of that knowledge. It is therefore perhaps not a matter for surprise that Torrance should use this term in Christological contexts: "Here we are faced with another fundamental characteristic of the truth of God as it is in Jesus: it is both divine and human. Knowledge of it is, accordingly, bipolar."

Some recent studies have confirmed the positive results which can be achieved from such an exploration. Christian orthodoxy has always held that Jesus Christ must be thought of as being truly divine and truly human. This simultaneous assertion of "two natures in one subject" clearly parallels Bohr's views on the complementarity of wave and particle models of light and matter. Yet it is not simply the classical Christological definitions as such which illustrates the importance of complementarity in theology, but the manner in which these emerged during the patristic period. In what follows, I propose to explore the development of Christology during the patristic period, and note the manner in which Bohr-type concerns can be seen as playing a significant role in this highly significant matter.

In what follows, we shall consider two of the parallels noted by Loder and Neidhardt between Bohr and Barth, and explore the manner in which the evolution of classic Christology conforms to a similar pattern.

First, Loder and Neidhardt note that that the phenomenon to be explained should be allowed to disclose how it can be known, and avoid reducing the phenomenon to known forms. As noted earlier, Bohr's reflections on complementarity were forced upon him by the experimental evidence which accumulated during the period 1905–25. Much simpler ways of visualizing the situation could have been put forward (and, as the development of quantum theory over this period indicates, were indeed adduced). Yet the simplicity of these models foundered against the experimental evidence, which ineluctably led Bohr to the conclusion that two apparently mutually exclusive ways of conceiving quantum phenomena were required.

The development of Christology during the period 100–451 shows this concern to have been of overwhelming importance. This same theme of allowing the phenomenon (if we may be allowed to use this term to refer to the complex amalgam of "historical testimony and religious experience") to dictate its own interpretation can be discerned throughout the development of patristic Christology. Simplistic reductionist modes of representing the identity and significance of Jesus of Nazareth foundered on the phenomena which they were required to represent. In particular, the model of Jesus of Nazareth as a purely human figure (generally held to be found in the Ebionite heresy) or as a purely divine figure (generally held to be found in the Docetic heresy) were regarded as quite inadequate. Both the representation of Jesus in the New Testament and the manner in which the Christian church incorporated Jesus into its life of prayer and worship required a more complex understanding of his identity and significance than either of these simpler models were able to offer.

The suggestion that some third model could be invoked to explain the phenomenon of Jesus of Nazareth was rejected as unsatisfactory. The debate over the teachings of Apollinarius of Laodicea led to agreement that there was no "intermediate state," no "*tertium quid*," interposing between the two natures. The patristic period witnessed a decisive rejection of any attempt to explain Jesus in terms which involved the construction of a mediating or hybrid concept between divinity and humanity. There is a direct Christological parallel with Bohr's insistence on the completeness of the principle of complementarity. As with Bohr's complementary accounts of waves and particles, the Chalcedonian approach to Christology affirmed that the approach offered by the "two natures" doctrine was complete (in that only two such models or natures are needed) and *complementary* (in that only one of these mutually exclusive models or natures can apply at any one time).

Patristic writers (such as Pope Leo I) often offered developed understandings of which aspects of the ministry of Jesus of Nazareth were to be attributed to his human, and which to his divine, nature. Such approaches were open to misunderstanding, in that they could be interpreted to mean that Jesus was divine only when acting in certain manners, and human only when acting in others. The assertion of more ontological manners of affirming both the humanity and divinity of Jesus can be understood as a means of avoiding this potentially vulnerably way of conceiving the identity of Jesus. Our point, however, concerns the development of patristic theology, not the form of its final statements.

Second, Loder and Neidhardt noted that both Bohr and Barth affirmed that the phenomenon (whether revelatory or quantum) discloses itself as an irreducible bipolar relationship which imposes itself upon the knower, and thus requires representation in terms of either the complementarity or dialectic of classical forms. The Christological issue of critical importance was that the biblical portrayal of Jesus of Nazareth at times suggested that he behaved or functioned as God, at others as human. This can be seen clearly stated in the famous letter written by Pope Leo I to Flavian, patriarch of Constantinople on June 13, 449, which is usually referred to as the "Tome of Leo." In this letter, Leo set out the prevailing Christological consensus within the Latin-speaking western church. The letter was later elevated to a position of authority by the Council of Chalcedon (451), which recognized it as a classic statement of Christological orthodoxy.

Patristic writers such as Athanasius argued that the total thrust of the biblical witness to and Christian experience of Jesus of Nazareth required him to be conceptualized as both divine and human. For example, Athanasius makes the point that it is only God who can save. God, and God alone, can break the power of sin, and bring us to eternal life. An essential feature of being a creature is that one requires to be redeemed. No creature can save another creature. Only the creator can redeem the creation. Having emphasized that it is God alone who can save, Athanasius then makes the logical move which the Arians found difficult to counter. The New Testament and the Christian liturgical tradition alike regard Jesus Christ as Saviour. Yet, as Athanasius emphasized, only God can save. So how are we to make sense of this?

The only possible solution, Athanasius argues, is to accept that Jesus is God incarnate. The logic of his argument at times goes something like this:

1 No creature can redeem another creature.
2 According to Arius, Jesus Christ is a creature.
3 Therefore, according to Arius, Jesus Christ cannot redeem humanity.

At times, a slightly different style of argument can be discerned, resting upon the statements of Scripture and the Christian liturgical tradition.

1 Only God can save.
2 Jesus Christ saves.
3 Therefore Jesus Christ is God.

Salvation, for Athanasius, involves divine intervention. Athanasius thus draws out the meaning of John 1: 14 by arguing that the "word became flesh": in other words, God entered into our human situation, in order to change it.

A second point that Athanasius makes is that Christians worship and pray to Jesus Christ. This represents an excellent case study of the importance of Christian practices of worship and prayer for Christian theology. By the fourth century, prayer to and adoration of Christ were standard features of the way in which public worship took place. Athanasius argues that if Jesus Christ is a creature, then Christians are guilty of worshipping a creature instead of God – in other words, they had lapsed into idolatry. Christians, Athanasius stresses, are totally forbidden to worship anyone or anything except God himself. Athanasius thus argued that Arius seemed to be guilty of making nonsense of the way in which Christians prayed and worshipped. Athanasius, argued that Christians were right to worship and adore Jesus Christ, because by doing so, they were recognizing him for what he was – God incarnate.

It was this awareness that Jesus of Nazareth required to be understood in both divine and human terms which eventually led to what is known as the "Chalcedonian definition of faith" – the famous assertion that Jesus is truly divine and truly human. Maurice Wiles summarizes the reasons for this development as follows:

On the one hand was the conviction that a saviour must be fully divine; on the other was the conviction that what is not assumed is not healed. Or, to put the matter in other words, the source of salvation must be God; the locus of salvation must be humanity. It is quite clear that these two principles often pulled in opposite directions. The Council of Chalcedon was the church's attempt to resolve, or perhaps rather to agree to live with, that tension. Indeed, to accept both principles as strongly as did the early church is already to accept the Chalcedonian faith.

Pressure on space limits our confirmation of the convergence between the other factors noted by Loder and Neidhardt and those which can be discerned as shaping doctrinal development in the early church. It is, however, important to notice that many of the arguments set out during the early patristic period for the "dual nature" of Christ are primarily functional. In other words, the focus of the arguments can be seen to rest on what it is that Jesus of Nazareth achieved. There is no doubt that patristic writers drew ontological conclusions from their functional analysis. In other words, if Jesus truly behaved as God, then the case could be made that he was God. A number of modern writers have argued that it is not necessary to draw such ontological conclusions (which may reflect a particular interest in ontology in the patristic period); it is quite possible to rest content with the assertion that Jesus behaves in divine and human manners.

It is also instructive to ask why complementary approaches were adopted in the first place in relation to both quantum phenomena and Christology. The pressure for clarification of the nature of quantum phenomena came from experimental observations which precipitated a theoretical crisis, demonstrating that existing conceptualities simply could not account for the phenomena. The pressure for clarification of the nature of Jesus of Nazareth arose through a growing awareness, fueled by intense debate and controversy, that Jesus simply could not be described in terms of any one existing idea. In each case, the temptation to reduce the phenomena to existing notions was resisted, on account of the serious distortions introduced. To explain the phenomenon, either new use had to be made of existing categories, or radically new categories had to be introduced. Bohr's approach was to retain existing categories ("classic models"), while recognizing that such ordinary language can have specialized extensions which allow it to illuminate other domains.

The present chapter has explored some aspects of the way in which the natural sciences and religion use analogies and models to depict reality. It will be clear that we have thus far been considering general aspects of the natural sciences in their relation to religion. It is now appropriate to consider some of the specific issues raised by individual natural sciences. The chapter which follows introduces some of the religious issues raised by developments in the fields of physics, biology, and psychology.

For further reading

Achinstein, P. "Light Hypotheses." *Studies in History and Philosophy of Science* 18 (1987): 293–337.

Atkins, P. W. *Physical Chemistry*. 5th edn. Oxford: Oxford University Press, 1994.

——, and R. S. Friedman. *Molecular Quantum Mechanics*. 3rd edn. Oxford: Oxford University Press, 1997.

Barbour, I. G. *Myths, Models and Paradigms: A Comparative Study in Science and Religion*. New York: Harper & Row, 1974.

Ben-Menahem, Y. "Models of Science: Fictions or Idealizations?" *Science in Context* 2 (1988): 163–75.

Brody, N., and P. Oppenheim. "The Application of Bohr's Principle of Complementarity to the Mind-Body Problem." *Journal of Philosophy* 66 (1969): 97–113.

Bunge, M. "Analogy in Quantum Theory: From Insight to Nonsense." *British Journal for the Philosophy of Science* 18 (1967): 265–286.

Burstein, M. H. "Combining Analogies in Mental Models." *Analogical Reasoning*. Ed. D. H. Helman. Dordrecht, Holland: Kluwer Academic Publishers, 1988, pp. 179–203.

Cantor, G. "The Reception of the Wave Theory of Light in Britain: A Case Study Illustrating the Role of Methodology in Scientific Debate." *Historical Studies in the Physical Sciences* 6 (1975): 109–32.

Duce, P. P. "Complementarity in Perspective." *Science and Christian Belief* 8 (1996): 145–55.

Folse, H. *The Philosophy of Niels Bohr: The Framework of Complementarity*. Amsterdam: North Holland, 1985.

Gehart, M., and A. M. Russell. *Metaphoric Process: the Creation of Scientific and Religious Understanding*. Fort Worth: Christian University Press, 1984.

Hesse, M. B. "Models and Analogy in Science." *Encyclopaedia of Philosophy*. Ed. Paul Edwards. Vol. 5. New York & London: Macmillan, 1967, pp. 354–9.

Kaiser, C. B. "Christology and Complementarity." *Religious Studies* 12 (1976): 37–48.

——. "Quantum Complementarity and Christological Dialectic." *Religion and Science: History, Method, Dialogue*. Ed. W. Mark Richardson and Wesley J. Wildman. New York: Routledge, 1996, pp. 291–8.

Kruger, C. B. "The Doctrine of the Knowledge of God in the Theology of Thomas F. Torrance." *Scottish Journal of Theology* 43 (1990): 366–89.

Loder, J. E., and W. J. Neidhardt. *The Knight's Move: The Relational Logic of the Spirit in Theology and Science*. Colorado Springs: Helmers & Howard, 1992.

——, and ——. "Barth, Bohr and Dialectic." *Religion and Science: History, Method, Dialogue*. Ed. W. Mark Richardson and Wesley J. Wildman. New York: Routledge, 1996, pp. 271–89.

MacKay, D. M. "'Complementarity' in Scientific and Theological Thinking." *Zygon* 9 (1974): 225–44.

Mascall, E. L. *Existence and Analogy*. London: Darton, Longman & Todd, 1966.

May, R. M. "Simple Mathematical Models with Very Complicated Dynamics." *Nature* 261 (1976): 459–67.

McFague, S. *Metaphorical Theology: Models of God in Religious Language*. London: SCM, 1983.

McGuire, J. E. "Atoms and the 'Analogy of Nature': Newton's Third Rule of Philosophizing." *Studies in History and Philosophy of Science* 1 (1970): 3–58.

Oser, F. K., and K. H. Reich. "The Challenge of Competing Explanations: The Development of Thinking in Terms of Complementarity of Theories." *Human Development* 30 (1987): 178–86.

Plotnitsky, A. *Complementarity: Anti-Epistemology after Bohr and Derrida*. Durham, NC: Duke University Press, 1994.

Porter, A. P. "Science, Religious Language and Analogy." *Faith and Philosophy* 13 (1996): 113–20.

Ramsey, I. T. *Models and Mystery*. London: Oxford University Press, 1964.

Scharlemann, R. P. "Theological Models and Their Construction." *Journal of Religion* 53 (1973): 65–82.

Seng, K. P. "The Epistemological Significance of Homoousion in the Theology of Thomas F. Torrance." *Scottish Journal of Theology* 45 (1992): 341–66.

Soskice, J. M. *Metaphor and Religious Language*. Oxford: Clarendon Press, 1985.

Torrance, T. F. *Theological Science*. Oxford: Oxford University Press, 1969.

——. *Reality and Scientific Theology: Theology and Science at the Frontiers of Knowledge*. Edinburgh: Scottish Academic Press, 1985.

Vaught, C. G. "Metaphor, Analogy and the Nature of Truth." *New Essays in Metaphysics*. Ed. Robert C. Neville. Albany, NY: State University of New York Press, 1987, pp. 217–36.

8

Issues in Science and Religion

The theme of "science and religion" is made more complicated by the fact that both "science" and "religion" refer to a variety of possibilities. As we have already seen, "religion" can refer to a variety of completely different belief-systems. In practice, the religion which is most widely studied in this respect is Christianity, which has had the closest relationship with and greatest impact upon the development of the natural sciences in the western world. Judaism and Islam have also been involved in this development, although to a lesser extent. One of the most interesting questions to be debated within the history of science is whether the fact that the three religions to have had the most significant impact on the development of the natural sciences are monotheistic (that is, believing in one God).

The importance of being aware of differences between the religions when discussing the theme of "science and religion" can be seen by considering Sigmund Freud's account of the origins of religion in primitive peoples. Freud's argument (which we shall explore at pp. 210–5) focuses on God as an idealized father figure. It is true that Christianity and Judaism portray God in terms of a "heavenly father". For example, the Lord's Prayer, widely used by Christians in public worship and private prayer, begins with the words: "Our Father in heaven." Yet eastern religions, particularly certain forms of Buddhism, do not think of God in this manner. Freud's theory thus rests on an inaccurate and simplistic generalization concerning what "religion" means.

Yet it is also important to appreciate that there are significant differences between the individual natural sciences, which are often obscured by talking in simple terms about "science" in general. Each of the natural sciences has a quite distinct way of understanding its goals, evaluating evidence and formulating research strategy. Thus physics, biology, and psychology are all regarded as natural sciences, despite their clear differences. Even within a single scientific discipline, there are also significant differences on a number of matters of considerable importance. For example, most natural scientists are committed to what is recognizably a form of "realism" – that is, that there is a world which exists independent of our thought. Yet it is easily shown that there are so many different types of realism in use that different scientists understand the term to mean very different things.

Given this diversity within the natural sciences, it seemed right to spend some time looking at three major scientific disciplines, and explore the way in which they relate to our theme. We have chosen three quite distinct areas of scientific research for this purpose, each of which has religious significance: physics and cosmology, in which we shall focus on some aspects of modern cosmological thinking; biology, in which we shall consider the impact of various forms of Darwinianism on religious thought; and psychology, in which we shall look at various approaches to understanding the origins and significance of religion.

Physics and Cosmology

It is generally thought that modern physics and cosmology offer the most important and fruitful possibilities for dialogue between the sciences and religion. The theme of "the ordering of the universe" has, as we have already seen (pp. 122–4), major significance when viewed in the light of a doctrine of creation, which understands the world to possess an ordering and rationality having its origins in the mind of God. Major contributions to an understanding of the way in which modern theoretical physics relates in a positive manner to Christianity have been set out by John Polkinghorne and Charles A. Coulson, and we shall consider them in a later chapter (see pp. 210–12; 218–21). However, two other contributions of importance, coming from very different perspectives, may be noted at this point.

1   Paul Davies, Professor of Mathematical Physics at the University of Adelaide has explored the complexity of the issues raised by modern cosmology. In his *God and the New Physics* (1984) and *The Mind of God* (1992), Davies explicitly identifies the religious dimen-

sions of this research. While Davies does not approach his subject from what might be called a "conventional theistic perspective," it is clear that he is sympathetic to a religious understanding of the universe.

2 Fritjof Capra researched high-energy physics, before becoming interested in the parallels between modern physics and eastern mysticism. His account of these similarities, published as *The Tao of Physics* (1976) became a best-seller. To its critics, the parallels which are identified are perhaps more superficial than Capra allows, resting on verbal rather than conceptual similarities.

It is generally agreed that two of the most important issues to emerge from modern cosmological research relate to "the big bang" and what is now widely known as "the anthropic principle." We shall consider these in what follows.

The "Big Bang"

The question of the origin of the universe is without doubt one of the most fascinating areas of modern scientific analysis and debate. That there are religious dimensions to this debate will be clear. Sir Bernard Lovell, the distinguished British pioneer of radio astronomy, is one of many to note that discussion of the origins of the universe inevitably raises fundamentally religious questions. More recently, Paul Davies, professor of physics at the University of Adelaide, South Australia, has drawn attention to the implications of the "new physics" for thinking about God, especially in his widely-read book *God and the New Physics*.

The origins of the "big bang" theory may be argued to lie in the general theory of relativity proposed by Albert Einstein. Einstein's theory was proposed at a time when the scientific consensus favored the notion of a static universe. The equations which Einstein derived to describe the effects of relativity were interpreted by him in terms of a gravitional and levitational equilibrium. However, the Russian metereologist Alexander Friedman noticed that the solutions to the equations which he himself derived pointed to a rather different model. If the universe was perfectly homogeneous and expanding, then the universe must have expanded from a singular initial state at some point in the past characterized by zero radius, and infinite density, temperature and curvature. Other solutions to the equations suggested a cycle of expansion and contraction. The analysis was disregarded, probably because it did not conform to the consensus viewpoint within the scientific community. All that began to change with the astronomical observations of Edwin Hubble (1889–1953), which led him to interpret the red shifts of galactic spectra in terms of an expanding universe.

A further major development took place (largely by accident, it has to be said) in 1964. Arno Penzias and Robert Wilson were working on an experimental microwave antenna at the Bell Laboratories in New Jersey. They were experiencing some difficulties: irrespective of the direction in which they pointed the antenna, they found that they picked up a background hissing noise which could not be eliminated. Their initial explanation of this phenomenon was that the pigeons roosting on the antenna were interfering with it. Yet even after the enforced removal of the offending birds, the hiss remained. It was only a matter of time before the full significance of this irritating background was appreciated. It could be understood as the "afterglow" of a primal explosion – a "big bang" – which had been proposed in 1948 by George Gamow, Ralph Alpher and Robert Herman. This thermal radiation corresponded to photons molving about randomly in space, without discernible source, at a temperature of 2.7 K. Taken alongside other pieces of evidence, this background radiation served as significant evidence that the universe had a beginning (and caused severe difficulties for the rival "steady state" theory advocated by Thomas Gold and Hermann Bondi, with theoretical support from Fred Hoyle).

It is now widely agreed that the universe had a beginning. This immediately points to at least some level of affinity with the Christian idea that the universe was created. It is thus of considerable importance to note the deeply religious questions which are raised by modern cosmology. We may explore these points by considering Stephen Hawking's *Brief History of Time*, an important book which is clearly alert to the philosophical and theological issues raised by modern cosmology. It needs to be noted, however, that the general perception of Hawking's own views has been somewhat skewed by an introduction by Carl Sagan, which suggests that Hawking's work leaves no place for a God. In view of the fact that many readers of the work appear to have got no further than this preface, it is important to note its genera tenor:

This is also a book about God ... or perhaps about the absence of God. The word God fills these pages. Hawking embarks on a quest to answer Einstein's famous question about whether God had any choice in creating the universe. Hawking is attempting, as he explicitly states, to understand the mind of God. And this makes all the more unexpected the conclusion of the effort, at least so far: a universe with no edge in space, no beginning or end in time, and nothing for a Creator to do.

It is fair to argue that this is not an accurate summary of Hawking's conclusions, nor of the general tone of the work. When a reader of an early draft of *Brief History* suggested that it left no place for God, Hawking replied that he "had left the question of the existence of a Supreme Being completely open."

As we have noted, the belief that the universe had a "beginning" does not necessarily imply that it was "created." However, the implication has certainly been stressed by a number of writers, such as Stanley L. Jaki. One of the factors which has been of particular importance in focusing this debate has been the "anthropic principle," to which we now turn.

The anthropic principle

The term "anthropic principle" is used in a variety of ways by different writers; nevertheless, the term is generally used to refer to the remarkable degree of "fine-tuning" observed within the natural order. The Australian physicist Paul Davies argues that the remarkable convergence of certain fundamental constants is laden with religious significance. "The seemingly miraculous concurrence of numerical values that nature has assigned to her fundamental constants must remain the most compelling evidence for an element of cosmic design." The most accessible introduction to the principle is widely agreed to be the 1986 study of John D. Barrow and Frank J. Tipler, entitled *The Anthropic Cosmological Principle*. The basic observation which underlies the principle may be stated as follows:

One of the most important results of twentieth-century physics has been the gradual realization that there exist invariant properties of the natural world and its elementary components which render the gross size and structure of virtually all its constituents quite inevitable. The size of stars and planets, and even people, are neither random nor the result of any Darwinian selection process from a myriad of possibilities. These, and other gross features of the Universe, are the consequences of necessity; they are manifestations of the possible equilibrium states between competing forces of attraction and compulsion. The intrinsic strengths of these controlling forces of Nature are determined by a mysterious collection of pure numbers that we call the *constants of Nature*.

The importance of this point can be seen from an important review article published in 1979 in the journal *Nature* by B. J. Carr and M. J. Rees. Carr and Rees pointed out how most natural scales – in particular, the mass and length scales – are determined by a few physical constants. They concluded that "the possibility of life as we know it evolving in the Universe depends on the values of a few physical constants – and is in some respects remarkably sensitive to their numerical values." The constants which assumed a particularly significant role were the electromagnetic fine structure constant, the gravitational fine structure constant, and the electron-to-proton mass ratio.

Examples of the "fine tuning" of fundamental cosmological constants include the following:

1 If the strong coupling constant was slightly smaller, hydrogen would be the only element in the universe. Since the evolution of life as we know it is fundamentally dependent on the chemical properties of carbon, that life could not have come into being without some hydrogen being converted to carbon by fusion. On the other hand, if the strong coupling constant were slightly larger (even by as much as 2 percent), the hydrogen would have been converted to helium, with the result that no long-lived stars would have been formed. In that such stars are regarded as essential to the emergence of life, such a conversion would have led to life as we know it failing to emerge.

2 If the weak fine constant was slightly smaller, no hydrogen would have formed during the early history of the universe. Consequently, no stars would have been formed. On the other hand, if it was slightly larger, supernovae would have been unable to eject the heavier elements necessary for life. In either case, life as we know it could not have emerged.

3 If the electromagmetic fine structure constant was slightly larger, the stars would not be hot enough to warm planets to a temperature sufficient to maintain life in the form in which we know it. If smaller, the stars would have burned out too quickly to allow life to evolve on these planets.

4 If the gravitational fine structure constant were slightly smaller, stars and planets would not have been able to form, on account of the

gravitational constraints necessary for coalescence of their constituent material. If stronger, the stars thus formed would have burned out too quickly to allow the evolution of life (as with the electromagnetic fine structure constant).

This evidence of "fine-tuning" has been the subject of considerable discussion among scientists, philosophers, and theologians. It will be clear that the considerations are actually quite anthropocentric, in that the observations derive their significance partly on account of their assumption that life is carbon-based.

So what is the religious significance of this? There is no doubt that these coincidences are immensely interesting and thought-provoking, leading at least some natural scientists to posit a possible religious explanation for these observations. "As we look out into the Universe and identify the many accidents of physics and astronomy that have worked together to our benefit, it almost seems as it the Universe must in some sense have known that we were coming" (Freeman Dyson, as cited in J. Barrow, and F. J. Tipler, *The Anthropic Cosmological Principle*. Oxford, Oxford University Press, 1986, p. 318). It must be stressed, however, that this does not command general assent within the scientific community, despite its obvious attractions to a significant subset of that community which endorses the notion of a creator God.

The anthropic principle, whether stated in a weak or strong form, is strongly consistent with a theistic perspective. A theist (for example, a Christian) with a firm commitment to a doctrine of creation will find the "fine-tuning" of the universe to be an anticipated and pleasant confirmation of his religious beliefs. This would not constitute a "proof" of the existence of God, but would be a further element in a cumulative series of considerations which is at the very least consistent with the existence of a creator God. This is the kind of argument set forth by F. R. Tennant in his important study *Philosophical Theology* (1930), in which the term "anthropic" is thought to have been used for the first time to designate this specific type of teleological argument:

The forcibleness of Nature's suggestion that she is the outcome of intelligent design lies not in particular cases of adaptedness in the world, nor even in the multiplicity of them . . . [but] consists rather in the conspiration of innumerable causes to produce, either by united and reciprocal action, and to maintain, a general order of Nature. Narrower kinds of teleological arguments, based on surveys of restricted spheres of fact, are much more precarious than that for which the name of "the wider teleology" may be appropriated in that the comprehensive design-argument is the outcome of synopsis or conspection of the knowable world.

This does not mean that the factors noted above constitute irrefutable evidence for the existence or character of a creator God; few religious thinkers would suggest that this is the case. What would be affirmed, however, is that they are consistent with a theistic worldview; that they can be accommodated with the greatest of ease within such a world-view; that they reinforce the plausibility of such a worldview for those who are already committed to them; and that they offer apologetic possibilities for those who do not yet hold a theistic position.

But what of those who do not hold a religious viewpoint? What status might the "anthropic principle" have in relation to the longstanding debate about the existence and nature of God, or the divine design of the universe? Peter Atkins, a physical chemist with stridently anti-religious views, notes that the "fine-tuning" of the world may appear to be miraculous; however, he argues that, on closer inspection, a purely naturalist explanation may be offered.

Perhaps the most significant discussion of this point may be found in the major work by Barrow and Tipler on this theme, which we shall explore in what follows. The basis argument deployed by Barrow and Tipler is that there is no need to seek any further explanation of the existence of the universe as it presently exists, in that if it was not as it presently is, we would not be able to observe it:

The enormous improbability of the evolution of intelligent life in general and *Homo sapiens* in particular at any randomly chosen point in space–time does *not* mean we should be amazed we in particular exist here. This would make as much sense as Elizabeth II being amazed she is Queen of England. Even though the possibility of a given Briton being monarch is about 10^{-8}, *someone* must be. Only for the person who is monarch is it possible is it possible to ask, "how improbable is it that I should be monarch?" Similarly, only if an intelligent species of a particular kind does evolve in a given space–time location is it possible for its members to ask how probable it was for intelligent life of some form to evolve there.

Barrow and Tipler here make the foundational assumption (which they do not seem to explicitly justify) that our existence as human observers is itself an adequate basis for explaining the fundamental features of the universe. The argument set out above takes the following form:

1   There are roughly 10^8 people in England.

2   One of these people is the monarch.
3   There is therefore a 10^{-8} probability of any one of these people being the monarch.
4   Therefore it should not be a cause for surprise to that one person to find that they are the monarch. Someone has to be.

The argument is not especially persuasive, in that it rests upon the conceded plausibility of an existing situation to render plausible a much more complex and contested situation. In effect, the argument presupposes an analogy between one person in Great Britain having to be the monarch, given the current constitutional situation of that country (a matter of contingency, not necessity) and the emergence of humanity in the universe. The analogy is vulnerable at critical points. To explore this matter in more detail, let us consider a central feature of the argument: the role of the observer.

In opening their extensive presentation of the anthropic principle, Barrow and Tipler stress the importance of the observer in the analysis of the universe:

The basic features of the Universe, including such properties as its shape, size, age and laws of change, must be *observed* to be of a type that allows the evolution of observers, for if intelligent life did not evolve in an otherwise possible universe, it is obvious that no one would be asking the question for the observed shape, size, age and so forth of the Universe. At first sight such an observation might appear true but trivial. However, it has far-reaching implications for physics. It is a restatement of the fact that any observed properties of the Universe that may initially appear astonishingly improbable, can only be seen in their true perspective after we have accounted for the fact that certain properties of the Universe are necessary prerequisites for the evolution and existence of any observers at all.

It will be clear that the basic line of argument here is that the fact that anyone is doing any observing at all reflects the fact that the universe possesses certain features which permits the evolution of life forms capable of observing at least some of those features.

This argument has been challenged by many religious writers, perhaps most notably by Richard Swinburne. Swinburne offers the following analogy which has an important point to make concerning the existence of an *observer*:

Suppose that a madman kidnaps a victim and shuts him in a room with a card-shuffling machine. This machine shuffles ten packs of cards simultaneously and then draws a card from each pack and exhibits simultaneously the ten cards. The kidnapper tells the victim that he will shortly set the machine to work and it will exhibit the first draw, but that unless the draw consists of an ace of hearts from each pack, the machine will simultaneously set off an explosion which will kill the victim, in consequence of which he will not see which cards the machine drew. The machine is then set to work, and to the amazement and relief of the victim the machine exhibits an ace of hearts drawn from each pack. The victim thinks that this extraordinary fact needs an explanation in terms of the machine having been rigged in some way. But the kidnapper, who now reappears, casts doubt on this suggestion. "It is hardly surprising," he says, "that the machine only draws aces of hearts. You could not possibly see anything else. For you would not be here to see anything at all, if any other card had been drawn." But of course the victim is right and the kidnapper is wrong. There is indeed something extraordinary in need of explanation in ten aces of hearts being drawn. The fact that this peculiar order is a necessary condition of the draw being perceived at all makes what is perceived no less extraordinary and in need of explanation.

Swinburne's point is that the existence of an observer has no bearing on the probability of the events being observed. If a series of highly improbable events give rise to an observer who can note this improbability, they are nonetheless improbable.

So what is the connection between the anthropic principle and natural theology? The theistic philosopher William Lane Craig argues that, once the basic philosophical fallacy noted by Swinburne is eliminated from Barrow and Tipler's work, the volume "becomes for the design argument in the twentieth century what Paley's *Natural Theology* was in the nineteenth" – that is, "a compendium of the data of contemporary science which point to a design in nature inexplicable in natural terms, and therefore pointing to the Divine Designer." Perhaps there is a degree of overstatement here; nevertheless, this is unquestionably how a theist would read the evidence assembled in this important volume. It does not prove anything, in the rigorous sense of that term. Nevertheless, it is clearly consistent with a theistic interpretation of the world.

Biology

From our discussion of the religious aspects of modern cosmology, it will be clear that the physical sciences offer significant and positive grounds for dialogue between science and religion. The situation is quite different in relation to the biological sciences, which we shall consider in the present section. One of the most fundamental questions concerns the origins of humanity, and the implications of, for example, a Darwinian answer to this question for a Christian understanding of human nature.

Charles Darwin (1809–1882)

By the eighteenth century, it had become clear that at least some degree of regularity or ordering could be observed within the world of plant and animal life. One of the most significant interpretations of the observation of ordering within the natural world is due to the eighteenth-century Swedish naturalist Carl von Linné (1707–78), more generally known by the Latinized form of his name, "Linnaeus."

Linnaeus argued that the diversity within the plant and animal kingdoms could be organized into a number of distinct groups or "species." Linnaeus" taxonomic system is grounded in the assumption that creation is fixed and rational. The basis of this assumption (which resonates with both an assumption of an orderly world, capable of rational investigation through acute observation and logical categorization, resonates with both supports the Christian doctrine of creation and the Enlightenment belief in the harmony and rationality of the world.

One of the most fundamental assumptions underlying Linnaeus" analysis is the "fixity of species." In other words, there has not been a significant change in the species. While Linnaeus did not hold that the world had been created in the time scale suggested by certain biblical passages, such as Genesis 1–2, he certainly believed that it had been created in more or less its present form. It is this assumption that would be challenged by Darwin, although evidence which pointed to certain species having become extinct had been noted long before then.

We have already noted some of the central features of the Darwinian controversy (see pp. 21–5), and it is not our intention to cover this ground again. Rather, we need to understand the specific issues raised by Darwin's theory of natural selection which were of direct religious importance. The four most significant themes of Darwin's theories, as set out in his *The Origin of Species* (1859) and *Descent of Man* (1871) are the following:

1 Linnaeus was incorrect to assert the "fixity of species." The evidence suggests that both animal and plant species are subject to

change and development. As a result, certain species which exist today did not exist in the more distant past, but came into existence by a process of evolution. Conversely, many species which existed in the past are now extinct. Some of thse are known only through the fossil record; others, whose existence can be inferred from the present diversity of species, appear to have left no fossil evidence at all. This evolutionary approach challenged the view, which had become widespread in much Protestant theology, that the biblical accounts of creation could only be interpreted in terms of a once-for-all act which permanently established an unchanging natural order.

2   Darwin's theory suggested that the process of evolution had taken place through a massive struggle for existence, in the course of which a number of species had been eliminated through competition. Perhaps Darwin's account of this battle for survival was colored by his reading of Thomas Robert Malthus" *Essay on the Principles of Population* (1798), which depicted a struggle for existence precipitated by limited food resources. However, the element of wastage seemed to come into conflict with the notion of divine providence. How, some asked, could a wise and good God allow such waste to take place? In effect, Darwin's theory of natural selection seemed to raise many of the difficulties associated with the traditional problem of evil. If God is omnipotent and good, why is there evil and suffering in the world? The new twist given to this familiar conundrum by Darwin lay in the extension of the suffering of the world from the present natural order to the process by which that present order came into being.

3   A further development of this point related to the apparent randomness of the evolutionary process. Darwin's theory seemed to some of its critics – perhaps most notably the Princeton theologian Charles Hodge (1797–1878) – to imply that plants and animals (including humanity) came into existence by accident. Darwin's account of natural selection, linked with the notion of "the survival of the fittest," seemed to imply that development took place through a series of accidental and random events, in which the guiding hand of God was conspicuously absent. How, Hodge wondered, could this be reconciled with the idea of God designing the world, when significant parts of the natural order seemed to have come into being without divine involvement?

4   Perhaps the most significant religious difficulty concerned the

place of humanity. As Darwin delicately hinted in *The Origin of Species*, and stated explicitly in *The Descent of Man*, humanity owed its origins and characteristics to precisely the same natural processes as those which brought other plant and animal species into being. Humanity was not exempt from this process, but was merely its most distinguished product to date. Human beings were descended from other forms of life, and owed their dominance to their superior ability to survive. This stood in stark contrast to traditional Christian ideas concerning the special creation of humanity (set out in Genesis 1–2), and especially the notion that, in some manner (traditionally set out in the concept of "the image of God in humanity"), human nature was distinct from and superior to the remainder of the natural order. Darwin did not dispute that humanity was superior to the remainder of the natural order; his account of how that superiority emerged, however, seemed to be totally incompatible with traditional religious thinking on the matter.

Charles Darwin, 1809–1982

Key works:
The Origin of Species (1859)
The Descent of Man (1871)

Key ideas:
Animal and plant types have evolved, and are not fixed.
Present-day species are descended from other species, some of which are now extinct.
The "struggle for existence" means that the best-adapted species survive in the competition for existence.
Humanity cannot be considered to be distinct from other animals, but has also evolved from earlier forms.

Key secondary studies:
Dennett, D. C. *Darwin's Dangerous Idea: Evolution and the Meaning of Life*. New York: Simon & Schuster, 1995.
Durant, J. *Darwinism and Divinity*. Oxford and New York: Basil Blackwell, 1985.
Hull, D. L. *Darwin and his Critics*. Cambridge, MA: Harvard University Press, 1973.
Moore, J. R. *The Post-Darwinian Controversies: A Study of the Protestant Struggle to come to terms with Darwin in Great Britain and America, 1870–1900*. Cambridge: Cambridge University Press, 1979.

On the basis of this brief account of the significance of Darwin's theory of natural selection, it will be clear that a significant challenge had been raised to traditional religious thinking. So what are its implications? In what follows, we shall explore two totally different lines of thought. According to one, the Darwinian theory of evolution (modified according to insights gained from molecular biology) eliminates belief in God. We shall explore this viewpoint as it is expounded by the Oxford molecular biologist Richard Dawkins. According to the second, Darwinianism obliges Christian theology to rethink the manner in which God governs the natural order – but not the fundamental belief that God created the world. This viewpoint, which is often referred to as "theistic evolutionism," has attracted many supporters, and will be considered later in this section. We turn first to consider the strongly anti-religious approach of Richard Dawkins.

Neo-Darwinism: Richard Dawkins

In his influential and widely discussed book *The Blind Watchmaker*, Dawkins deals with the appearance of design within the world, which has led many to draw religious conclusions. For Dawkins, while these conclusions may be understandable, they remain mistaken and unfounded.

This [appearance of design] is probably the most important reason for the belief, held by the vast majority of people that have ever lived, in some kind of supernatural deity. It took a very great leap of the imagination for Darwin and Wallace to see that, contrary to all intuition, there is another way and, once you have understood it, a far more plausible way, for complex "design" to arise out of primeval simplicity.

The title of Dawkin's work is inspired by an analogy used by William Paley, one of the more noted advocates of the "argument from design." Paley argues that the world is like a watch, which shows evidence of design and construction (see p. 99). Just as the existence of a watch points to a watchmaker, so the appearance of design in nature (evident, for example, in the human eye) points to a designer. Dawkins, while appreciating Paley's imagery, regards it as fatally flawed. The whole idea of "design" or "purpose" is out of place.

Paley drives his point home with beautiful and reverent descriptions of the dissected machinery of life, beginning with the human eye . . . Paley's argument is made with passionate sincerity and is informed by the best biological scholarship of his day, but it is wrong, gloriously and utterly wrong . . . Natural selection, the blind, unconscious, automatic process which Darwin discovered, and which we now know is the explanation for the existence and apparently purposeful form of all life, has no purpose in mind. It has no mind and no mind's eye. It does not plan for the future. It has no vision, no foresight, no sight at all. If it can be said to play the role of watchmaker in nature, it is the *blind* watchmaker.

The process of natural selection is thus seen as unguided and undirected, "selecting" in the sense that certain natural forces tend to lead to the failure of certain species to establish themselves in the face of intense competition with other species, fighting for existence in the same environment.

This strongly anti-teleological tone can be found in a number of earlier works by noted molecular biologists, perhaps most significantly Jacques Monod's *Chance and Necessity*, in which he argued that evolutionary change took place by chance and was perpetuated by necessity. However, it is fair to suggest that Dawkins develops the religious aspects of this to a far greater extent than Monod. The two main religious conclusions which Dawkins draws in his analysis can be set out as follows.

1   One of the primary functions of religion is *explanatory*. Religions offer explanations of the way the world is, and hence are to be regarded as "scientific theories" of a certain type. As he puts it in *The Extended Phenotype* (1982), "God and natural selection . . . are the only two workable theories we have of why we exist." The explanation offered by the "hypothesis of God" is, Dawkins argued, to be rejected as inferior to that offered by natural selection. Religious explanations were once credible; however, they are so no longer, and should therefore be abandoned as outdated and unjustified.

2   Where the natural sciences offer theories which are justified with reference to evidence, the religions offer theories which are counter to the evidence. Faith is thus unwarranted and unsubstantiated belief. Dawkins developed this theme with particular vigour in a lecture delivered on April 15, 1992, to the Edinburgh International Science Festival. Faith, he argued, "is the great cop-out, the great excuse to evade the need to think and evaluate evidence. Faith is belief in spite of, even perhaps because of, the lack of evidence." At times, Dawkins is perhaps a little less cautious in his language, suggesting that faith is "a

kind of mental illness" or "one of the world's great evils, comparable to the smallpox virus but harder to eradicate."

It is no easy matter to respond to these points in the space available. Writers from a Christian perspective have challenged both assumptions as showing a worrying absence of knowledge of Christian thought. For example, the philosophy of religion deals at length with the grounds of faith. The contribution of writers such as Alvin Plantinga and Richard Swinburne to the question of the warrants and grounds of faith makes it clear that it is quite unacceptable to suggest that faith is "the great excuse to evade the need to think and evaluate evidence" or that it is "belief in spite of, even perhaps because of, the lack of evidence." Dawkin's more polemical writings are perhaps directed towards an audience which lacks familiarity with the Christian intellectual tradition, and hence prepared to accept his assertions without question.

Evolutionary theism

The Darwinian controversies showed that many Christian theologians regarded Darwin's ideas as hostile to Christian faith. Did not *The Origin of Species* call into question aspects of the Genesis creation account? And did not *The Descent of Man* further challenge that account, and also call into question the Christian idea of humanity as the height of God's creation?

There is no doubt that many accepted these criticisms. Others, however, saw in the mysterious process of evolution nothing less than the providential guiding hand of God, leading the creation on to higher states of consciousness and development – a viewpoint generally known as "theistic evolution." Henri Bergson and Pierre Teilhard de Chardin are excellent examples of philosophers and theologians who found the idea of biological evolution profoundly attractive. We shall discuss Teilhard de Chardin's ideas in the following chapter; in what follows, we shall consider some nineteenth-century conservative Protestant responses to Darwin which show an awareness of the possibility of integrating a Christian theology of providence with the Darwinian concept of an evolving world.

Henry Ward Beecher (1818–87) is an excellent example of a writer originally sympathetic to Calvinism who came to adopt a form of theistic evolution. In his 1885 work *Evolution and Religion*, Beecher set out his vision of an complex evolutionary process guided by God. Was not this much more impressive and suggestive of design than a single original act of creation?

If single acts [of creation] would evince design, how much more a vast universe, that by inherent laws gradually builded itself, and then created its own plants and animals, a universe so adjusted that it left by the way the poorest things, and steadily wrought towards more complex, ingenious and beautful results! Who designed this mighty machine, created matter, gave to it its laws, and impressed upon it that tendency which has brought forth the almost infinite results on the globe, and wrought them into a perfect system?

For Beecher, God providentially ordained that the animal origins of humanity should gradually be eliminated, so that its superior spiritual and moral capacity could be established.

If the whole theory of evolution is but a slow decree of God, and if he is behind and under it, then the solution not only becomes natural and easy, but it becomes sublime, that in that waiting experiment which was to run through the ages of the world, God had a plan by which the race should steadily ascend, and the weakest become the strongest ... and the good in men become stronger than the animal in them.

One of the most noted conservative Protestant thinkers of the period was also a theistic evolutionist. Benjamin B. Warfield, professor of theology at Princeton Theological Seminary, had established a formidable reputation of Protestant Orthodoxy, especially in relation to the inspiration of Scripture. For Warfield, there was "no question as to the compatibility of the Darwinian form of the hypothesis of evolution with Christianity." Divine design could be seen in the laws within which the natural process operated. In an 1888 essay on Darwin, Warfield set out his view that the Darwinian doctrine of natural selection could easily be accommodated by evangelicals as a natural law operating under the aegis of the general providence of God. A similar view was taken by other writers, including several who contributed to the volumes entitled *The Fundamentals*, which are widely seen as marking the origins of the "fundamentalist" movement in North America.

Psychology

A third area of particular importance in relation to the theme of science and religion focuses on the discipline of psychology. The work of

Sigmund Freud illustrates the potential relevance of psychology in relation to, for example, explaining the origins of religious belief. Freud himself was convinced that the origins of religious belief lay in certain deep-rooted delusions. Other writers, including William James, offered more appreciative and positive approaches to religion. In what follows, we shall explore some psychological approaches to religion, and note their importance for our theme.

Ludwig Feuerbach (1804–1872)

It may seem a little strange to begin a discussion of the complex interaction of psychology and religion by dealing with a writer who is not regarded as a pyschologist. However, Feuerbach's analysis of religious experience has had considerable influence within western thought, and can be argued to have influenced Freud at several points of importance. We shall therefore open our discussion with a brief account of Feuerbach's ideas, indicating their significance for our theme.

Feuerbach's most influential work is *The Essence of Christianity* (1841), in which he argues that the idea of God arises understandably, but mistakenly, from human experience. Religion in general is simply the projection of the desires and longings of human nature onto an illusory transcendent plane. Human beings mistakenly objectify their own feelings. They interpret their subjective experience as an awareness or experience of God, whereas it is in fact nothing other than an experience of themselves. God is the longing of the human soul personified.

According to Feuerbach, we yearn for a supernatural being that will satisfy all our desires and dreams. It is therefore the most natural of things that, by doing so, we should invent such a being. For Feuerbach, the doctrine of the resurrection of Christ is nothing more than an echo of the deep human longing for immediate certainty of personal immortality. God is simply a projection of the human will. Scripture tells us that God created human beings in his image; Feuerbach declares that we, in turn, have made God in our image. "Humanity is the beginning, the centre and the end of religion". God is a human wish fulfilled and sustained by an illusion. Christianity is a fantasy world inhabited by people who have failed to realize that when they think that they are talking about God, they are simply disclosing their own innermost hopes and fears.

It is important to realize that Feuerbach was writing at a time in which the influence of the great German liberal theologian Friedrich Schleiermacher (1736–1834) was at its zenith. Schleiermacher's theological system rests upon an analysis of human experience, supremely the general human experience of being dependent (which Schleiermacher interprets in a Christian manner as "being dependent upon God"). Whatever the merits of this approach might be, it runs the risk of making the reality of God dependent upon the religious experiences of the pious believer. Theology becomes anthropology, as an understanding of God becomes reduced to an understanding of human nature.

Feuerbach's analysis is widely regarded as being a brilliant critique of this approach. For Schleiermacher, the existence of God is held to be grounded in human experience. But, as Feuerbach emphasizes, human experience might be nothing other than experience of *ourselves*, rather than of God. We might simply be projecting or objectifying our own experiences, and calling the result "God" – where we ought to realize that they are simply experiences of our own very human natures. Feuerbach's approach can thus be argued to represent a devastating critique of humanity-centered ideas of Christianity. Given the wide influence of these ideas in western European academic circles during the nineteenth century, it is little surprise that Feuerbach's ideas were so significant.

It is, however, important to note that Feuerbach generalizes hopelessly about religions. He assumes (without any cogent argument or appeal to scholarship) that all the world religions have the same basic core components, which can all be explained on the basis of his atheistic projection theory. All gods, and hence all religions, are simply projections of human desires. But what of the non-theistic religions – those world religions, such as Theravada Buddhism, which explicitly deny the existence of a god?

Perhaps the most serious objection to Feuerbach's hypothesis relates to the logic of his analysis. At the heart of Feuerbach's atheism is his belief that God is only a projected longing. Now it is certainly true that things do not exist because we desire them. But it does not follow from this that, because we desire something, it does not exist, or cannot exist for this reason. The noted German logician Eduard von Hartmann drew attention to this point a century ago in his monumental study *The History of Logic*:

It is perfectly true that nothing exists merely because we wish it, but it is not true that something cannot exist if we wish it. However, Feuerbach's entire critique of religion and the proof of his atheism rest upon this single argument – a logical fallacy.

Feuerbach's arguments, directed against religious belief, turn out to have reflexive implications, in that they suggest that Feuerbach's anti-religious beliefs might lie within him – specifically, in his own longing for autonomy.

Nevertheless, Feuerbach's argument that religious experience can be interpreted, not as experience of God but as experience of one's inner longings, has clear implications for the psychology of religion. If religion is understood to be a human creation, it can be explained along the kind of reductionist lines set out by Feuerbach. Perhaps the most important early development of this approach can be seen in the writings of Karl Marx, especially his 1844 political and economic manuscripts, in which Marx argued that religion is a reflection of the material world: "religion is just the imaginary sun which seems to human beings to revolve around them, until they realize that they themselves are the centre of their own revolution." In other words, God is simply a projection of human concerns. Human beings "look for a superhuman being in the fantasy reality of heaven, and find nothing their but their own reflection." Marx locates the origin of religion in socioeconomic alienation, and its continuing appeal in a form of spirit-ual intoxication which renders the masses incapable of recognizing their situation, and doing something about it. Religion is a comfort, "the opiate of the masses," which enables people to tolerate their economic alienation. If there were no such alienation, there would be no need for religion. The division of labor and the existence of private property introduce alienation and estrangement into the economic and social orders.

Materialism affirms that events in the material world bring about corresponding changes in the intellectual world. Religion is thus the result of a certain set of social and economic conditions. Change those conditions, so that economic alienation is eliminated, and religion will cease to exist. It will no longer serve any useful function. Unjust social conditions produce religion, and are in turn supported by religion. "The struggle against religion is therefore indirectly a struggle against *the world* of which religion is the spiritual fragrance".

Marx thus argues that religion will continue to exist, as long as it meets a need in the life of alienated people. A revolution in the real world is thus needed to get rid of religion, both in terms of the factors which cause it on the one hand, and sustain it on the other. Marx thus argues that when a non-alienating economic and social environment is brought about through communism, the needs which gave rise to religion will vanish. And with the elimination of those material needs, spiritual hunger will also vanish.

Feuerbach had argued that religion was the projection of human needs, an expression of the "uttered sorrow of the soul." Marx argues that it is not enough to explain how religion arises on account of sorrow and injustice. It is necessary to change that world, the causes of religion can be removed. It is important to note that Marx regards Feuerbach as correct in his analysis of the origins of religion, even if he failed to discern how an understanding of those origins might lead to its eventual elimination. It is this insight which underlies his often quoted eleventh thesis on Feuerbach: "the philosophers have only interpreted the world, in various ways; the point, however, is to change it."

Ludwig Feuerbach (1804–1872)

Key work:
The Essence of Christianity (1841)

Key theme:
Religion is the projection of human desires onto an imaginary objective plane

Key secondary studies:
Harvey, V. A. *Feuerbach and the Interpretation of Religion.* Cambridge: Cambridge University Press, 1995.
Wartofsky, M. *Feuerbach.* Cambridge: Cambridge University Press, 1982.

However, our interest lies especially with the use made by Sigmund Freud of this general intellectual foundation laid for the critique of religion. It is probably fair to say that Feuerbach's "projection" or (to use its popular designation) "wish-fulfillment" theory is best known today in its Freudian variant, rather than in Feuerbach's original version. In view of the importance of Freud to our theme, we may consider his ideas in a little detail at a later stage. Our attention is first claimed by the earlier work by the noted American writer William James, widely regarded as a pioneer in the scientific study of religion.

William James (1842–1910)

William James studied at Harvard University, where he subsequently became professor of psychology (1887–97) and then philosophy (1897–1907). His most influential work was based on his Gifford Lectures at Edinburgh University, which were published under the title *The Varieties of Religious Experience* (1902). Although other writers, such as F. D. E. Schleiermacher, had addressed the issue of religious experience before him, James brought to his task a more rigorously empirical and analytical way of thinking. Yet James is aware that experience is a private matter, which is not easily open to public description:

Feeling is private and dumb, and unable to give an account of itself. It allows that its results are mysteries and enigmas, declines to justify them rationally, and on occasion is willing that they should even pass for paradoxical and absurd. Philosophy takes just the opposite attitude. ... To redeem religion from unwholesome privacy, and to give public status and universal right of way to its deliverances, has been reason's task. ... As moderator amid the clash of hypotheses, and mediator among the criticisms of one man's construction by another, philosophy will always have much to do ... [These lectures] are a laborious attempt to extract from the privacies of religious experience some general facts which can be defined in formulas upon which everybody may agree.

James' pioneering effort to construct an empirical study of the phenomenon of religious experience is still widely regarded as an authoritative, balanced and finely observed study of religious experience.

James makes it clear that his primary interest is personal religious experience, rather than the type of religious experiences which are associated with institutions. "In critically judging of the value of religious phenomena, it is very important to insist on the distinction between religion as an individual personal function, and religion as an institutional, corporate or tribal product."

So what is it about "experiences" which determine whether they are religious or not? James answers this critically important question by asserting that religious experience is distinguished qualitatively from other modes of experience: "The essence of religious experiences, the thing by which we finally must judge them, must be that element or quality in them which we can meet nowhere else." In general terms, James argues that two primary features of mystical experience can be defined, one of which is to be stated in negative, and the other in positive, terms. Such experience is, in the first place, incapable of being expressed in purely verbal forms; and in the second, is "noetic," in that it appears to relate to some form of knowledge. Yet James is aware that such statements could be understood to refer to "moral" experiences as well. How can a purely religious experience be defined? It is clear that James regards religious experience as imparting a new quality to life. He speaks of religious experience raising "our centre of personal energy," and giving rise to "regenerative effects unattainable in other ways." God is to be conceived of as "the deepest power in the universe" who can be "conceived under the form of a mental personality." While clearly lacking the analytical rigour which some might expect, it is clear that James is working with two fundamental insights at this point. First, that an experience of "God" or "the divine" is existentially transformative, leading to the renewal or regeneration of individuals. Second, that any attempt to codify or formulate these experiences will fail to do justice to them. A number of intellectual responses are possible; none of them, however, is adequate.

It must be stressed that James sees his primary task as offering an empirical account of personal religious experience, and is reluctant to venture far beyond his designated topic. Nevertheless, it is also clear that he sees there as being some link between religious experience and the existence of God, even if he is reluctant to speculate on the precise nature of that link. Well-read in philosophy, James was aware of the problematic character of the "proofs" of God's existence. Might not another way – and perhaps a more reliable approach – lie to hand in the phenomenon of religious experience? At several points in the *Varieties of Religious Experience*, James draws a distinction between "theory" and "experience," regarding the former as the outcome of reflection on the latter.

When we survey the whole field of religion, we find a great variety in the thoughts that have prevailed there; but the feelings on the one hand and the conduct on the other are almost always the same for Stoic, Christian and Buddhist saints are practically indistinguishable in their lives. The theories which Religion generates, being thus variable, are secondary; and if you wish to grasp her essence, you must look to the feelings and the conduct as being the more constant elements.

Theology, according to James, thus owes both its origins and form to experience. "In a world in which no religious feeling had ever existed, I doubt whether any philosophic theology would ever have been framed."

So what is the significance of James to our study? One major theme to emerge from his study is that organized religion has relatively little to offer those interested in religious experience. It trades in "second hand" experience, where what needs to be studied is fresh and vital, often being perceived as a threat to the settled ways of organized religion:

A genuine first hand religious experience . . . is bound to be a heterodoxy to its witnesses, the prophet appearing as a lonely madman. If his doctrine proves contagious enough to spread to any others, it becomes a definite and labelled heresy. But, if it still proves contagious enough to triumph over persecution, it becomes itself an orthodoxy; and when religion has become an orthodoxy, its way of inwardness is over; the spring is dry; the faithful live at second hand exclusively, and stone prophets in their turn.

This suggests that empirical study of religious experience is best carried on outside the sphere of organized religion – an assertion which has had considerable impact on the scientific study of the phenomenon of religious experience. Subsequent empirical studies have not provided substantiation of this suggestion; nevertheless, it is important to appreciate that James' approach was an important stimulus to work in this area.

William James, 1842–1910

Key works:
The Varieties of Religious Experience (1902)
The Will to Believe (1897)

Key themes:
Distinction between "personal" and "institutional"; religious experience.
Genuine religious experience often appears as heterodoxy.
The validity of religious experience as a category in its own right.

Key secondary studies:
Feinstein, H. M. *Becoming William James*. Ithaca, NY: Cornell University Press, 1984.
Lash, N. *Easter in Ordinary: Reflections on Human Experience and the Knowledge of God*. Charlottesville, VA: University of Virginia Press, 1988.
Vanden Burgt, R. J. *The Religious Philosophy of William James*. Chicago: Nelson-Hall, 1981.

One of the most significant aspects of James" work is that it does not attempt to reduce religious experience to social or psychological categories, but attempts to describe the phenomena in a manner which respects their integrity. This heightens the contrast between James and Freud, to whom we now turn.

Sigmund Freud (1856–1939)

It is widely agreed that Freud's discussion of religion is one of his most significant contributions to the debate on science and religion. It is also widely agreed that Freud's approach to religion is totally unsympathetic in tone, and strongly reductionist in approach. *Totem and Taboo* (1913) considers how religion has its origins in society in general; *The Future of an Illusion* (1927) deals with deals with the psychological origins (Freud often uses the term "psychogenesis" here) of religion in the individual. For Freud, religious ideas are "illusions, fulfilments of the oldest, strongest and most urgent wishes of mankind". Similar ideas were developed in a later work, *Moses and Monotheism* (1939), published at the end of his life.

To understand Freud at this point, we need to examine his theory of repression. These views were first made generally known in *The Interpretation of Dreams* (1900), a book which was generally ignored by the critics and the general reading public. Freud's thesis here is that dreams are wish-fulfilments. They are disguised fulfilments of wishes that are repressed by the consciousness (the ego), and are thus displaced into the unconsciousness. In *The Psychopathology of Everyday Life* (1904), Freud argued that these repressed wishes intrude into everyday life at a number of points. Certain neurotic symptoms, dreams, or even small slips of the tongue or pen – so-called "Freudian slips" – reveal unconscious processes.

The task of the psychotherapist is to expose these repressions which have such a negative effect on life. Psychoanalysis (a term coined by Freud) aims to lay bare the unconscious and untreated traumatic experiences, by assisting the patient to raise them up into consciousness. Through persistent questioning, the analyst can identify repressed traumas which are having so negative an effect upon the patient, and enable the patient to deal with them by bringing them into the open.

As we noted earlier, Freud's views on the origin of religion need to be considered in two stages: first, its origins in the development of human history in general, and second, its origins in the case of the individual person. We may begin by dealing with his account of the psychogenesis of religion in the human species in general, as it is presented in *Totem and Taboo*.

Developing his earlier observation that religious rites are similar to the obsessive actions of his neurotic patients, Freud declared that religion was basically a distorted form of an obsessional neurosis. His studies of obsessional patients (such as the "Wolf Man') led him to argue that such disorders were the consequence of unresolved developmental issues, such as the association of "guilt" and "being unclean" which he associated with the "anal" phase in childhood development. He suggested that aspects of religious behavior (such as the ritual cleansing ceremonies of Judaism) could arise through similar obsessions.

Freud argued that the key elements in all religions included the veneration of a father figure and a concern for proper rituals. Freud traces the origins of religion to the Oedipal complex. At some point in the history of the human race, Freud argues (without substantiation), the father figure had exclusive sexual rights over females in his tribe. The sons, unhappy at this state of affairs, overthrew the father figure, and killed him. Thereafter, they are haunted by the secret of parricide, and its associated sense of guilt. Religion, according to Freud, has its origins in this prehistorical parricidal event, and for this reason has guilt as a major motivating factor. This guilt requires purging or expiation, for which various rituals were devised.

Freud summarized his views on the matter as follows in his autobiography:

The father of the primal horde, since he was an unlimited despot, had seized all the women for himself; his sons, being dangerous to him as rivals, had been killed or driven away. One day, however, the sons came together and united to overwhelm, kill and devour their father, who had been their enemy but also their ideal. After the deed they were unable to take over their heritage since they stood in one another's way. Under the influence of failure and remorse they learned to come to an agreement among themselves; they banded themselves into a clan of brothers by the help of the ordinances of totemism, which aimed at preventing a repetition of such a deed, and they jointly undertook to forgo the possession of the women on whose account they had killed their father. They were then driven to finding foreign women, and this was the origin of the exogamy which is so closely bound up with totemism. This totem meal was the festival commemorating the fearful deed from which man's sense of guilt (or "original sin') sprang and which was the beginning at once of social organiza-tion, religion and ethical restrictions.

Freud thus argues that religion has its ultimate origins in the Oedipus complex of the human race as a whole, centering initially on aggression toward, and subsequently veneration of, a father figure.

The emphasis within Christianity upon the death of Christ and the veneration of the risen Christ seemed to Freud to be a superb illustration of this general principle. "Christianity, having arisen out of a father-religion, became a son-religion. It has not escaped the fate of having to get rid of the father." The "totem meal," he argued, had its direct counterpart in the Christian celebration of communion.

Freud's account of the social origins of religion is not taken with great seriousness, and is often regarded as a "period piece," bearing witness to the highly optimistic and somewhat simplistic theories which were emerging in the aftermath of the general acceptance of the Darwinian theory of evolution. His account of the origins of religion in the individual is, however, more significant. Once more, the theme of the veneration of a "father figure" emerges as significant. Interestingly, Freud's account of the development of religion in individuals seems not to rest upon careful study of the actual development of such views in children, but an observance of similarities (often rather superficial ones, it has to be said) between some adult neuroses and some religious beliefs and practices, particularly those of Judaism and Roman Catholicism.

In an essay on a childhood memory of Leonardo da Vinci (1910), Freud sets out his explanation of individual religion:

Psychoanalysis has made us familiar with the intimate connection between the father-complex and belief in God; it has shown us that a personal God is, psychologically, nothing other than an exalted father, and it brings us evidence every day of how young people lose their religious beliefs as soon as their father's authority breaks down. Thus we recognize that the roots of the need for religion and in the parental complex.

The veneration of the father figure has its origins in childhood. When going through its oedipal phase, Freud argues, the child has to deal with anxiety over the possibility of being punished by the father. The child's response to this threat is to venerate the father, identify with him, and to project what it knows of the father's will in the form of the superego.

Freud explored the origins of this projection of an ideal father figure in *The Future of an Illusion*. Religion represents the perpetuation of a piece of infantile behavior in adult life. Religion is simply an immature response to the awareness of helplessness, by going back to one's childhood experiences of paternal care: "my father will protect me; he is in control." Belief in a personal God is thus little more than an infantile delusion, the projection of an idealized father figure.

Sigmund Freud (1856–1939)

Key works relating to psychology and religion:
Totem and Taboo (1913)
The Future of an Illusion (1927)
Moses and Monotheism (1939)

Key themes:
Religion as an infantile delusion.
God as idealized projection of father figure.
Religious rituals as forms of obsessional disorders.

Key secondary studies:
Küng, H. *Freud and the Problem of God*. New Haven, CT: Yale University Press, 1979.
Preus, S. J. *Explaining Religion: Criticism and Theory from Bodin to Freud*. New Haven, CT: Yale University Press, 1987.
Ricoeur, P. *Freud and Philosophy: An Essay on Interpretation*. New Haven, CT: Yale University Press, 1970.

Yet Freud's highly negative approach to religion was not the only view on the matter to emerge from early psychoanalytic circles. Carl Gustav Jung (1875–1961) was the son of a Swiss pastor, who was closely associated with Freud from 1907. In 1914, Jung resigned as president of the International Psychoanalytical Society, an action which signalled his growing distance from Freud on a number of matters, particularly the latter's emphasis upon the libido. As we noted earlier (p. 201),

Freud is noted for a hostile and reductionist approach to religion. Jung is generally regarded as being more sympathetic to religion than Freud, and clearly wished to distance himself from Freud's reductionism. While Jung remained sympathetic to Freud's belief that the "image of God" is essentially a human projection, he located its origins increasingly in the "collective unconscious." Humans are naturally religious; it is not something which they "invent." Perhaps more significantly, he stressed the positive aspects of religion, particularly in relation to an individual's progress towards wholeness and fulfilment.

This present chapter has surveyed some of the religious issues which are raised by specific scientific disciplines. It is, however, important to note that a number of individual scholars have made significant contributions to the discussion of the relation of science and religion, from both sides of the discussion.

In the next chapter, we shall consider seven such individuals, and the significance of their contributions. Given the rapid pace of developments within the field, discussion will center on individuals whose works have been published since 1950.

For further reading

Barbour, I. G. *Issues in Science and Religion*. Englewood Cliffs: Prentice-Hall, 1966.

——. *Religion in an Age of Science*. San Francisco: HarperSanFrancisco, 1990.

Barrow, J., and F. J. Tipler. *The Anthropic Cosmological Principle*. Oxford: Oxford University Press, 1986.

Bradley, J. "Across the River and Beyond the Trees: Feuerbach's Relevance to Modern Theology." *New Studies in Theology*. Ed. S. W. Sykes and D. Holmes. London: Duckworth, 1980, pp.139–61.

Craig, W. L. "Barrow and Tipler on the Anthropic Principle vs. Divine Design." *British Journal for Philosophy of Science* 38 (1988): 389–95.

——. "Theism and Big Bang Cosmology." *Australasian Journal of Philosophy* 69 (1991): 492–503.

——. "Creation and Big Bang Cosmology." *Philosophia Naturalis* 31 (1994): 217–24.

Dennett, D. C. *Darwin's Dangerous Idea: Evolution and the Meaning of Life*. New York: Simon & Schuster, 1995.

Drees, W. B. *Beyond the Big Bang: Quantum Cosmologies and God*. La Salle: Open Court, 1990.

Hawking, S. *A Brief History of Time: From the Big Bang to Black Holes*. New York: Bantam Books, 1988.

Hull, D. L. *Darwin and his Critics*. Cambridge, MA: Harvard University Press, 1973.

Küng, H. *Freud and the Problem of God*. New Haven, CT: Yale University Press, 1979.

Moore, J. R. *The Post-Darwinian Controversies: A Study of the Protestant Struggle to come to terms with Darwin in Great Britain and America, 1870–1900*. Cambridge: Cambridge University Press, 1979.

Preus, S. J. *Explaining Religion: Criticism and Theory from Bodin to Freud*. New Haven, CT: Yale University Press, 1987.

Ricoeur, P. *Freud and Philosophy: An Essay on Interpretation*. New Haven, CT: Yale University Press, 1970.

Smith, Q. "Atheism, Theism and Big Bang Cosmology." *Australasian Journal of Philosophy* 69 (1991): 48–66.

Wartofsky, M. *Feuerbach*. Cambridge: Cambridge University Press, 1982.

Watts, F., and M. Williams. *The Psychology of Religious Knowing*. Cambridge: Cambridge University Press, 1988.

Wittgenstein, L. *Lectures and Conversations on Aesthetics, Psychology and Religious Belief*. Oxford: Blackwell, 1966.

9

Case Studies in Science and Religion

One of the most fascinating aspects of the dialogue between "science and religion" is the manner in which it has brought together a rich diversity of writers from different fields. Some of the most significant writers to contribute to our understanding of this area began their scholarly careers in the natural sciences, and then found themselves being drawn to explore the religious implications of their work. Others began as specialists in the field of religious thought, and found themselves drawn to study the natural sciences on account of a growing awareness of the importance of the distinctive contributions of the sciences to religion.

The present chapter offers a brief survey of seven twentieth-century writers of importance to our theme. Five can be regarded as scientists turned theologians: Ian R. Barbour (physics); Charles A. Coulson (theoretical chemistry); Arthur Peacocke (molecular biology); John Polkinghorne (theoretical physics); and Pierre Teilhard de Chardin (paleontology). Two are "theologians turned scientists": Wolfhart Pannenberg and Thomas F. Torrance, both of whom are systematic theologians of distinction. Some of the writers to be surveyed here develop ideas which we have already touched upon in earlier sections – such as natural theology, the anthropic principle, or critical realism; readers may therefore find it helpful to have read the material in earlier chapters of this work beforehand.

Ian G. Barbour (1923–)

Ian G. Barbour is widely regarded as one of the most important and positive influences on the growing interest in the interface between science and religion. Barbour was born on October, 5 1923 in Beijing, China, and initially focussed his studies on the field of physics, gaining his Ph.D. from the University of Chicago in 1950. His first academic appointment was at Kalamazoo College, Michigan, as professor of physics. However, he had a strong interest in religion, which he was able to pursue through studies at Yale University, leading to a BD in 1956. He served for many years in various roles, including Chairman of the Department of Religion and Professor of Physics, at Carleton College, Northfield, Minnesota (1955–81). He finally became Winifred and Atherton Bean Professor of Science, Technology and Society at the college (1981–6). His concern to relate science and religion developed during the 1960s, and led to the publication of the book for which he is best known – *Issues in Science and Religion* (1966). This book reflected his experience of teaching in both the areas of science and religion – teaching interests which he was able to maintain throughout most of his academic career. During the 1970s, Barbour developed his interests further through a program on ethics, public policy and technology, which identified and engaged with a series of religious issues.

Issues in Science and Religion is widely regarded as an authoritative, clearly written, and learned book introduced many to the fascinating questions which were associated with this field. Since then, Barbour has authored or edited a series of works dealing with issues on the interface of science and religion (most notably *Religion in an Age of Science*, which appeared in 1990, based on the Gifford lectures given at the University of Aberdeen in 1989). He is widely regarded as the doyen of dialogue in this field, and was honored for this by the American Academy of Religion in 1993.

However, it is important to appreciate that Barbour has done more than encourage dialogue in this field. He has given considerable attention to the development of an intellectual basis for the facilitation and consolidation of this dialogue, and has found the ideas developed in what is known as "process thought" or "process theology," especially helpful in this regard. We have already set out the basic features of process thought in an earlier chapter (see pp. 105–9). In what follows, we shall explore the particular use which Barbour makes of this approach in relation to the field of science and religion.

The key aspect of process theology which Barbour appropriates is the rejection of the classic doctrine of God's omnipotence: God is one agent among many, not the sovereign Lord of all. As Barbour points out, process affirms "a God of persuasion rather than compulsion . . . who influences the world without determining it." Process theology thus locates the origins of suffering and evil within the world to a radical limitation upon the power of God. God has set aside (or simply does not possess) the ability to coerce, retaining only the ability to persuade. Persuasion is seen as a means of exercising power in such a manner that the rights and freedom of others are respected. God is obliged to persuade every aspect of the process to act in the best possible manner. There is, however, no guarantee that God's benevolent persuasion will lead to a favorable outcome. The process is under no obligation to obey God. As Barbour comments, process theology thus calls into question "the traditional expectation of an absolute victory over evil."

God intends good for the creation, and acts in its best interests. However, the option of coercing everything to do the divine will cannot be exercised. As a result, God is unable to prevent certain things happening. Wars, famines, and holocausts are not things which God desires; they are, however, not things which God can prevent, on account of the radical limitations placed upon the divine power. God is thus not responsible for evil; not can it be said, in any way, that God desires or tacitly accepts its existence. The metaphysical limits placed upon God are such as to prevent any interference in the natural order of things.

Barbour finds this approach (especially as it is set out in the writings of A. N. Whitehead) valuable in illuminating the manner in which science and religion interact. It allows God to be seen as present and active within nature, working within the limits and constraints of the natural order. It would be fair to categorize Barbour as a "panentheist" at this point (meaning "God includes and penetrates all things," and not to be confused with "pantheism," the view that "all things are divine"). Perhaps the most interesting way in which Barbour uses the distinctive ideas of process thought relates to the theory of evolution. Barbour argues that the evolutionary process is influenced by – but *not* directed by – God. This allows him to deal with the fact that the evolutionary process appears to have been long, complex and wasteful. "There have been too many blind alleys and extinct species and too much waste, suffering and evil to attribute every event to God's specific will." God influences the process for good, but cannot dictate precisely what form it will take.

Yet Barbour also offers criticism of process thought at points where he feels that it is inadequate, particularly in relation to its treatment of the inanimate world. In his *Religion in an Age of Science* (1990), he comments:

The Whiteheadian analysis does not present any direct inconsistency with contemporary science. Creativity is said to be either totally absent (in the case of stones and inanimate objects, which are aggregates without integration or unified experience) or so attenuated that it would escape detection (in the case of atoms). A vanishingly small novelty and self-determination in atoms is postulated only for the sake of metaphysical consistency and continuity. But does process philosophy allow adequately for the radical diversity among levels of activity in the world and the emergence of genuine novelty at all stages of evolutionary history? Could greater emphasis be given to emergence and the contrasts between events at various levels, while preserving the basic postulate of metaphysical continuity?

Summary

Ian G. Barbour (1923–)
Area of Specialization: Physics

Key writings on science and religion:
Issues in Science and Religion (1966)
Religion in an Age of Science (1990)

Significant Secondary Studies:
Polkinghorne, J. *Scientists as Theologians: A Comparison of the Writings of Ian Barbour, Arthur Peacocke and John Polkinghorne* London: SPCK, 1996.

The March 1996 (vol. 31, no. 1) edition of the leading journal *Zygon* included a number of significant articles dealing with Barbour's contribution to religion and science.

Charles A. Coulson (1910–1974)

Charles Alfred Coulson was born on December, 13 1910, in the English country town of Dudley, in Worcestershire. In 1928, at the age of 17, he went up to Trinity College, Cambridge, to study mathematics. During his time at Cambridge University, he became heavily involved in student Christian activities, especially through a group organized by the local Methodist church. He once wrote that he experienced God for the first time in a personal manner during his first weeks at Cambridge. His deep interest in Christianity developed further during his time as an undergraduate, and caused his father to worry that he was neglecting his academic work.

In the event, that anxiety proved to be misplaced. Coulson gained first-class honors in each of the three parts of the Cambridge tripos – Mathematics Part I (1929), Mathematics Part II (1930), and Physics Part II (1931). He developed a particular interest in quantum theory, and its application to chemistry. He was appointed Professor of Theoretical Physics at Kings College, London, in 1947, and went on to become Rouse Ball Professor of Mathematics at Oxford University in 1952. In 1972, he became the first Professor of Theoretical Chemistry at Oxford. Among his most significant scientific works, we may note *Valence* (1952) and *The Shape and Structure of Molecules* (1973).

It was already known that he was suffering from cancer at the time of his appointment to the new Oxford chair. It was thought that an operation in 1970 to remove cancerous growth had been successful. Sadly, the tumour had not been fully removed. He died in his sleep on January, 7, 1974.

In addition to a substantial corpus of writings dealing with aspects of physics, chemistry and mathematics, Coulson wrote a number of works specifically dealing with the relation of the sciences and Christian belief. The two most important such writings are the Riddell Memorial Lectures, published as *Christianity in an Age of Science* (1953) and the John Calvin McNair lectures, published as *Science and Christian Belief* (1955). It is clear that Coulson's religious beliefs were deeply shaped by his father, to whose memory he dedicated the work on science and religion for which he is best remembered – *Science and Christian Belief*.

Coulson's major contribution to the discussion of the relation of science and religion lies in his vigorous and insistent rejection of the notion of a "God of the gaps." The "gaps" in question could be described as explanatory lacunae – in other words, gaps in our understanding. Coulson was alarmed at the tendency of some religious writers to propose that what could not at present be explained was to be put down to the action or influence of God.

For Coulson, this was a vulnerable and unjustified strategy. It was vulnerable on account of scientific progress. What might be unexplained today might find an explanation tomorrow. "When we come to the scientifically unknown, our correct policy is not to rejoice because we have found God: it is to become better scientists." Coulson was fond of quoting Henry Drummond on the pointlessness of an appeal to such gaps: "There are reverent minds who ceaselessly scan the fields of nature and the books of science in search of gaps – gaps which they fill up with God. As if God lived in gaps!" Coulson insisted that God was to be discerned through the ordering and beauty of the world, not hiding in its recesses.

A God who is obliged to conceal his actions of providence so that we cannot see him, a God who hides his presence in Nature behind the law of large numbers, is a God for whom I have no use. He is a God who leaves Nature still unexplained, while he sneaks in through the loopholes, cheating both us and Nature with his disguised "room for manouevre."

For Coulson, the biblical account of creation points to the universe possessing and demonstrating a meaningful and ordered pattern, which can be uncovered by the natural sciences. It is in this area that Coulson sees a strong convergence between science and Christianity. Rather than seek God in those things which cannot be explained, Coulson argues that God is to be found in the remarkable beauty and ordering of the world. "We can trace in what we call the Order of Nature the working out of an almost unbelievably grand purpose."

Summary

Charles A. Coulson, 1910–1974
Area of Specialization: Theoretical Chemist

Key writings on science and religion:
Science and Christian Belief (1955)
Christianity in an Age of Science (1953)

Significant secondary studies:
Hawkin, D. and E. *The World of Science: The Religious and Social Thought of C. A. Coulson* London: Epworth Press, 1989.

Wolfhart Pannenberg (1928–)

Wolfhart Pannenberg was born in 1928 in Stettin (then part of Germany; now included in Poland), and began theological studies after the Second World War at the University of Berlin. His early theological studies were subsequently based at Göttingen and Basle, where he completed his doctoral thesis on the doctrine of predestination of the noted medieval scholastic theologian John Duns Scotus (published in 1954). His first teaching appointment was at the University of Heidelberg, where he remained until called to a vacant chair of systematic theology at the *Kirchliche Hochschule* at Wuppertal (1958–61) as a colleague of Jürgen Moltmann. After a period at the University of Mainz (1961–8), he moved to the University of Munich, where he has remained.

Pannenberg is an example of a professional theologian who developed an interest in the natural sciences. Initially, Pannenberg's interests lay in the area of the importance of the philosophy of history. These issues were explored throughout the 1960s, when the predominance of Marxism in German intellectual culture made an examination of the role of history particularly significant. Marxism emphasized the importance of the correct interpretation of history, and Pannenberg responded by arguing for the grounding of theology in what he termed "universal history." His views on this issue were developed and justified in the 1961 volume *Offenbarung als Geschichte* ("Revelation as History"), edited by Pannenberg, in which these ideas are explored at some length. This volume established Pannenberg as a leading young theologian of the period. This reputation was further consolidated by his 1968 work on Christology, in which he set out an approach to the identity and significance of Jesus of Nazareth which made a particular appeal to the resurrection as a public historical event.

Pannenberg's early essay "Dogmatic Theses on the Doctrine of Revelation" opens with a powerful appeal to universal history:

History is the most comprehensive horizon of Christian theology. All theological questions and answers have meaning only within the framework of the history which God has with humanity, and through humanity with the whole creation, directed towards a future which is hidden to the world, but which has already been revealed in Jesus Christ.

These crucially important opening sentences sum up the distinctive features of Pannenberg's theological program at this stage in his career. Christian theology is based upon an analysis of universal and publicly accessible history. For Pannenberg, revelation is essentially a public and universal historical event which is recognized and interpreted as an "act of God."

Pannenberg's argument takes the following form. History, in all its totality, can only be understood when it is viewed from its endpoint. This point alone provides the perspective from which the historical process can seen in its totality, and thus be properly understood. However, where Marx argued that the social sciences, by predicting the goal of history to be the hegemony of socialism, provided the key to the interpretation of history, Pannenberg declared that this was provided only in Jesus Christ. The end of history is disclosed in advance (or, to use the jargon, proleptically) in the history of Jesus Christ. In other words, the end of history, which has yet to take place, has been disclosed in advance of the event in the person and work of Christ.

Perhaps the most distinctive, and certainly the most discussed, aspect of this work is Pannenberg's insistence that the resurrection of Jesus is an objective historical event, witnessed by all who had access to the evidence. Whereas Bultmann treated the resurrection as an event within the experiential world of the disciples, Pannenberg declares that it belongs to the world of universal public history. Revelation is not something that takes place in secret. It is "open to anyone who has eyes to see. It has a universal character." Any concept of revelation which implies that revelation is either opposed to or distinct from natural knowledge is in danger of lapsing into a form of Gnosticism. The distinctively Christian understanding of revelation lies in the way in which publicly available events are interpreted. Thus the resurrection of Jesus, he argues, was a publicly accessible event. But what did it *mean*? Christian revelation concerns the distinctively Christian way of understanding that event, and its implications for our understanding of God.

During the 1970s, however, Pannenberg began to express an interest in the way in which theology relates to the natural sciences. Two papers dating from the period 1971–2 focus on the approach of Pierre Teilhard de Chardin, and show a clear interest in the general issue of the formulation of a "theology of nature." In one sense, this can be seen as a direct extension of his earlier interest in history. Just as he appealed to the publicly observable sphere of history in his theological analysis of the 1960s, so he appeals to another publicly observable sphere – the world of nature – from the 1970s onwards. Both history and the natural world are available to scrutiny by anyone; the critical question concerns how they are to be understood. In his essay "Contingency and Natural Law," Pannenberg draws attention to the way in which these two spheres of history and nature interact, exploring in particular the idea of a "history of nature."

Pannenberg is clear that the natural sciences and theology are distinct disciplines, with their own understandings of how information is gained and assessed. Nevertheless, both relate to the same publicly observable reality, and they therefore have potentially complementary insights to bring. The area of the "laws of nature" is a case in point, in that Pannenberg believes that the provisional explanations for such laws offered by natural scientists have a purely provisional status, until they are placed on a firmer theoretical foundation by theological analysis. There is thus a clear case to be made for a creative and productive dialogue between the natural sciences and religion; indeed, had this taken place in the past, much confusion and tension could have been avoided.

Much would have been gained with the insight that the themes of theology and the reality that natural sciences describe must not stand side by side without relationship. Rather, it must be possible and meaningful to think of reality as a whole with the inclusion of nature as a process of a history of God with his creatures. . . . It is clear that faith in God has to be gained in other areas of life than that of scientific knowledge, but the significance of the idea of God for an interconnected understanding of nature is just as clear.

Summary

Wolfhart Pannenberg, 1928–
Area of Specialization: Systematic Theology

Key writings on science and religion:
Toward a Theology of Nature: Essays on Science and Faith (1993), a useful collection which brings together seven major essays published over the period 1970–89.

Significant secondary studies:
Braaten, C. E., and Clayton, P. *The Theology of Wolfhart Pannenberg* Minneapolis, MN: Augsburg Press, 1988.

Hefner, P. "The Role of Science in Pannenberg's Theological Thinking." *Zygon* 24 (1989): 135–51.

Russell, R. J. "Contingency in Physics and Cosmology: A Critique of the Theology of Wolfhart Pannenberg." *Zygon* 23 (1988): 23–43.

Arthur Peacocke (1924–)

Arthur Peacocke went up to Exeter College, Oxford University in 1942 to study chemistry. At that stage, the Oxford University chemistry course lasted four years. After the initial three years of teaching, the final year consisted of a substantial research project. Peacocke chose to work under Sir Cyril Hinshelwood in the Physical Chemistry Laboratory for this final year of his undergraduate work, and remained with him for his doctoral research. Although Hinshelwood was a physical chemist who had received the Nobel Prize for his work on chemical kinetics (that is, the study of the rates of chemical reactions), he subsequently extended his interests to include the growth rates of living organisms. Peacocke's doctoral work focused on the manner in which bacterial growth was inhibited by certain chemical substances.

After his doctoral work, Peacocke accepted a lectureship in physical chemistry at the University of Birmingham, England, where he further developed an interest in aspects of the physical chemistry of DNA. During his time at Birmingham, Peacocke developed his interests in Christian theology by studying for the Bachelor of Divinity, offered by the University of Birmingham. Reading the works of leading English theologians of the time (such as William Temple, Ian Ramsey and G. W. H. Lampe) encouraged him to explore further the relation of science and religion. After a period as a lecturer at Oxford University and fellow of St Peter's College (1968–73), he accepted the position of Dean of Clare College, Cambridge, which allowed him to develop his interest in the interface of science and religion. He is currently director of the Ian Ramsey Centre at Oxford, which has a special interest in fostering study of issues at the interface of science and religion. Peacocke is particularly noted for his "sacramental parentheism" – the view that the transcendence of God acts in, with and under the processes of the world. In this section, however, we shall focus on his important discussion of realism.

His first major publication in the field of science and religion was the result of being invited to deliver the Bampton Lectures at Oxford in 1978. These were published the following year, with the title *Creation and the World of Science*. A stream of publications followed, focusing on aspects of the relationship of religion and science in general, and the biological sciences in particular. One of Peacocke's most distinctive concerns is his belief that Christian theology needs to respond to the challenges posed by the natural sciences in the modern period. His own work can be seen as representing exactly such a response.

In common with many of those working at the interface of science and religion, Peacocke argues the case for "critical realism." Noting that some recent writers have argued that the natural sciences are "sociologically and ideologically conditioned," Peacocke stresses that they attempt to give account of something which cannot be regarded as conditioned in this manner. Science and theology alike use imagery in an attempt to offer a reliable and responsible picture of the world as it really is.

I think that both science and theology *aim* to depict reality; that they both do so in metaphorical language with the use of models; and that their metaphors and models are revisable within the context of the continuous communities which have generated them. This philosophy of science ("critical realism") has the virtue of being the implicit, though often not articulated, working philosophy of working scientists who aim to depict reality but know only too well their fallibility in doing so.

Theology also aims to depict reality using models or analogies.

Theology, the intellectual formulation of religious experience and beliefs, also employs models which may be similarly described. I urge that a critical realism is also the most appropriate and adequate philosophy concerning religious language and theological propositions. Theological concepts and models should be regarded as partial, adequate and revisable but necessary and, indeed, the only ways of referring to the reality that is named as "God" and God's dealings with humanity.

It will thus be clear that Peacocke believes that both science and religion operate on the basis of a "critical realism," in which models are "partial, adequate, revisable and necessary" means of depicting reality. Each of these terms merits a little further exploration.

- *Partial.* Theological models can only allow access to part of the greater reality which they depict. Peacocke thus recognizes that there are limits on what can be known of reality, whether scientific or religious, on account of the mode of representation which has to be used in the process of depiction.

- *Adequate*. Peacocke here draws attention to the fact that these models are good enough to allow us to know about the reality which is depicted. The fact that such knowledge does not derive *directly* from reality is not to be seen as implying that it is somehow substandard or second-rate.

- *Revisable*. In the natural sciences, models are revised in the light of an accumulation of experimental knowledge which indicates that the model requires revision. Peacocke also suggests that religious models can be revised in the same way. Perhaps this is one of the more controversial aspects of his analysis, in that many more traditional religious thinkers would hold that the religious models are "given" – what is revisable is the interpretation which we place upon them.

- *Necessary*. A distinction is generally made between "naïve realism" and "critical realism", with the former holding that it is possible to know reality *directly* and the latter that it is necessary to know it *indirectly*, through models.

Summary

Arthur R. Peacocke, 1924 –
Area of Specialization: Molecular Biology

Key writings on science and religion:
Creation and the World of Science (1979)
Theology for a Scientific Age (1993)
God and Science – A Quest for Christian Credibility (1996)

Significant Secondary Studies:
Polkinghorne, J. *Scientists as Theologians: A Comparison of the Writings of Ian Barbour, Arthur Peacocke and John Polkinghorne* London: SPCK, 1996.

Russell, R. J. "The Theological-Scientific Vision of Arthur Peacocke," *Zygon* 26 (1991), 505–17.

John Polkinghorne (1930–)

One of the most significant contributions to the dialogue between natural science and religion is due to John Polkinghorne. Polkinghorne's expertise is in the area of theoretical physics. He eventually went on to become Professor of Mathematical Physics at the University of Cambridge. In 1979, he resigned his chair in order to become a country priest in the Church of England. After a period spent ministering in two parishes in the south of England, he returned to Cambridge in 1986 to become Dean of Trinity Hall. Three years later, he was appointed President of Queen's College, a position which he retained until his retirement in 1997.

One of Polkinghorne's most significant achievements is to establish a firm place for natural theology in apologetics and theology. Natural theology is, in Polkinghorne's view, perhaps the most important bridge between the worlds of science and religion. Polkinghorne directs attention to the ordering of the world, which is disclosed particularly clearly in the physical sciences. He argues that one of the most significant achievements of modern science has been its demonstration of the ordering of the world. It has disclosed an intelligible and delicately balanced structure, which raises questions which transcend the scientific, and provoke an intellectual restlessness which can only be satisfied through an adequate explanation.

Polkinghorne is quite clear that exploring or speaking of the ordering of the world in this way does not fall into the discredited "God of the Gaps" approach. It was once thought that there were certain gaps in scientific understanding, which could never be filled by subsequent scientific investigation. It therefore seemed to make apologetic sense to invoke God to explain such gaps. These "gaps," however, kept getting filled through scientific inquiry, with the result that God gradually got squeezed out of a series of steadily decreasing gaps. As we have seen, Charles A. Coulson made a similar point earlier (see p. 211).

Polkinghorne argues that a more credible approach is to concentrate upon the scientifically given, rather than the scientifically open. Science discloses the world as having a tightly-knit and intricately interconnected structure, which requires to be explained. Yet, paradoxically, the natural sciences are unable to answer such questions, even though this would appear to be an essential aspect of the project of understanding the world. The central question to be considered is the following: where does the ordering of the world come from? An obvious answer, widely canvassed in more secular circles, might be that there is no order within the world, save that which we impose upon it. It is a construct of the order-loving human mind, resting upon no adequate basis in reality.

Attractive though this belief might initially seem, it rests upon a series of historical improbabilities. Time and time again, it is the neat and ordered theories of human beings which have come to grief against the sheer intractability of the observational evidence. The ordering which the human mind seeks to impose upon the world proves incapable of explaining it, forcing the search for a better understanding. The ordering imposed by the human mind is thus constantly being compared with that disclosed in the world, to be amended where it is inadequate.

One feature of the ordering of the universe which has attracted especial attention, and which is dealt with fully in Polkinghorne's works, is the *anthropic principle* (see pp. 181–6). In order for creation to come into being, a very tightly-connected series of conditions had to apply. Polkinghorne thus draws attention to

our increasing realization that there is a delicate and intricate balance in its structure necessary for the emergence of life. For example, suppose things had been a little different in those crucial first three minutes when the gross nuclear structure of the world got fixed as a quarter helium and three quarter's hydrogen. If things had gone a little faster, all would have been helium; and without hydrogen how could water (vital to life) have been able to form?

After listing other aspects in which a significant degree of fine-tuning is indicated, Polkinghorne points to the way in which such considerations lay the foundations for the Christian belief in God. They do not necessarily give rise to that belief; they are, none the less, consistent with it, raising important and disturbing questions which the religious apologist is in a position to exploit.

Having thus laid the foundations of what we might call a "general theistic apologetic" (in other words, an argument for the existence of some divine being in general), Polkinghorne argues that this general idea of a divine being requires to be supplemented with reference to the specifics of the Christian revelation. Having devoted several chapters in his work *The Way the World Is* to a survey of some pointers towards the existence of God, he notes:

The kinds of consideration outlined in the preceding chapters would, I think, incline me to take a theistic view of the world. By themselves that is about as far as they would get me. The reason why I take my stand within the Christian community lies in certain events which took place in Palestine nearly two thousand years ago.

Summary

John Polkinghorne, 1930–
Area of Specialization: Theoretical Physics

Key writings on science and religion:
The Way the World Is (1983)
Science and Creation (1988)

Significant Secondary Studies:
Avis, P. D. L. "Apologist from the World of Science: John Polkinghorne, FRS." *Scottish Journal of Theology* 43 (1990): 485–502.

Polkinghorne, J. *Scientists as Theologians: A Comparison of the Writings of Ian Barbour, Arthur Peacocke and John Polkinghorne* London: SPCK, 1996.

Pierre Teilhard de Chardin (1881–1955)

One of the most remarkable contributions to the twentieth-century debate over the relation of science and religion was made by the distinguished French paleontologist Pierre Teilhard de Chardin. Teilhard de Chardin joined the Society of Jesus (also known as the "Jesuits") in 1899. He initially studied theology, but found himself increasingly attracted to the natural sciences, particularly geology and palaeontology. He was part of a team which worked in China, and uncovered the fossilized remains which are often referred to as "Peking man." After his work in China, he settled in the United States, where he remained to his death. During his lifetime, Teilhard de Chardin published a number of scientific papers. Despite having given considerable thought to the relation of science and religion, he was not able to gain permission from his religious superiors to publish his writings in this field, partly because they were regarded as of dubious orthodoxy.

Teilhard de Chardin's death in 1955 opened the way to the publication of these writings. Within months of his death, the first major work appeared. *Le phénomène humaine* ("The human phenomenon") was written during the years 1938–40. It finally appeared in French in 1955, and in English translation in 1959. This was followed by *Le milieu divin* was originally written in 1927, and appeared in French in 1957. The title is notoriously difficult to translate into English, on account of the rich connotations of the French word *milieu*. (The English word "medium" conveys at least some of these, but not all.) This difficulty led to the work appearing under two different titles in translation. It was published in English under its original French title in London in 1960, and under the title *The Divine Milieu* in New York. These two works, taken together, set out a remarkable fusion of evolutionary biology, philosophical theology and spirituality, which captured the imagination of many working in the field of science and religion.

Teilhard de Chardin viewed the universe as an evolutionary process which was constantly moving towards a state of greater complexity and higher levels of consciousness. Within this process of evolution, a number of critically important transitions (generally referred to as "critical points") can be discerned. For Teilhard, the origination of life on earth and the emergence of human consciousness are two particularly important thresholds in this process. These "critical points" are like rungs on a ladder, leading to new stages in a continuous process of development. The world is to be seen as a single continuous process – a "universal interweaving" of various levels of organization. Each of these levels has its roots in earlier levels, and its emergence is to be seen as the actualization of what was potentially present in earlier levels. Teilhard de Chardin thus does not consider that there is a radical dividing line between consciousness and matter, or between humanity and other animals. The world is a single evolving entity, linked together as a web of mutually interconnected events, in which there is a natural progression from matter to life to human existence to human society.

For some of his critics, this seems to suggest that there is some way in which matter can be thought of as "rational." Teilhard de Chardin's stress on the potential of lower levels flowering or becoming actualized in later levels leads him to the conclusion that, since matter has the potential to become "conscious," it can therefore be thought of as being "conscious" in some manner. There must therefore have been a "rudimentary consciousness" which "precedes the emergence of life" in the physical matter of the universe. Teilhard de Chardin expresses this idea in the following manner: "there is a Within to things." In other words, there is some form of biological layer lying within the fabric of the universe. This biological layer may be "attenuated to the uttermost" in the early stages of the evolutionary process, but its existence is necessary to explain the emergence of consciousness in later periods. It is important to note how this conclusion arises from his insistence that there are no radical discontinuities or innovations within the evolutionary process, which proceeds in a constantly progressive manner. New phases are to be thought of in terms of crossing thresholds, not breaking with earlier stages.

This clearly raises the question of how God is involved in evolution. It is clear that Teilhard de Chardin places considerable emphasis on the theme of the consummation of the world in Jesus Christ, an idea which is clearly stated in the New Testament (especially the letters to the Colossians and Ephesians: see Colossians 1: 15–20; Ephesians 1: 9–10, 22–23), and which was developed with particular enthusiasm by some Greek patristic writers, including Origen. Teilhard de Chardin develops this theme with particular reference to a concept which he calls "Omega" (after the final letter of the Greek alphabet). In his earlier writings, he tends to think of Omega primarily as the point towards which the evolutionary process is heading. The process clearly represents an upward ascent; Omega defines, so to speak, its final destination. It will be clear that Teilhard de Chardin regards evolution as a teleological and directional process. As his thinking developed, however, he began to integrate his Christian understanding of God into his thinking about Omega, with the result that both the directionality of evolution and its final goal are explained in terms of a final union with God.

Teilhard de Chardin is not as lucid in his discussion of this point as might be hoped, and there are some difficulties in understanding him at points. However, the main points in his later thinking appear to be the following. Omega is to be seen as a force which attracts the evolutionary process towards it. It is "the Prime Mover ahead," the principle which "moves and collects" the process. Unlike gravity, which attracts downwards, Omega is "an inverse process of gravitation" which attracts the evolutionary process upwards, so that it may finally ascend into union with God. The entire direction of the evolutionary process is thus not defined by its point of departure, by where it started from, but by its goal, by its final objective, which is Omega.

Teilhard de Chardin argues that the existence of Omega is suggested, but not proved, by scientific analysis. "This pole Omega is reached only by extrapolation; it remains of its nature an assumption and a conjecture." Yet it is confirmed and given substance by the Christian revelation. It is argued that the New Testament theme of all things finding their goal in Christ (which, as we noted, is clearly stated in the letters to the Colossians and Ephesians) provides a theological underpinning for this religious interpretation of evolution. "Far from overshadowing Christ, the universe can find only in him the guarantee of its stability." Jesus Christ, as God incarnate, is therefore understood as the ground and goal of the entire process of cosmic evolution. "In place of the vague focus of convergence demanded as a terminus for evolution, we now have the well-defined personal reality of the Incarnate Word, in whom all things hold together." If all things are to be "summed up in Christ" (Ephesians 1: 9–10), then Christ is to be seen as the final goal of the evolving cosmos.

The overall vision that Teilhard de Chardin sets out is thus that of a universe in the process of evolution – a massive organism which is slowly progressing towards its fulfilment through a forward and upward movement. God is at work within this process, directing it from inside – yet also at work *ahead* of the process, drawing it towards himself and its final fulfilment. In a paper entitled "What I believe," Teilhard de Chardin set out his cosmic vision in four terse statements:

1 I believe that the universe is in evolution.
2 I believe that evolution proceeds toward the spiritual.
3 I believe that the spiritual is fully realized in a form of personality.
4 I believe that the supremely personal is the universal Christ.

Teilhard de Chardin has evoked admiration and amusement in about equal measure. Many have found themselves fascinated by the vision which he offers of a universe converging towards its final goal. Others have found his ideas lacking intellectual rigor, and hopelessly optimistic in terms of the final outcome of cosmic evolution. Nevertheless, he remains a fascinating example of a twentieth-century writer who found points of connection between his scientific and religious thinking.

Summary

Pierre Teilhard de Chardin (1881–1955)
Field of Specialization: Palaeontology

Key writings on science and religion:
The Phenomenon of Man (1959).
Le milieu divin (1960) also known as *The Divine Milieu*.

Significant secondary studies:
Cuénot, C. *Teilhard de Chardin: A Biographical Study*. London: Burnes & Oates, 1965.

Lyons, J. A. *The Cosmic Christ in Origen and Teilhard de Chardin*. Oxford: Oxford University Press, 1982.

Mooney, C. F. *Teilhard de Chardin and the Mystery of Christ*. London: Collins, 1966.

Thomas F. Torrance (1913–)

Torrance was born on August 30, 1913, at Chengdu, in the Szechuan region of China, to missionary parents. He was initially educated at the Chengdu Canadian Mission School (1920–7), before returning to Scotland to continue his education at Bellshill Academy (1927–31). He then entered the University of Edinburgh, gaining his MA in Classical Languages and Philosophy in 1934, and his BD (with specialization in systematic theology) in 1937. He subsequently undertook further research work at Oxford and Basle, and was awarded a doctorate from Basle for a study of the doctrine of grace in the writings of some early Christian theologians. After a year spent as Professor of Systematic Theology at Auburn Theological Seminary in New York State (1938–9), he was ordained as a Presbyterian minister, and served as Parish Minister at Alyth, in Perthshire 1940–7, including a period spend on chaplaincy Service with the British Army during the Second World War. After a second period of ministry at Beechgrove Parish Church, Aberdeen (1947–50), Torrance was appointed Professor of Church History, at Edinburgh University and New College. In 1952, he was appointed Professor of Christian Dogmatics at Edinburgh, and remained in this position until his retirement in 1979.

Torrance is widely regarded as the most significant British theologian of the present century, and it is therefore particularly importance to note his interest in the relation of the natural sciences and Christian theology. Among his major writings to deal with the theme, the following are widely regarded as being of particular significance.

- *Theological Science* (1969), which was based on the Hewett Lectures delivered in 1959 at Union Theological Seminary, New York.
- *Reality and Scientific Theology: Theology and Science at the Frontiers of Knowledge* (1985), based on the Harris Lectures at the University of Dundee in 1970.

He was awarded the Templeton Prize for Progress in Religion in 1978 in recognition of his major contribution to the dialogue between the two disciplines. Torrance argued that there was a "hidden traffic between theological and scientific ideas of the most far-reaching significance for both theology and science . . . [which shows that they] have deep mutual relations." Of the various convergences which Torrance identifies, the most important is that both result from a posteriori reflection on an independent reality which they attempt to describe in their respective manners.

Torrance draws a careful and critical distinction between "religion" and "theology." The distinction is important, as many discussions of the interaction of religious and scientific ways of thinking often treat the issues of "science and religion" and "science and theology" as synonymous – different ways of speaking about the same thing. Drawing partly on a Barthian perspective, Torrance insists that this is unacceptable. "Religion" is to be understood as concerning human consciousness and behavior. Religion is essentially a human creation. Theology, on the other hand, has to do with our knowledge of God.

Theology is the unique science devoted to knowledge of God, differing from other sciences by the uniqueness of its object which can be apprehended only on its own terms and from within the actual situation it has created in our existence in making itself known. . . . As a science theology is only a human endeavour in quest of the truth, in which we seek to apprehend God as far as we may, to understand what we apprehend, and to speak clearly and carefully about what we understand.

Both theology and the natural sciences are thus determined by the reality of the object which is to be apprehended. They cannot set out from preconceptions of their own devising, but must allow their inquiry to be guided by the independent reality which they are seeking to understand.

Christian theology arises out of the actual knowledge of God given in and with concrete happenings in space and time. It is knowledge of the God who actively meets us and gives Himself to be known in Jesus Christ – in Israel, in history, on earth. It is essentially positive knowledge, with articulated content, mediated in concrete experience. It is concerned with fact, the fact of God's self-revelation; it is concerned with God Himself who just because He really is God always comes first. We do not therefore begin with ourselves or our questions, nor indeed can we choose where to begin; we can only begin with the facts prescribed for us by the actuality of the subject positively known.

Torrance is thus critical of the use of *a priori* notions in both science and theology, believing that both should respond to the objective reality with which they are confronted, and which they are required to describe. Theology and the natural sciences are to be seen as *a posteriori* activities, conditioned by what is given.

Torrance argues that both theology and the natural sciences are thus committed to some form of realism, in that they deal with a reality whose existence is prior to their attempts to comprehend it. Both require openness to the way things are, and that their modes of inquiry are conformed to the nature of the reality which they encounter.

We are concerned in the development of scientific theories to penetrate into the comprehensibility of reality and grasp it in its mathematical harmonies or symmetries or its invariant structures, which hold good independently of our perceiving: we apprehend the real world as it forces itself upon us through the theories it calls forth from us. Theories take shape in our minds under the pressure of the real world upon us. ... This is the inescapable "dogmatic realism" or a science pursued and elaborated under the compelling claims and constraints of reality.

In the case of the natural sciences, the "reality" is the natural order; in the case of theology, it is the Christian revelation.

The basic convictions and fundamental ideas with which our knowledge of God is built up arise on the ground of evangelical and liturgical experience in the life of the Church, in response to the way God has actually taken in making himself known to mankind through historical dialogue with Israel and the Incarnation of his Son in Jesus Christ and continues to reveal himself to us through the Holy Scriptures. Scientific theology or theological science, strictly speaking, can never be more than a refinement and extension of the knowledge informed by those basic convictions and fundamental ideas, and it would be both empty of material content and empirically irrelevant it it were cut adrift from them.

It will be clear that Torrance's approach is grounded in an approach which stresses the priority of God's self-revelation. This is seen as an objective reality, independent of human rational activity. Although Torrance is no uncritical supporter of Barth, this would unquestionably be one area in which he identifies with Barth's agenda. This means that the approach adopted by Torrance would not find favor with religious thinkers who regard theology as reflection on human experience, or who adopt a postmodern stance, according to which there is no such objective reality in the first place.

Yet Torrance must be seen as developing Barth's theological program in a manner which is fundamentally more friendly and receptive towards the natural sciences. Where Barth tended to be dismissive of any dialogue between theology and the natural sciences, Torrance noted that such a dialogue had considerable potential. His argument that natural theology had a role within systematic theology which paralleled the use made by Einstein of geometry is particularly important in this respect. For many, Torrance's decisive modification of Barth's position at this critical juncture constitutes one of his most significant contributions to the discussion of the relation between science and religion, and opens the way to a genuine and significant dialogue between natural and special revelation.

Summary

Thomas F. Torrance, 1913–
Area of Specialization: Christian theology

Key writings on science and religion:
Theological Science (1969)
Reality and Scientific Theology (1985)

Significant Secondary Studies:
Kruger, C. B. "The Doctrine of the Knowledge of God in the Theology of Thomas F. Torrance", *Scottish Journal of Theology* 43 (1990): 366–389.

Weightman, C. *Theology in a Polanyian Universe: The Theology of Thomas Torrance*. New York: Peter Lang, 1994.

Conclusion

This work has aimed to introduce some of the themes which students will encounter in the study of science and religion. It is inevitable that this introduction will have raised more questions than it answers, and that its discussion of many complex questions need to be followed through in much greater detail and to a greater depth. The suggestions for further reading aim to allow and encourage readers to develop their interest in this fascinating subject.

For further reading

Achtemeier, P. M. "The Truth of Tradition: Critical Realism in the Thought of Alasdair MacIntyre and T. F. Torrance." *Scottish Journal of Theology* 47 (1994): 335–74.

Avis, P. D. L. "Apologist from the World of Science: John Polkinghorne, FRS." *Scottish Journal of Theology* 43 (1990): 485–502.

Barbour, I. G. *Issues in Science and Religion*. Englewood Cliffs: Prentice-Hall, 1966.

——. *Technology, Environment, and Human Values*. New York: Praeger, 1980.

——. "Ways of Relating Science and Theology." *Physics, Philosophy and Theology*. Ed. R. J. Russell, W. R. Stoeger and G. V. Coyne. Vatican City: Vatican Observatory, 1988, pp. 21–48.

——. *Religion in an Age of Science*. San Fransisco: HarperSanFransisco, 1990.

Chardin, P. T. de. *The Phenomenon of Man*. New York: Harper, 1959.

Coulson, C. A. *Christianity in an Age of Science*. London: Oxford University Press, 1953.

——. *Science and Christian Belief*. Oxford: Oxford University Press, 1955.

Hefner, P. "The Role of Science in Pannenberg's Theological Thinking." *Zygon* 24 (1989): 135–51.

Kruger, C. B. "The Doctrine of the Knowledge of God in the Theology of Thomas F. Torrance." *Scottish Journal of Theology* 43 (1990): 366–89.

Morrison, J. D. "Heidegger, Correspondence Truth and the Realist Theology of Thomas Forsyth Torrance." *Evangelical Quarterly* 59 (1997): 139–55.

Pannenberg, W. *Theology and the Philosophy of Science*. Philadelphia: Westminster, 1973.

——. *Toward a Theology of Nature: Essays on Science and Faith*. Philadelphia: Westminster/John Knox, 1993.

Peacocke, A. *Creation and the World of Science*. Oxford and New York: Oxford University Press, 1979.

——. *The Sciences and Theology in the Twentieth Century*. Notre Dame, IN: University of Notre Dame Press, 1981.

Peacocke, A. R. *God and the New Biology*. San Fransisco: Harper & Row, 1986.

Polkinghorne, J. *Science and Providence: God's Interaction with the World*. Boston, MA: Shambhala, 1989.

——. *Scientists as Theologians: A Comparison of the Writings of Ian Barbour, Arthur Peacocke and John Polkinghorne*. London: SPCK, 1996.

Rudwick, M. J. S. "Senses of the Natural World and Senses of God: Another Look at the Historical Relation of Science and Religion." *The Sciences and Theology in the Twentieth Century*. Ed. Arthur R. Peacocke. London: Oriel Press, 1981, pp. 241–61.

Russell, R. J. "Contingency in Physics and Cosmology: A Critique of the Theology of Wolfhart Pannenberg." *Zygon* 23 (1988): 23–43.

Seng, K. P. "The Epistemological Significance of Homoousion in the Theology of Thomas F. Torrance." *Scottish Journal of Theology* 45 (1992): 341–66.

Torrance, T. F. *Theological Science*. Oxford: Oxford University Press, 1969.

——. *Reality and Scientific Theology: Theology and Science at the Frontiers of Knowledge*. Edinburgh: Scottish Academic Press, 1985.

Worthing, M. W. *Foundations and Functions of Theology as Universal Science: Theological Method and Apologetic Praxis in Wolfhart Pannenberg and Karl Rahner*. Frankfurt am Main/Berlin: Peter Lang, 1996.

Bibliography

Achtemeier, P. M. "The Truth of Tradition: Critical Realism in the Thought of Alasdair MacIntyre and T. F. Torrance." *Scottish Journal of Theology* 47 (1994): 355–74.

Attfield, R. "Science and Creation." *Journal of Religion* 58 (1978): 37–47.

Austin, W. H. *The Relevance of Natural Science to Theology*. London: Macmillan, 1976.

Avis, P. D. L. "Apologist from the World of Science: John Polkinghorne, FRS." *Scottish Journal of Theology* 43 (1990): 485–502.

Banner, M. C. *The Justification of Science and the Rationality of Religious Belief*. Oxford and New York: Oxford University Press, 1990.

Barbour, I. G. *Issues in Science and Religion*. Englewood Cliffs: Prentice-Hall, 1966.

——. *Myths, Models and Paradigms: A Comparative Study in Science and Religion*. New York: Harper & Row, 1974.

——. "Ways of Relating Science and Theology." *Physics, Philosophy and Theology*. Ed. R. J. Russell, W. R. Stoeger and G. V. Coyne. Vatican City: Vatican Observatory, 1988, pp. 21–48.

——. *Religion in an Age of Science*. San Francisco: HarperSanFrancisco, 1990.

——. "Experiencing and Interpreting Nature in Science and Religion." *Zygon* 29 (1994): 457–87.

Barr, J. *Biblical Faith and Natural Theology*. Oxford: Clarendon Press, 1993.

Barth, K., and E. Brunner. *Natural Theology*. London: SCM Press, 1947.

Blackwell, R. J. *Galileo, Bellarmine and the Bible*. Notre Dame, IN: University of Notre Dame Press, 1991.

Blaisdell, M. "Natural Theology and Nature's Disguises." *Journal of the History of Biology* 15 (1982): 163–89.

Bouma-Prediger, S. "Creation as the Home of God: The Doctrine of Creation in the Theology of Jürgen Moltmann." *Calvin Theological Journal* 32 (1997): 72–90.

Brooke, J. H. "Science and the Fortunes of Natural Theology: Some Historical Perspectives." *Zygon* 24 (1989): 3–22.

——. *Science and Religion: Some Historical Perspectives*. Cambridge and New York: Cambridge University Press, 1991.

Brown, H. "Alvin Plantinga and Natural Theology." *International Journal for Philosophy of Religion* 30 (1991): 1–19.

Burhoe, R. W. *Toward a Scientific Theology*. Belfast/Ottawa: Christian Journals, 1981.

Butler, D. "God's Visible Glory: The Beauty of Nature in the Thought of John Calvin and Jonathan Edwards." *Westminster Theological Journal* 52 (1990): 13–26.

Byrne, P. A. "Berkeley, Scientific Realism and Creation." *Religious Studies* 20 (1984): 453–64.

Cairns, D. "Thomas Chalmer's Astronomical Discourses: A Study in Natural Theology." *Scottish Journal of Theology* 9 (1956): 410–21.

Cartwright, N. "Comments on Wesley Salmon's "Science and Religion"." *Philosophical Studies* 33 (1978): 177–83.

Clarke, B. L. "Natural Theology and Methodology." *New Scholasticism* 57 (1983): 233–52.

Clayton, P. *Explanation from Physics to Theology: An Essay in Rationality and Religion*. New Haven, CT: Yale University Press, 1989.

Cohen, I. B. *The Newtonian Revolution*. Cambridge: Cambridge University Press, 1980.

Cole-Turner, R. *The New Genesis: Theology and the Genetic Revolution*. Louisville, KY: Westminster/John Knox, 1993.

Cooper, K. J. "Scientific Method and the Appraisal of Religion." *Religious Studies* 21 (1985): 319–29.

Corr, C. A. "The Existence of God, Natural Theology and Christian Wolff." *International Journal for Philosophy of Religion* 4 (1973): 105–18.

Cosslett, T. *Science and Religion in the Nineteenth Century*. Cambridge and New York: Cambridge University Press, 1984.

Crombie, A. C. *Augustine to Galileo: the History of Science A.D. 400–1650*. London: Falcon Press, 1952.

Davis, E. B. "God, Man and Nature: The Problem of Creation in Cartesian Thought." *Scottish Journal of Theology* 44 (1991): 325–48.

——. "Fundamentalism and Folk Science Between the Wars." *Religion and American Culture* 5 (1995): 217–48.

Davis, S. T. "Theology, Verification and Falsification." *International Journal for Philosophy of Religion* 6 (1975): 23–39.

Dawkins, R. "Is Science a Religion?" *The Humanist* January/February (1997): 26–9.

Deason, G. B. "The Protestant Reformation and the Rise of Modern Science." *Scottish Journal of Theology* 38 (1985): 221–40.

Dennett, D. C. *Darwin's Dangerous Idea: Evolution and the Meaning of Life*. New York: Simon & Schuster, 1995.

Dowey, E. A. *The Knowledge of God in Calvin's Theology*. New York: Columbia University Press, 1952.

Draper, J. W. *History of the Conflict between Religion and Science*. New York: Daniel Appleton, 1874.

Drees, W. B. *Religion, Science and Naturalism*. Cambridge and New York: Cambridge University Press, 1995.

Durant, J. *Darwinism and Divinity*. Oxford and New York: Basil Blackwell, 1985.

Eaves, L. "Spirit, Method and Content in Science and Religion: The Theological Perspective of a Geneticist." *Zygon* 24 (1989): 185–215.

Evans, L. T. "Darwin's Use of the Analogy between Artificial and Natural Selection." *Journal of the History of Biology* 17 (1984): 113–40.

Ferre, F. *Hellfire and Lightning Rods: Liberating Science, Technology, and Religion*. Maryknoll, NY: Orbis, 1993.

Fisch, H. "The Scientist as Priest: A Note on Robert Boyle's Natural Theology." *Isis* 44 (1953): 252–65.

Funkenstein, A. *Theology and the Scientific Imagination from the Middle Ages to the Seventeenth Century*. Princeton: Princeton University Press, 1986.

Gale, B. G. *Evolution without Evidence: Charles Darwin and The Origin of Species*. Albuquerque: University of New Mexico Press, 1982.

Garrison, J. W. "Newton and the Relation of Mathematics to Natural Philosophy." *Journal of the History of Ideas* 48 (1987): 609–27.

Gascoigne, J. "From Bentley to the Victorians: The Rise and Fall of British Newtonian Natural Theology." *Science in Context* 2 (1988): 219–56.

——. *Cambridge in the Age of the Enlightenment: Science, Religion and Politics from the Restoration to the French Revolution*. Cambridge and New York: Cambridge University Press, 1989.

Gehart, M., and A. M. Russell. *Metaphoric Process: the Creation of Scientific and Religious Understanding*. Fort Worth: Christian University Press, 1984.

Gilbert, J. "Burhoe and Shapley: A Complementarity of Science and Religion." *Zygon* 30 (1995): 531–39.

Gilkey, L. *Religion and the Scientific Future: Reflections on Myth, Science, and Theology*. New York: Harper & Row, 1970.

——. "Nature, Reality and the Sacred: A Meditation in Science and Religion." *Zygon* 24 (1989): 283–98.

Gill, J. H. "Kant, Analogy and Natural Theology." *International Journal for Philosophy of Religion* 16 (1984): 19–28.

Gillespie, N. C. *Charles Darwin and Special Creation*. Chicago: University of Chicago Press, 1979.

——. *Charles Darwin and the Problem of Creation*. Chicago: University of Chicago Press, 1979.

Gilley, S., and A. Loades. "Thomas Henry Huxley: The War between Science and Religion." *Journal of Religion* 61 (1981): 285–308.

Gillispie, C. C. *Genesis and Geology: A Study in the Relations of Scientific Thought, Natural Theology and Social Opinion in Great Britain, 1790–1850*. Harvard Historical Studies 58. Cambridge, MA: Harvard University Press, 1996.

Gingerich, O. "Is there a Role for Natural Theology Today?" *Science and Theology: Questions at the Interface*. Ed. M. Rae, H. Regan and J. Stenhouse. Edinburgh: T. & T. Clark, 1994, pp. 29–48.

Goldman, S. L. "On the Interpretation of Symbols and the Christian Origins of Modern Science." *Journal of Religion* 62 (1982): 1–20.

Grant, E. *The Foundations of Science in the Middle Ages: Their Religious, Institutional and Intellectual Contexts*. Cambridge: Cambridge University Press, 1996.

Gregersen, N. H. "Theology in a Neo-Darwinian World." *Studia Theologica* 48 (1994): 125–49.

Gregory, F. *Nature Lost? Natural Science and the German Theological Traditions of the Nineteenth Century*. Cambridge, MA: Harvard University Press, 1992.

Hall, A. R. *Isaac Newton: Adventurer in Thought*. Cambridge: Cambridge University Press, 1996.

Hefner, P. "Theology's Truth and Scientific Formulation." *Zygon* 23 (1988): 263–79.

——. "The Role of Science in Pannenberg's Theological Thinking." *Zygon* 24 (1989): 135–51.

Hendry, G. *The Theology of Nature*. Philadelphia: Westminster Press, 1980.

Hesse, M. "Criteria of Truth in Science and Theology." *Religious Studies* 11 (1975): 385–400.

Hudson, W. D. "Theology and the Intellectual Endeavour of Mankind." *Religious Studies* 21 (1985): 21–37.

Hull, D. L. *Darwin and his Critics*. Cambridge, MA: Harvard University Press, 1973.

Huyssteen, W. v. "Experience and Explanation: The Justification of Cognitive Claims in Theology." *Zygon* 23 (1988): 247–61.

——. *Theology and the Justification of Faith: Constructing Theories in Systematic Theology*. Grand Rapids, MI: Eerdmans, 1989.

Inwagen, P. v. "Genesis and Evolution." *Reasoned Faith: Essays in Philosophical Theology*. Ed. Eleonore Stump. Ithaca, NY: Cornell University Press, 1993, pp. 93–127.

Jacob, M. C. *The Newtonians and the English Revolution 1689–1720*. London: Harvester, 1976.

Kaiser, C. B. "Calvin, Copernicus and Castellio." *Calvin Theological Journal* 21 (1986): 5–31.

Kempsey, D. S. "Religious Influences in the Rise of Modern Science." *Annals of Science* 24 (1968): 199–226.

Klaaren, E. *Religious Origins of Modern Science*. Grand Rapids, MI: Eerdmans, 1977.

Klauber, M. "Jean-Alphonse Turrettini (1671–1737) on Natural Theology: The Triumph of Reason over Revelation at the Academy of Geneva." *Scottish Journal of Theology* 47 (1994): 301–25.

Kuhn, T. S. *The Copernican Revolution*. New York: Random House, 1959.

Langford, J. R. "Science, Theology and Freedom: A New Look at the Galileo Case." *On Freedom*. Ed. Leroy S. Rouner. Notre Dame, IN: University of Notre Dame Press, 1989, pp. 108–25.

Livingstone, D. N. "The Idea of Design: The Vicissitudes of a Key Concept in the Princeton Response to Darwin." *Scottish Journal of Theology* 37 (1984): 329–57.

——. *Darwin's Forgotten Defenders: The Encounter between Evangelical Theology and Evolutionary Thought*. Grand Rapids, MI: Eerdmans, 1987.

——. "Darwinism and Calvinism: The Belfast-Princeton Connection." *Isis* 83 (1992): 408–28.

Loder, J. E., and W. J. Neidhardt. "Barth, Bohr and Dialectic." *Religion and Science: History, Method, Dialogue*. Eds. W. Mark Richardson and Wesley J. Wildman. New York: Routledge, 1996, pp. 271–89.

Long, E. T. "Experience and Natural Theology." *Philosophy of Religion* 31 (1992): 119–32.

MacIntosh, J. J. "Robert Boyle's Epistemology: the Interaction between Scientific and Religious Knowledge." *International Studies in the Philosophy of Science* 6 (1992): 91–121.

MacKay, D. M. " 'Complementarity' in Scientific and Theological Thinking." *Zygon* 9 (1974): 225–44.

Manuel, F. E. *The Religion of Isaac Newton*. Oxford: Clarendon Press, 1974.

Mascall, E. L. *Christian Theology and Natural Science: some Questions on their Relations*. London: Longmans Green, 1956.

Mayr, E. "The Concept of Finality in Darwin and after Darwin." *Scientia* 118 (1983): 99–117.

McFague, S. *Metaphorical Theology: Models of God in Religious Language*. London: SCM, 1983.

McGrath, A. E. *The Foundations of Dialogue in Science and Religion*. Oxford/ Cambridge, MA: Blackwell, 1998.

McOuat, G., and M. P. Winsor. "J. B. S. Haldane's Darwinism in its religious context." *British Journal for History of Science* 28 (1995): 227–31.

Millar, P. D. "Cosmology and World Order in the Old Testament: The Divine

Council as Cosmic-Political Symbol." *Horizons in Biblical Theology* 9 (1987): 53–78.

Moore, J. R. *The Post-Darwinian Controversies: A Study of the Protestant Struggle to come to terms with Darwin in Great Britain and America, 1870–1900.* Cambridge: Cambridge University Press, 1979.

——. "Evangelicals and Evolution: Henry Drummond, Herbert Spencer and the Naturalisation of the Spiritual World." *Scottish Journal of Theology* 38 (1985): 383–417.

Murphy, N. "Relating Theology and Science in a Postmodern Age." *CTNS Bulletin* 7.4 (1987): 1–10.

——. *Theology in the Age of Scientific Reasoning.* Ithaca, NY: Cornell University Press, 1990.

Murphy, N. C. "Acceptability Criteria for Work in Theology and Science." *Zygon* 22 (1987): 279–97.

Nebelsick, H. *Theology and Science in Mutual Modification.* Belfast/Ottawa: Christian Journals, 1981.

Newton-Smith, W. H. *The Rationality of Science.* London: Routledge & Kegan Paul, 1981.

Numbers, R. L. "George Frederick Wright: From Christian Darwinist to Fundamentalist." *Isis* 79 (1988): 624–45.

O'Higgins, J. "Hume and the Deists." *Journal of Theological Studies* 22 (1971): 479–501.

Pagels, H. R. *The Cosmic Code: Quantum Physics and the Language of Nature.* Harmondsworth: Penguin, 1984, p. 83.

Pannenberg, W. *Theology and the Philosophy of Science.* Philadelphia: Westminster, 1973.

——. *Toward a Theology of Nature: Essays on Science and Faith.* Philadelphia: Westminster/John Knox, 1993.

Peacocke, A. *The Sciences and Theology in the Twentieth Century.* Notre Dame, IN: University of Notre Dame Press, 1981.

——. *Theology for a Scientific Age: Being and Becoming Divine and Human.* London: SCM Press, 1993.

—— *God and Science – A Quest for Christian Credibility.* London: SCM Press, 1996.

Pedersen, O. *Galileo and the Council of Trent.* Vatican City: Specolo Vaticana, 1983.

Peters, K. E. "Empirical Theology in the Light of Science." *Zygon* 27 (1992): 297–325.

Peters, T. "Theology and the Natural Sciences." *The Modern Theologians: An Introduction to Christian Theology in the Twentieth Century.* Ed. David F. Ford. 2nd edn. Oxford/Cambridge, MA: Blackwell, 1997, pp. 649–68.

Polkinghorne, J. *One World: The Interaction of Science and Theology.* Princeton: Princeton University Press, 1986.

——. *Scientists as Theologians: A Comparison of the Writings of Ian Barbour, Arthur Peacocke and John Polkinghorne*. London: SPCK, 1996.

—— *Belief in God in an Age of Science*. New Haven: Yale University Press, 1998.

Poole, M. "A Critique of Aspects of the Philosophy and Theology of Richard Dawkins." *Science and Christian Belief* 6 (1994): 41–59.

Porter, A. P. "Science, Religious Language and Analogy." *Faith and Philosophy* 13 (1996): 113–20.

Postman, N. *Technopoly: The Surrender of Culture to Technology*. New York, Vintage, 1993, p. 71.

Ramsey, I. T. *Religious Language. An Empirical Placing of Theological Phrases*. London: SCM, 1957.

Ratzsch, D. "Abraham Kuyper's Philosophy of Science." *Calvin Theological Journal* 27 (1992): 277–303.

Raven, C. E. *Natural Religion and Christian Theology*. 2 vols. Cambridge: Cambridge University Press, 1953.

Reich, K. H. "The Relation between Science and Theology: The Case for Complementarity Revisited." *Zygon* 25 (1990): 369–90.

——. "The Doctrine of the Trinity as a Model for Structuring the Relations between Science and Theology." *Zygon* 30 (1995): 383–405.

——. "A Logic-Based Typology of Science and Theology." *Journal of Interdisciplinary Studies* 7 (1996): 149–67.

Richards, R. J. *Darwin and the Emergence of Evolutionary Theories of Mind and Behaviour*. Chicago: University of Chicago Press, 1987.

Richardson, W. M., and W. J. Wildman. "Religion and Science: History, Method, Dialogue." New York: Routledge, 1996.

Robbins, J. W. "Science and Religion: Critical Realism or Pragmatism?" *International Journal for Philosophy of Religion* 21 (1987): 83–94.

Roberts, J. H. *Darwinism and the Divine in America*. Madison: University of Wisconsin Press, 1988.

Rolston, H. *Science and Religion: A Critical Survey*. Philadelphia: Temple University Press, 1987.

Ruse, M. *Taking Darwin Seriously: a Naturalistic Approach to Philosophy*. Oxford: Basil Blackwell, 1986.

Russell, B. *Religion and Science*. London: Oxford University Press, 1935.

Russell, R. J., W. R. Stoeger, and G. V. Coyne. *Physics, Philosophy and Theology: A Common Quest for Understanding*. Vatican City State: Vatican Observatory, 1988.

——, N. Murphy, and A. Peacocke. *Chaos and Complexity: Scientific Perspectives on Divine Action*. Vatican City State: Vatican Observatory and Berkeley: Center for Theology and Natural Sciences, 1995.

Salmon, W. C. "Religion and Science: A New Look at Hume's Dialogues." *Philosophical Studies* 33 (1978): 143–76.

Schilling, H. K. *Science and Religion*. New York: Charles Scribner's Sons, 1962.

Schlesinger, G. *Religion and Scientific Method*. Dordrecht, Holland: D. Reidel, 1977.

Schmitt, C. B. "Galilei and the Seventeenth-Century Text Book Tradition." *Novità celesti e crisi del sapere: atti del convegno internazionale di studi galileiani.* Ed. P. Galluzzi. Florence: Giunti Barbera, 1984, pp. 217–28.

Schoen, E. L. *Religious Explanations: A Model from the Sciences*. Durham, NC: Duke University Press, 1985.

——. "The Roles of Prediction in Science and Religion." *International Journal for Philosophy of Religion* 29 (1991): 1–31.

Schrader, D. E. "Karl Popper as a Point of Departure for a Philosophy of Theology." *International Journal for Philosophy of Religion* 14 (1983): 193–201.

Schroeder, G. L. *The Science of God: The Convergence of Scientific and Biblical Wisdom*. New York: Free Press, 1998.

Soskice, J. "Theological Realism." *The Rationality of Religious Belief*. Ed. W. J. Abraham and S. Holtzer. Oxford and New York: Clarendon Press, 1987, pp. 105–19.

Stanesby, D. *Science, Reason, and Religion*. London and New York: Routledge, 1988.

Sulloway, F. J. "Darwin's Conversion: The Beagle Voyage and its Aftermath." *Journal of the History of Biology* 15 (1982): 325–96.

Tennant, F. R. *Philosophical Theology*. 2 vols. Cambridge: Cambridge University Press, 1930.

Torrance, T. F. *Theological Science*. Oxford: Oxford University Press, 1969.

——. *The Ground and Grammar of Theology*. Belfast: Christian Journals Ltd, 1980.

——. *Reality and Scientific Theology: Theology and Science at the Frontiers of Knowledge*. Edinburgh: Scottish Academic Press, 1985.

Toulmin, S. *The Return to Cosmology: Postmodern Science and the Theology of Nature*. Berkeley, CA: University of California Press, 1982.

Tracy, D., and N. Lash. *Cosmology and Theology*. New York: Seabury, 1983.

Tumbleson, R. D. "'Reason and Religion': The Science of Anglicanism." *Journal of the History of Ideas* 57 (1996): 131–56.

Turner, F. M. "Rainfall, Plagues and the Prince of Wales: A Chapter in the Conflict of Science and Religion." *Journal of British Studies* 13 (1974): 46–65.

——. "The Victorian Conflict between Science and Religion: A Professional Dimension." *Isis* 69 (1978): 356–76.

Ward, K. *Rational Theology and the Creativity of God*. Oxford: Blackwell, 1982.

Warfield, B. B. *Studies in Theology*. New York: Oxford University Press, 1932.

Watts, F. "Are Science and Religion in Conflict?." *Zygon* 32 (1997): 125–38.

Welch, C. "Dispelling Some Myths about the Split between Theology and Science in the Nineteenth Century." *Religion and Science: History, Method, Dialogue*. Ed. W. Mark Richardson and Wesley J. Wildman. New York: Routledge, 1996, pp. 29–40.

Westfall, R. S. *Science and Religion in Seventeenth-Century England*. Ann Arbor, MI: University of Michigan Press, 1973.

——. "Galileo and the Jesuits." *Metaphysics and Philosophy of Science in the Seventeenth and Eighteenth Centuries*. Ed. R. S. Woolhouse. Dordrecht: Kluwer, 1988, pp. 45–72.

Westman, R. S. "Three Responses to the Copernican Theory: Johannes Praetorius, Tycho Brahe, and Michael Maestlin." *The Copernican Achievement*. Ed. Robert S. Westman. London: University of California Press, 1975, pp. 285–345.

White, A. D. *A History of the Warfare of Science with Theology in Christendom*. 2 vols. London: Macmillan, 1896.

White, R. "Calvin and Copernicus: The Problem Reconsidered." *Calvin Theological Journal* 15 (1980): 233–43.

Wicken, J. S. "Theology and Science in the Evolving Cosmos: A Need for Dialogue." *Zygon* 23 (1988): 45–55.

Wilkinson, D. A. "The Revival of Natural Theology in Contemporary Cosmology." *Science and Christian Belief* 2 (1990): 95–115.

Wisan, W. L. "Galileo's Scientific Method: A Reexamination." *New Perspectives on Galileo*. Ed. Robert E. Butts and Joseph C. Pitt. Dordrecht: D. Reidel, 1978, pp. 1–57.

——. "Galileo and God's Creation." *Isis* 77 (1986): 473–86.

Worthing, M. W., *God, Creation and Contemporary Physics*. Minneapolis: Fortress Press, 1998.

Young, F. " 'Creatio ex Nihilo': A Context for the Emergence of the Christian Doctrine of Creation." *Scottish Journal of Theology* 44 (1991): 139–51.

Young, R. M. "Darwin's Metaphor: Does Nature Select?" *Monist* 55 (1971): 442–503.

——. *Darwin's Metaphor: Nature's Place in Victorian Culture*. Cambridge: Cambridge University Press, 1985.

——. "Darwin's Metaphor and the Philosophy of Science." *Science as Culture* 16 (1993): 375–403.

Sources of Citations

All important citations in the text have been sourced, to allow users to read them in their original context and in greater depth.

Chapter 1

Page 5
van Bavel, T. "The Creator and the Integrity of Creation in the Fathers of the Church." *Augustinian Studies* 21 (1990): 1–33.

Page 10
John Calvin. *Institutes of the Christian Religion*, I.v.i–ii.

Pages 12–13
Blackwell, R. J. *Galileo, Bellarmine and the Bible*. Notre Dame, IN: University of Notre Dame Press, 1991, pp. 94–5.

Page 14
Chadwick, O. *From Bossuet to Newman: The Idea of Doctrinal Development*. Cambridge: Cambridge University Press, 1957, p. 20.

Page 20
Alexander, H. G. *The Leibniz-Clark Correspondence*. Manchester: Manchester University Press, 1956, p. 14.

Page 24
Darwin, C. *The Origin of Species*. Harmondsworth: Penguin, 1968, p. 205.

Pages 24–5
Lucas, J. R. "Wilberforce and Huxley: A Legendary Encounter." *Historical Journal* 22 (1979): 313–30. Quote at pp. 313–14.

Chapter 2

Page 30
Cobb, J., "Beyond Pluralism." *Christian Uniqueness Reconsidered*. Ed. G.D. D'Costa. Maryknoll, NY: Orbis, 1990, pp.81–84.

Chapter 3

Page 60
McGrath, A. E. *The Christian Theology Reader*. Oxford/Cambridge, MA: Blackwell, 1995, p. 17

Page 62
McGrath, A. E. *The Christian Theology Reader*. Oxford/Cambridge, MA: Blackwell, 1995, pp. 16–7.

Page 64
Fraassen, B. C. van. *The Scientific Image*. Oxford: Oxford University Press, 1980, pp. 202–3.

Page 65
Newton-Smith, W. H. *The Rationality of Science*. London: Routledge & Kegan Paul, 1981, p. 25.

Page 66
Polkinghorne, J. *One World: The Interaction of Science and Theology*. Princeton: Princeton University Press, 1986, p. 47.

Pages 68–9
Quine, W. V. O. *From a Logical Point of View*. Cambridge, MA: Harvard University Press, 1953, pp. 42–3.

Page 73
Ayer, A. J. *Logical Positivism*. New York: Free Press, 1959, pp. 63–4.

Page 74
Schilpp, P. A. *The Philosophy of Rudolph Carnap*. Lasalle, IL: Open Court, 1963, p. 8.

Pages 74–5
Crombie, I. M. "Theology and Falsification." *New Essays in Philosophical Theology*. Ed. Anthony Flew and Alasdair MacIntyre. London: SCM Press, 1955, p. 126.

Page 75
Hick, J. "Theology and Verification." *The Existence of God*. Ed. John Hick. London: Macmillan, 1964, pp. 260–1.

Page 76
Popper, K. R. *Conjectures and Refutations: The Growth of Scientific Knowledge*. London: Routledge & Kegan Paul, 1963, p. 281.

Pages 76–7
Popper, K. R. *Realism and the Aim of Science*. London: Hutchinson, 1983, pp. 162–3.

Page 77
Popper, K. R. *The Logic of Scientific Discovery*. New York: Science Editions, 1961, pp. 40–1.

Page 81
Kuhn, T. *The Structure of Scientific Revolutions*. Chicago: University of Chicago Press, 1962, p. 150.

Page 82
Kuhn, T. *The Structure of Scientific Revolutions*. Chicago: University of Chicago Press, 1962, p. 77.

Chapter 4

Page 90
McGrath, A. E. *The Christian Theology Reader*. Oxford/Cambridge, MA: Blackwell, 1995, p. 8.

Page 91
McGrath, A. E. *The Christian Theology Reader*. Oxford/Cambridge, MA: Blackwell, 1995, p. 9.

Pages 95–6
McGrath, A. E. *The Christian Theology Reader*. Oxford/Cambridge, MA: Blackwell, 1995, pp. 10–12.

Page 97
Craig, W. L. *The Kalam Cosmological Argument*. London: Macmillan, 1979, p. 149.

Page 99
McGrath, A. E. *The Christian Theology Reader*. Oxford/Cambridge, MA: Blackwell, 1995, pp. 10–12.

Pages 100–1
William Paley, *Works*, ed. E. Paley, 6 vols. London: Rivington, 1830, vol. 4, pp. 16, 34–5.

Chapter 5

Page 118
Augustine. *Saint Augustine: Confessions*. Trans. Henry Chadwick. Oxford: Clarendon Press, 1991, pp. 229–30.

Page 118
Davies, P. *The Mind of God: Science and the Search for Ultimate Meaning*. London: Penguin, 1992, p. 50.

Page 121
Guardini, R. *Letters from Lake Como: Explorations in Technology and the Human Race*. Grand Rapids, MI: Eerdmans, 1994, p. 46.

Page 123
O'Donovan, O. *Resurrection and Moral Order*. Grand Rapids, MI: Eerdmans, 1986, pp. 31–2.

Pages 123–4
O'Donovan, O. *Resurrection and Moral Order*. Grand Rapids, MI: Eerdmans, 1986, pp. 36–7.

Page 126
Davies, P. *The Mind of God: Science and the Search for Ultimate Meaning*. London: Penguin, 1992, pp. 82–3.

Chapter 6

Pages 130–1
Torrance, T. F. *The Ground and Grammar of Theology*. Belfast: Christian Journals Ltd, 1980, pp. 90–1.

Pages 131–2
Torrance, T. F. *Reality and Scientific Theology: Theology and Science at the Frontiers of Knowledge*. Edinburgh: Scottish Academic Press, 1985, p. 41.

Page 132
Torrance, T. F. *Reality and Scientific Theology: Theology and Science at the Frontiers of Knowledge*. Edinburgh: Scottish Academic Press, 1985, p. 39.

Pages 135–6
Polkinghorne, J. *Science and Creation: The Search for Understanding*. London: SPCK, 1988, p. 20.

Page 137
Edwards, J. *The Images of Divine Things*. Ed. Perry Millar. New Haven, CT: Yale University Press, 1948, pp. 61–9.

Page 138
Weinberg, S. *Dreams of a Final Theory: The Search for the Fundamental Laws of Nature*. London: Hutchinson Radius, 1993, p. 119.

Page 138
Dirac, P. "The Evolution of the Physicist's Picture of Nature." *Scientific American* 208 (1963): 45–53, p. 47.

Pages 141–2
Fisch, H. "The Scientist as Priest: A Note on Robert Boyle's Natural Theology." *Isis* 44 (1953): 252–65, p. 258.

Chapter 7

Page 144
Polkinghorne, J. *Reason and Reality*. London: SPCK, 1991, p. 20.

Page 150
Aquinas, T. *Summa contra Gentiles*. Trans. Anton C. Pegis. 5 vols. Notre Dame, IN: University of Notre Dame Press, 1975, vol. 1, 138–9.

Page 153
McGrath, A. E. *The Christian Theology Reader*. Oxford/Cambridge, MA: Blackwell, 1995, p. 180.

Page 155
McFague, S. *Models of God*. Philadelphia: Fortress Press, 1987, pp. 32–4.

Page 156
Barbour, I. G. *Myths, Models and Paradigms: The Nature of Scientific and Religious Language*. New York: Harper & Row, 1974, p. 15.

Page 158
Darwin, F., and A. C. Seward. *More Letters of Charles Darwin*. 2 vols. London: John Murray, 1903, vol. 1, 267–8

Pages 160–1
Hayter, M. *The New Eve in Christ*. London: SPCK, 1987, pp. 87--92

Page 161
Pannenberg, W. *Systematic Theology*. 3 vols. Grand Rapids, MI: Eerdmans, 1991, vol. 1, pp. 260–1.

Page 161
Hayter, M. *The New Eve in Christ*. London: SPCK, 1987, pp. 87–92

Page 161
McFague, S. *Models of God*. Philadelphia: Fortress Press, 1987, pp. 122–3.

Page 161
Caird, G. *The Language and Imagery of the Bible*. London: Duckworth, 1980, p. 80.

Page 162
Julian of Norwich. *Revelations of Divine Love*. Harmondsworth: Penguin, 1958), pp. 151, 174.

Page 169
Torrance, T. F. *Theological Science*. Oxford: Oxford University Press, 1969, pp. 26–7.

Page 173
Wiles, M. F. *The Making of Christian Doctrine*. Cambridge: Cambridge University Press, 1967, p. 106.

Chapter 8

Pages 180–1
Hawking, S. *A Brief History of Time: From the Big Bang to Black Holes*. New York: Bantam Books, 1988, p. x.

Pages 181–2
Barrow, J., and F. J. Tipler. *The Anthropic Cosmological Principle*. Oxford: Oxford University Press, 1986, p. 5.

Pages 183–4
Tennant, F. R. *Philosophical Theology*. 2 vols. Cambridge: Cambridge University Press, 1930, vol. 2, p. 79.

Page 184
Barrow, J., and F. J. Tipler. *The Anthropic Cosmological Principle*. Oxford: Oxford University Press, 1986, p. 566.

Page 185
Barrow, J., and F. J. Tipler. *The Anthropic Cosmological Principle*. Oxford: Oxford University Press, 1986, pp. 1–2.

Pages 185–6
Swinburne, R. *The Existence of God*. Oxford: Clarendon Press, 1979, p. 138.

Page 190
Dawkins, R. *The Blind Watchmaker: Why the Evidence of Evolution reveals a Universe without Design*. New York: W. W. Norton, 1986, p. 15.

Pages 190–1
Dawkins, R. *The Blind Watchmaker: Why the Evidence of Evolution reveals a Universe without Design*. New York: W. W. Norton, 1986, p. 5.

Page 193
Beecher, H. W. *Evolution and Creation*. New York: Fords, Howard & Hulbert, 1885, p. 113.

Page 193
Beecher, H. W. *Evolution and Creation*. New York: Fords, Howard & Hulbert, 1885, p. 429.

Pages 195–6
von Hartmann, E. *Geschichte der Logik*. 2 vols. Leipzig, 1900, vol. 2, p. 444.

Page 198
James, W. *The Varieties of Religious Experience*. Cambridge, MA: Harvard University Press, 1985, pp. 341–2.

Pages 199–200
James, W. *The Varieties of Religious Experience*. Cambridge, MA: Harvard University Press, 1985, p. 397.

Page 200
James, W. *The Varieties of Religious Experience*. Cambridge, MA: Harvard University Press, 1985, pp. 268–70.

Pages 202–3
Freud, S. "An Autobiographical Study." *Complete Psychological Works of Sigmund Freud*. 24 vols. London: Hogarth Press, 1953–, vol. 20, p. 68.

Page 203
Freud, S. "Leonardo da Vinci and a Memory of his Childhood." *Complete Psychological Works of Sigmund Freud*. 24 vols. London: Hogarth Press, 1953–, vol. 11, p. 123

Chapter 9

Page 210
Barbour, I. G. *Religion in an Age of Science*. San Francisco: HarperSanFrancisco, 1990, p. 227.

Page 212
Coulson, C. A. *Science and Christian Belief*. Oxford: Oxford University Press, 1955, p. 21.

Page 213
Pannenberg, W. "Redemptive Event and History." *Basic Questions in Theology*. London: SCM Press, 1970, vol. 1, p. 15.

Page 215
Pannenberg, W. *Toward a Theology of Nature*. Louisville, KY: Westminster/John Knox Press, 1993, pp. 50–72.

Page 217
Peacocke, A. *God and Science: A Quest for Christian Credibility*. London: SCM Press, 1996, pp. 5–6.

Page 220
Polkinghorne, J. *The Way the World Is*. London: SPCK, 1983, p. 12.

Page 226
Torrance, T. F. *Theological Science*. Oxford: Oxford University Press, 1969, pp. 26–7.

Page 226
Torrance, T. F. *Reality and Scientific Theology: Theology and Science at the Frontiers of Knowledge*. Edinburgh: Scottish Academic Press, 1985, pp. 54–5.

Page 227
Torrance, T. F. *Reality and Scientific Theology: Theology and Science at the Frontiers of Knowledge*. Edinburgh: Scottish Academic Press, 1985, p. 85.

Index

THE INTELLECTUAL FOUNDATIONS OF DIALOGUE IN SCIENCE AND RELIGION

Alister E. McGrath

This book explores the way in which religions and the natural sciences differ from each other, yet converge in a number of areas. Focusing on Christianity as a case study, McGrath develops the agenda set out by Thomas F. Torrance in his 1969 work 'Theological Science'. Like Torrance, McGrath sees the need to examine the relation between Christian theology and the natural sciences at the level of method - that is to say, the way in which reality is apprehended, investigated and represented.

229 x 152mm / 6 x 9 in   272 pages
0-631-20853-4 hardback
0-631-20854-2 paperback
August 1998

TO ORDER CALL :
1-800-216-2522 (N. America orders only) or
24-hour freephone on 0500 008205
(UK orders only)

VISIT OUR RELIGION WEB SITE : http://www.blackwellpublishers.co.uk